Symbian OS
Platform Security

Symbian OS Platform Security

Software Development Using the Symbian OS Security Architecture

Craig Heath

With

**Andy Harker, Geoff Preston, Jonathan Dixon,
Mark Shackman, Matthew Allen, Michael Bruce,
Phil Spencer, Simon Higginson, Will Palmer**

Reviewed by

**Andy Harker, Antti Vähä-Sipilä, Corinne Dive-Reclus,
Ilhan Gurel, Jo Stichbury, Jonathan Dixon, Kal Patel,
Matthew Allen, Phil Spencer, Sami Lehtisaari,
Stephen Mansfield, Steve Matthews, Tim Band,
Martin de Jode**

Head of Symbian Press
Phil Northam

Managing Editor
Freddie Gjertsen

John Wiley & Sons, Ltd

Other Wiley Editorial Offices

John Wiley & Sons Inc., 111 River Street, Hoboken, NJ 07030, USA

Jossey-Bass, 989 Market Street, San Francisco, CA 94103-1741, USA

Wiley-VCH Verlag GmbH, Boschstr. 12, D-69469 Weinheim, Germany

John Wiley & Sons Australia Ltd, 42 McDougall Street, Milton, Queensland 4064, Australia

John Wiley & Sons (Asia) Pte Ltd, 2 Clementi Loop #02-01, Jin Xing Distripark, Singapore
129809

John Wiley & Sons Canada Ltd, 22 Worcester Road, Etobicoke, Ontario, Canada M9W 1L1

Wiley also publishes its books in a variety of electronic formats. Some content that appears
in print may not be available in electronic books.

Library of Congress Cataloging-in-Publication Data:

Heath, Craig.
  Platform security : software development using the Symbian OS security
architecture / Craig Heath, with Andy Harker . . . [et al.].
     p. cm.
Includes bibliographical references and index.
ISBN-13: 978-0-470-01882-8
ISBN-10: 0-470-01882-8 (pbk. : alk. paper)
1. Computer networks – Security measures. 2. World Wide Web – Security
measures. I. Title.
TK5105.59.H43 2006
005.8 – dc22

                                                         2005031924

British Library Cataloguing in Publication Data

A catalogue record for this book is available from the British Library
ISBN-13: 978-0-470-01882-8 (PB)
ISBN-10: 0-470-01882-8 (PB)

Typeset in 10/12pt Optima by Laserwords Private Limited, Chennai, India
Printed and bound in Great Britain by Bell & Bain, Glasgow
This book is printed on acid-free paper responsibly manufactured from sustainable forestry
in which at least two trees are planted for each one used for paper production.

Dedicated to the memory of my mother,
Iris Heath, who passed away peacefully
on 30th December 2005 aged 89.

Contents

Part 2 Application Development for Platform Security   43

Part 3 Managing Platform Security Attributes 155

About This Book

Symbian Press is delighted to bring you this book documenting the fruits of Symbian's platform security project. The project has been in development for several years, and at last we have the opportunity to present the enhanced features of the Symbian OS security architecture in public.

Symbian OS Platform Security describes the philosophy of platform security as well as its implementation. It documents the mechanisms Symbian has implemented to protect phone integrity, to protect sensitive data, and to control access to sensitive operations.

This book describes the context and need for platform security on mobile devices and the concepts that underlie the Symbian OS security architecture, such as the core principles of 'trust', 'capability' and 'data caging'. It goes on to explain how to develop applications on a secure platform: the development environment, how to write secure applications, servers and plug-ins, and how to share data safely between devices. The book also clarifies the concepts of application certification and signing, the industry 'gatekeepers' of platform security. All of this information will be vital to those wishing to develop or port applications to mass-market phones based on Symbian OS v9.

The content of this book will be useful for developers involved with Symbian OS at all levels, from activities based around device creation, to the creators of applications for commercially available Symbian OS phones, to security specialists involved in mobile phone procurement or the design of mobile network services based on Symbian OS phones.

Foreword

Tim Wright
Security Technologies, Vodafone Research and Development

In the 10 years I have been working in the field of mobile phone security, we have seen a vast increase in the power and flexibility of the programming environment available on mobile phones, moving towards the openness of the PC and the Internet. Over that same period there have been attempts, not to close down the open environments of the PC and the Internet but, at the very least, to 'tame' them. This taming needed to happen and needs to continue.

Fortunately, the growth in the functionality and openness of mobile phones happened in a controlled manner, with many factors working in favor of security. Firstly, over this period most mobile phones were, and still are, bought by network operators (for sale on to their subscribers) who imposed security requirements that have kept implementation standards high. Secondly, most data coming in to and out of mobile phones involves a network operator, who has both the reason and the power to take steps on the network side to curb the effects of viruses and worms on the client side. Finally, there was the simple fact that Symbian OS phones represented a small percentage of the total mobile phone population.

Some of these factors are changing. Surely the most significant is that the percentage of mobile phones based on Symbian OS and other open operating systems is set to increase significantly. Symbian OS will become a serious and worthwhile target for writers of malware. The increasing variety of short-range and long-range wireless interfaces means that there are many ways for data and applications to get onto a phone and the proportion that operators can control will decrease. Symbian OS is entering a bigger and less controlled world and needs to be able to look after itself.

Vodafone, therefore, very much welcome Symbian's introduction of the platform security architecture. It is Vodafone's hope that effective certification schemes for application developers, continued scrutiny and improvement of the most trusted parts of the Symbian OS, and complementary hardware security features for boot-time and run-time protection of the secure software will be used alongside platform security and help to ensure its long term success. Symbian OS can then be opened up to a wider range of application developers with the assurance that privileges can be allocated to code on the basis of the responsibility the developers will take, and that users and their phones can be protected from poor code and malicious intent.

This book provides background to the platform security architecture, which will be of interest to security professionals, and guidance to application developers on how best to take advantage of the improved security now available. Widespread adoption of these practices will benefit the whole mobile phone industry, including software vendors, semiconductor vendors, phone manufacturers, network operators, content providers and, not least, the phone user!

About the Authors

Craig Heath, Lead Author

Craig has been working in IT security since 1988, holding positions at the Santa Cruz Operation as security architect for SCO UNIX, and at Lutris Technologies as security architect for the Enhydra Enterprise Java Application Server. He joined Symbian in 2002, working in product management and strategy.

A member of The Open Group Security Forum (originally the X/Open Security Working Group) since 1993, sitting on the Steering Committee since 1999, he has contributed to several published security standards. These include XBSS (baseline system security requirements), XDAS (distributed audit) and XSSO (single sign-on). He has also participated in standards work within POSIX, IETF, the Java Community Process, and the Open Mobile Alliance. He graduated from the University of Warwick with a BSc. in computer science in 1984.

Craig is co-author of *Security Design Patterns* (**www.opengroup. org/bookstore/catalog/g031.htm**) and lead author of The Open Group *Guide to Digital Rights Management* (**www.opengroup.org/bookstore/ catalog/g052.htm**).

Andy Harker

With an honors degree in Electronic Systems, Andy has spent the last 17 years working in the telecommunications software arena on projects as diverse as FDDI-2, mobile presence and availability systems, distributed real-time middleware, and optical switching.

He joined Symbian in 2002, and designed and developed the Digital Rights Management infrastructure (Content Access Framework). He is now a Senior Technical Architect in the Crypto Services technology area which provides cryptographic, key and certificate management, authentication and software installation services into Symbian OS.

In his spare time, Andy enjoys tinkering with 3D-graphics rendering. When he wants to get away from a keyboard completely, he looks after 400 liters of water – complete with tropical fish. Occasionally, he also visits bigger fish in their native habitat if he's lucky enough to be away diving with his partner Rebecca and his SCUBA buddies.

Geoff Preston

Geoff joined Symbian in 2000 from Vodafone to lead the Product Test organization. Following a move to Marketing, Geoff introduced Symbian's Catalyst program, working with a range of partners to develop compelling third-party applications on top of Symbian OS. Recently, Geoff and his team have developed and delivered the industry-leading certification program, Symbian Signed. Geoff's background in mobile telephony, network topologies and operations mean he is actively involved with Symbian's operating partners and related standards forums.

Geoff studied in Hull, then lived in the Middle East, Far East and North America working on a range of communications systems. Geoff joined Motorola to work on their new GSM infrastructure and then joined a small UK network operator (Racal–Vodafone) to launch their new GSM network.

Geoff lives in Wiltshire and is married to Anne with whom he has a daughter, Thea.

Jonathan Dixon

Jonathan has spent the last seven years working for Symbian developing software in a range of technology areas and roles. After spending two years developing Symbian's Bluetooth and infrared protocol stacks, he spent a period researching a redesign of the Socket Server architecture that subsequently debuted in Symbian OS v9. For two years he worked as a Senior Technical Consultant within Symbian's Professional Services department, helping Symbian's licensees to ship mobile phone products such as the Sony Ericsson P910i, and the Motorola A1000. In the last 15 months, he has been working as a System Architect with an instrumental role in realizing Symbian's Platform Security implementation.

Jonathan graduated with a first class MEng. in Information Systems Engineering from Imperial College, London. He is a keen skier and cyclist, and spends whatever time he can cycle-touring or on long distance journeys with his wife Emma, and their beloved tandem, Dobbin. Jonathan thanks Keith Robertson for giving him so much to write about, teaching him how to approach it, and then letting him get on with it.

Mark Shackman

Mark graduated with a first class honors degree in Computing Studies, followed by a Masters in Digital Systems and finally a Postgraduate

Certificate of Education. After six years of teaching and a spell at Morgan Stanley, he joined Psion Software in 1997 as a Technical Author working on SDK content and installation technologies.

After the formation of Symbian, Mark joined the Connectivity Engineering group, with sole responsibility for authoring, producing, delivering and supporting the Connectivity SDK. He also wrote a chapter in Symbian's first book, *Professional Symbian Programming*. In 2001, Mark moved to the Kits team, becoming Technical Architect shortly afterwards, with the responsibility of introducing both the new Package Manager Kit format and subsequently the Component-Based Releases.

Mark transferred to the Symbian Developer Network in 2004, providing technical support to developers in the form of presentations, papers, books and tools.

Mark thanks Stephen Mansfield for review comments and corrections, and both Stephen and Jonathan Dixon for providing technical advice and suggestions. Thanks also to Colin Turfus and the Symbian Developer Network team for their ongoing support and to Hashem for everything else.

Matthew Allen

Matthew started work over a quarter of a century ago using 6th Edition Unix on a minicomputer, and punched cards and JCL on a mainframe. He has been working at the leading edge of technology ever since. Before joining Symbian's Security team in 2003, he worked on projects as varied as directory enquiry systems, Unix kernel ports, free space optical links, distributed processing frameworks, SS7 call processing and compiler development.

Matthew studied at Robinson College, Cambridge, where he gained an MA.

Matthew would like to thank both his father for bringing him up and his wife for putting up with the result.

Michael Bruce

In 1996 Michael Bruce graduated with an honors degree in Mechanical Engineering from the University of New South Wales (Sydney, Australia). After several years working on process automation in the manufacturing sector he emigrated to the UK, joining Symbian's Networking team in 2002. Later, after moving to the Security Team, he was one of the developers involved in the implementation of the new Platform Security Software Install. Recently he has moved to Marketing and has been responsible for providing the tools required by Symbian Signed to support Symbian OS v9.

When Michael is not at work he enjoys traveling, preferably to somewhere with snow so that he can pursue his passion for skiing.

Phil Spencer

Phil's involvement with Symbian OS began with its predecessor, which powered the original Psion PDAs. As one of the most successful authors of Psion 'shareware' in the early 1990s, Phil took a work experience position at Psion Software during the summer of 1998. One year later, having finishing his A Levels, he accepted a job as a 'Developer Consultant' at the newly-formed Symbian during his 'year out' before university. Responsible for providing support, advice and guidance to third party developers, Phil decided to extend his 'year out' to two years, and eventually began his Economics degree at the London School of Economics in September 2000, whilst continuing to work for Symbian.

Phil graduated with a BSc. Econ. (Hons) in summer 2004 and returned full-time to Symbian to become Head of Developer Content, managing the team responsible for delivering the necessary documentation and support to make Symbian OS accessible to developers, and ensuring compelling and innovative applications are available for Symbian OS phones.

Phil currently lives in London and outside work his biggest interest is travel. Phil would like to thank his close colleagues at Symbian and the Symbian Press team not only for providing much support and amusement, but also for helping him to retain a small degree of sanity whilst juggling work and study at university!

Simon Higginson

Simon Higginson joined Symbian's Technical Training Team as a Senior Developer Consultant in 1999. He has helped author a number of training courses for Symbian OS, including, most recently, a platform security course. His experience covers 19 years in the IT industry, working as a software developer for GST Professional Services and then consultant for Origin Automation Technology on the Cambridge Science Park.

Simon started his computing career on the York University computer while at school; after which he went on to read Natural Sciences and Computer Science at Churchill College, Cambridge. While writing Chapter 2 of this book, Simon amazingly found time to stand for the UK Parliament, and thanks the people of King's Lynn for giving him time to finish the job, by electing someone else!

Will Palmer

Will started working for Symbian in June 2000; firstly as a developer in local synchronization to the PC, then moving into remote synchronization development implementing SyncML. He stayed in this field while progressing from programmer through Technical Lead to Technology Architect, and also gained experience of OMA Device Management as a related technology. He is currently a Systems Architect specializing in device and settings management.

Will studied Electronic Engineering at Oxford Polytechnic, before training as a C++ programmer. He worked for a telematics company that sells vehicle-tracking software – developing the PC client–server architecture and also software for in-vehicle hand-held devices – before moving to Symbian to further his interest in telecommunications.

Will liked to travel until family life got the better of him. He is now blessed with two young sons who have helped him hone the communication and negotiation skills he needs in his professional life.

Author's Acknowledgements

Craig would like to thank:

The Symbian OS platform security architects, in particular Corinne Dive-Reclus, Mal Minhas, Keith Robertson and Andrew Thoelke, who deserve the bulk of the credit for the features this book describes. Other contributors from Symbian who had a significant influence on the design include Will Bamberg, Jonathan Harris and Dennis May. Credit is also due to the many Symbian engineers who worked on the implementation, integration and testing who are too numerous to list individually.

Our partners and customers who contributed to the design, including from Nokia, Timo Heikkinen, Janne Uusilehto and Antti Vähä-Sipila; from Sony-Ericsson, Johan Alm; from UIQ, Matthias Reik; from Vodafone, Steve Babbage and Tim Wright; from France Telecom, Didier Bégay; and from Orange, Tim Haysom.

My co-authors, Matthew Allen, Michael Bruce, Jonathan Dixon, Andy Harker, Simon Higginson, Will Palmer, Geoff Preston, Mark Shackman, and Phil Spencer who did most of the hard work.

My manager, Richard Wloch, and my co-authors' managers', Tim Bentley, Bruce Carney, Simon Garth, and Neil Hepworth for allowing us to devote significant amounts of our work days to preparing this book.

Other contributors of material or insightful comments, including Tim Band, Ilhan Gurel, Sami Lehtisaari, Stephen Mansfield, Steve Mathews, Kal Patel and Jo Stichbury,

Last but not least, Phil Northam and Freddie Gjertsen for making the process of producing this book easy and putting up with many missed deadlines!

Symbian Press Acknowledgements

Symbian Press wishes to thank Craig for his perseverance; Stephen Evans for, once again, being beneficent when we asked, 'can we have more resources please'; the LBC for tying us to our desks; and William because he surely deserves a mention.

We would also not like to thank Spencer for his mastery of eye-rolling.

PART 1

Introduction to Symbian OS Platform Security

1

Why a Secure Platform?

by Craig Heath

1.1 User Expectations of Mobile Phone Security

Mobile phones are perceived somewhat differently from desktop PCs and laptops, although, from a technical point of view, a smartphone is actually a general-purpose computing device. Users of mobile phones have rather different expectations than PC users regarding their device's security and reliability.

A mobile phone is essentially a personal item. It is not typically shared with other family members, and the fact that it is carried around in your pocket leads to a higher degree of trust in it as a reliable and secure repository for your personal data. It *feels* secure, just knowing it's right there with you. However, contrary to this natural feeling of security, it may, in fact, be exposed to attacks via Bluetooth, Wi-Fi, GPRS or other network connections, even while it is sitting in your pocket.

To address this disparity of perception (without increasing the paranoia of mobile phone users to match their feelings regarding PCs, which would probably be damaging for the whole mobile phone industry), Symbian believes it should provide higher levels of mobile phone security to match customers' existing expectations. Mobile phone users don't expect, for example, to have to install anti-virus software on their phones after they buy them and, if the industry does its job properly, they won't need to.

Mobile phone users also have clear expectations regarding the reliability of their phones which differ substantially from PC standards. They expect to be able to place and receive voice calls at any time; they don't expect 'blue screens' (unrecoverable errors) and they don't expect to have to reboot their phone at all, let alone daily.

The purpose of a mobile phone is, primarily, to be a delivery point for network services, so users really don't care whether their calendar is stored on the phone or on a remote server, or indeed is synchronized between the two. One consequence of this 'blurring' between the device and the network is that people are generally comfortable with device settings being managed remotely (typically by the mobile network operator). We expect that the controversy regarding the control of the device that has surrounded the work of the Trusted Computing Group (or TCPA as it was formerly known), dubbed 'treacherous computing' in [Stallman 2002], is unlikely to be as significant an issue, if and when similar technology is applied to mobile phones.

Lastly, and certainly not least, users expect the behavior of their mobile phones to be predictable – they don't want nasty surprises on their bill at the end of the month. This is demonstrated by the fact that people pay more for pay-as-you-go phones or for flat-rate services – they will pay a premium for predictability of billing.

1.2 What the Security Architecture Should Provide

Bearing in mind the security expectations of the mobile phone user, let's consider what properties the phone needs in order to deliver those expectations.

1.2.1 Privacy

Privacy is a property that is preserved by systems that exercise a duty of confidentiality when handling all aspects of private information. Various kinds of private information may be held on a mobile phone, particularly contact details and calendar entries, but also such things as recording a call being placed and the parties involved in the call. The security architecture needs to ensure that private information is not disclosed to unauthorized parties. This is in order to prevent misuse, either directly, as in the recent case of the disclosure of the American celebrity Paris Hilton's address book, or, for example, by using contact numbers held on the phone to spread malware to other devices.

1.2.2 Reliability

Reliability is the property of a system that ensures that the system does not perform in unexpected ways. This is often closely related to availability, which is the ability of a system to be ready to operate whenever it's needed. The security architecture needs to contribute to this by protecting the integrity of critical system components and configuration settings, thus ensuring that they are not changed by unauthorized parties.

It is also worth mentioning, in passing, that apart from the specific security functionality that is discussed in detail later in this book, Symbian OS was designed to provide resilience in the face of errors occurring in application software. Interestingly, this design also helps in protecting against security problems due to deliberate misuse of system services. Resilience may also be referred to as 'survivability'.

1.2.3   Defensibility

In addition to the general properties of reliability, availability and resilience, further steps can be taken to help defend against attacks from malware, financial fraud (such as unauthorized use of premium-rate SMS numbers) and the use of the device to attack the network (for example, by sending malformed packets or floods of requests). The security architecture needs to subject such actions to specific controls, which can be used to prevent or limit damage to both customers and networks.

1.2.4   Unobtrusiveness

As far as a mobile phone user is concerned, any security architecture and components should be as invisible as possible. As previously noted, mobile phone users are less paranoid about, and thus more confident in, the security of their devices than are PC users. This is generally a Good Thing [Sellar and Yeatman 1930]. We know that the majority of mobile phone users would prefer not to be bothered with decisions and information about security, that they would rather that, like a car or TV, the phone 'just works'. The security architecture, therefore, needs to handle as much as possible without explicit user interaction.

1.2.5   Openness

Symbian OS is just one of the components (albeit quite an important one!) that goes in to making a mobile phone. Symbian is part of a larger ecosystem (the value chain is discussed in more detail in Section 1.4) and our success is interdependent with the success of other suppliers – providers of software and hardware components that integrate with our OS. Reducing the openness, by 'locking down' the OS and preventing third parties from implementing software to run on phones, might provide a good defense, but it could at the same time destroy much of the value of Symbian OS as a platform to both third parties and customers. The security architecture needs to be open, so that suppliers are able to add their own components, and compelling third-party applications are available.

1.2.6   Trustworthiness

Trustworthiness is an elusive concept, but in any discussion of trust, the first question to ask is: Who is being trusted by whom to do what? In the case of Symbian OS, very briefly, the device manufacturer is being trusted by the user and by network service providers to provide a device that preserves the first three properties discussed above: privacy, reliability and defensibility. Specific threats to these properties are covered later, but first let's consider how the security architecture contributes, in general, to the trustworthiness of the device.

For the past 10 to 15 years, a lot of effort in the computer security field has been devoted to securing network boundaries, on the principle that if you stop bad things happening at your network border, then you won't need to worry about the level of security being applied to individual devices within your network. However, today there are trends towards 'boundaryless information flow' (as promoted by The Open Group [Holmes 2002]) and 'deperimeterization' (a similar concept, espoused by the Jericho Forum [Simmonds 2004]). The consequence of these trends is that placing controls at the network boundary is becoming ineffective – and a perfect example of this problem is the mobile phone. Today's smartphone may have several different network connections active at any time (Wi-Fi, Bluetooth, GPRS, etc.). Some of those connections may be inside an enterprise's network boundary, and other connections outside, both at the same time; and the device itself is likely to be holding commercially confidential information. The device itself, therefore, must be trusted to protect the information on it, and act securely with the networks it connects to, according to a well-defined security policy.

We believe that this reliance on the security properties of an individual computing device represents something of a comeback for the concept of 'trusted computer systems' in the sense of the 'orange book' [United States Department of Defense 1985]. There is a substantial body of knowledge about the design of trusted computer systems and Symbian has taken advantage of it (see Chapter 2).

1.3   Challenges and Threats to Mobile Phone Security

Having considered user expectations of security and, at a high level, what the security architecture of a mobile phone should provide, we must ask ourselves: What specific challenges are posed by the nature and environment of the mobile phone, and what threats does the security architecture need to counter?

1.3.1   The Scale of the Problem

Let's first consider the potential scale of the problem – there are a lot of mobile phones out there. As we can see from Figure 1.1, the total number of mobile phone subscribers at the end of 2004 was roughly 1.7 billion. (For comparison, the number of PCs in use at that time was

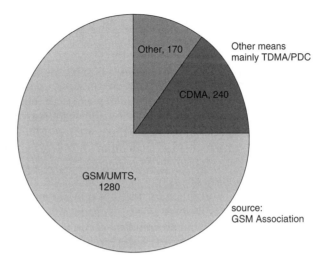

Figure 1.1   Global Mobile Phone Subscribers, Dec. 2004 (millions)

estimated at 820 million [Computer Industry Almanac 2005].) As a first approximation, we'll assume that each of these subscriptions represents one mobile phone. Figure 1.1 categorizes phones by the voice network technology used, but we need to consider categories of mobile phone based on their support for add-on software in order to consider security architecture requirements.

Table 1.1   Categories of Mobile Phone Platforms

Open OS (Native Execution)	Symbian OS Windows Mobile Palm OS
Layered Execution Environment	Java (including μITRON, Linux) BREW
Closed Platform	Proprietary real-time OS

The first category in Table 1.1 includes mobile phones that are based on an open operating system that allows execution of native binaries from third parties. This is probably the most attractive target for attackers because more public information is available regarding interfaces to these phones' system software and there are publicly available development kits for these devices which people can download and use to write software. These software development kits allow third parties to develop code that executes 'natively', in the same environment as the system software – this allows powerful and efficient add-on applications to be developed, but it does, at the same time, introduce a number of security concerns.

The second category in Table 1.1 includes phones that support lay-ered execution environments (that is, an execution environment that does not give third-party software direct access to native code). This category consists primarily of Java-capable phones using a variety of underlying plat-forms, including Nokia Series 40, in Japan μITRON (pronounced micro-eye-tron) and also, perhaps unexpectedly, Linux. The Linux phones that have appeared so far do not allow the execution of third-party native code; after-market applications for them are typically written in Java. We have also chosen to consider Qualcomm's BREW (Binary Run-time Environment for Wireless) platform in this category. It is hard to place in that, although it is an execution environment and not an operating system as such, it does allow third-party native code, but only under certain controlled circum-stances. Typically there are no public development kits available for phones in this category, but nevertheless security exploits have been reported – in October 2004 there was an exploit [Gowdiak 2004] demonstrated on a Nokia Series 40 phone which used a security vulnerability in the Java virtual machine to enable execution of arbitrary native code.

The third category in Table 1.1 includes all the rest – closed-platform mobile phones that don't allow third-party applications to be run on them. It is hard to create malware for this category, as for the second category, because the development tools are not available. Development tools do of course exist, but they are typically only used within the device man-ufacturers' facilities. Even without public availability of system interface information and development kits, such phones can still be vulnerable to denial of service attacks – for example, malformed SMS messages have been known to cause security problems for closed-platform phones.

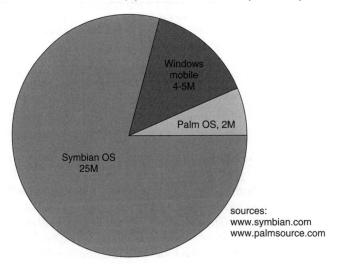

Figure 1.2   Open OS Mobile Phone Shipments up to December 2004

Let's consider in more detail the first category, open OS mobile phones.

Taking the numbers of units shipped up to the end of 2004, we see from Figure 1.2 that there were approximately 25 million mobile phones running Symbian OS. Although Microsoft does not release separate figures for Windows Mobile (sales are reported for all Windows CE devices, which includes PDAs and embedded systems), we estimate that there were somewhere between 4 and 5 million mobile phones shipped running Windows Mobile by the end of 2004. At the same time PalmSource's reported figures indicate that approximately 2 million mobile phones had been shipped running Palm OS.

The implication of this analysis is that, of the likely targets for mobile phone attackers, Symbian OS is the most attractive since it has the biggest target installed base and offers free public availability of interface documentation and development kits. Because of this, Symbian needed to take a lead in establishing a secure platform, while preserving the advantages of an open OS. Making it hard for third parties to write add-on applications for Symbian OS-based phones, although it might increase security, would be an unacceptable price to pay because it would limit access to markets.

1.3.2 Constraints on the Security Architecture

Mobile phones present some interestingly different challenges from typical desktop or server computer systems when implementing an effective security architecture.

Mobile phones are by their nature low-powered devices – low power in the sense of the speed or 'horsepower' of the processor and in the sense of minimizing the drain on the battery (to maximize talk and standby time). Because of this, there are not a lot of spare processor cycles available for any security checks that would introduce a run-time overhead. Even running such checks in otherwise idle processor time risks significantly decreasing the battery life (mobile phone software typically goes quiescent when not actively being used, which allows the processor to enter a power-saving mode).

Mobile phones also, typically, have limited storage, which discourages security solutions that might involve storing large databases of potentially relevant information such as virus signatures or certificate revocation lists. Although mobile phones with more storage are becoming available, our solution must be usable on lower-end devices, and the more storage that is free for user data, the better!

The possibilities for dialog with the user are also, typically, limited on a mobile phone – the screen is small and text entry may be slow and difficult by comparison with a PC monitor and keyboard. User prompts, therefore, have to be short and to the point and the security cannot depend on significant amounts of text entry such as pass-phrases.

To put it simply, you cannot afford to waste energy on anything.

1.3.3   The Challenge of Connectivity

As the technology of mobile phone networks develops and with the take-up of wireless LANs and other wireless short-link connection methods, mobile phones are increasingly being provided with many, potentially simultaneously active, data connections. Such connections include 3G/UMTS data (with speeds approaching that of typical domestic fixed broadband), 2.5G data (EDGE and GPRS), Wi-Fi (802.11b), Bluetooth and infrared. As mentioned previously, this multiplicity of connections is an example of the increasing ineffectiveness of controls at network boundaries. It is entirely possible that a modern phone could be communicating via Bluetooth to a company laptop on the company's internal network, while being directly connected to the internal network via a Wi-Fi LAN access point, and also accessing the Internet via the 3G phone network.

Each of those connections is a potential point of attack. In this example, Internet Protocol (IP) traffic is flowing over all the connections, so the mobile phone could potentially act as a gateway between the networks, bypassing firewalls and access controls that may be implemented only on the company's internal network. The security of the phone and the data on it must not depend on any particular connection that an attack may arrive on.

It's also worth noting here that it is in the nature of wireless connectivity to be unpredictable. Coverage can be lost altogether, or the actual physical network access point that you're connected to can change almost transparently when you're roaming – either going to another network cell or actually roaming to a different provider. The security architecture must not assume continuous connectivity. This is important when doing things such as revocation checks on digital signatures. It would be very annoying, for example, not to be able to install and play a game you had previously downloaded because you happen to be on the London Underground (which reportedly will not have mobile network coverage on the underground platforms until 2008) and, therefore, can't check a signature online with a Certificate Authority.

1.3.4   Malware and Device Perimeter Security

One of the most well-publicized security threats to open mobile phones is malware: trojans (malicious programs which masquerade as benign ones), worms (malicious programs which send copies of themselves to other devices) and viruses (malicious code which attaches itself to legitimate files and is carried along with them).

Malware targeting Symbian OS started to appear in June 2004 and over the following year we saw increasing numbers of new strains (13 in all). The first was Cabir, a worm that spreads via Bluetooth. It was stated by its authors to be a 'proof of concept', not intended to cause harm to mobile phone users, but to alert people to deficiencies in mobile phone security (Symbian's platform security project was well advanced by this point, so Symbian was well aware of the need for improved security without this reminder!) The worm's authors also released the source code, which resulted in many minor variants of the code being implemented and released 'into the wild'. One variant has been classified as a new strain (Mabir) as it includes the ability to spread via MMS messages as well as via Bluetooth.

We have also seen trojans such as Skulls, which appear to be harmless programs, however, when they are installed they corrupt configuration settings and cause legitimate applications to stop working. There has been, as of the time of writing, one virus, Lasco, which infects the installation files of legitimate applications.

One thing to note is that, thus far, none of this malware has been able to bypass the Symbian OS software install security controls. For the Cabir worm to infect a mobile phone, the user of the targeted phone has to explicitly acknowledge the three security-related dialogs shown in Figure 1.3.

Figure 1.3   Device Perimeter Security Prompts

The user first has to acknowledge that they want to receive this Bluetooth message; then, because the installation file is not signed by a trusted authority the user is warned that the source of the software cannot be verified; lastly, the user is presented with the name of the application (or of the malware, in this case) and has to confirm that they do want to install it. We call this the 'perimeter security' for the actual device itself – in order to get executable content on to the device you have to go through this install phase.

Perimeter security has been a feature of Symbian OS since the early versions, but it is not the complete answer to malware. Even though the user is required to make a deliberate, conscious step to allow malware to install itself on their phone, it is still found to some extent in the wild. Ed Felten of Princeton University is well known for saying, 'Given a choice between dancing pigs and security, users will pick dancing pigs every time' [McGraw and Felten 1999], and indeed why shouldn't they? Users are entitled to expect their mobile phones to help them defend against malicious attacks, and most people have no desire to become security experts.

We have not yet seen an explosive spread of mobile phone malware, certainly nothing on the scale of worms such as Code Red and Sasser in the PC world, and we have some reason to believe that we never will. The need for user confirmation before software installation significantly limits the rate of spread, and, referring back to the figures on the number of mobile phones in use, at the end of 2004 something less than 2% of all mobile phones were running Symbian OS, so, if you picked a random target, it probably wouldn't be susceptible. Nevertheless, the percentage of phones running Symbian OS will increase in future, and there is a risk of flaws in the device perimeter security which could be exploited, so Symbian's platform security architecture is designed to minimize risk from malware even after it has succeeding in installing onto the mobile phone.

1.4   How Symbian OS Platform Security Fits into the Value Chain

Having considered the high-level goals of our platform security architecture and reviewed the major challenges facing us, it is worth spending a little time considering how developers actually deliver something into the hands of the mobile phone user. There are several kinds of organization that contribute to the development of a mobile phone product, creating a 'value chain', and, as we have previously noted, there is significantly more to the user experience than the product delivered in the box by the device manufacturer – the phone is an end point for network services and a repository for after-market content. Symbian, as an OS vendor, has a crucial part to play in providing the building blocks to construct a secure solution, but it can't solve all the problems on its own.

All of the links in the value chain shown in Figure 1.4 have a part to play.

The OS vendor, their technology partners and the device manufacturer need to work together on improving platform security in the construction of a device. The OS and the device hardware need to be tightly integrated with technology from specialist security suppliers, such as anti-virus and firewall vendors, to make these components work effectively together and minimize the risk of things being overlooked.

After-market software vendors, content providers and content distributors – although not contributing to the mobile phone as it is sold to the user – still have an important part to play in building the user's trust in the security of the platform. In particular, the use of digital signatures helps to demonstrate that the supplier of the software, or other content, is willing to stand behind the quality and security of what they are delivering. There are several signing programmes for mobile phone software now

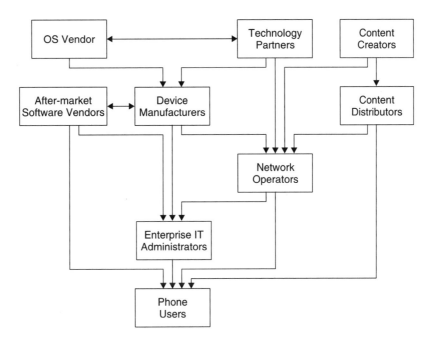

Figure 1.4   The Mobile Phone Value Chain

in place (we will discuss the Symbian Signed program in more detail in Chapter 9). The more content providers and software vendors that take advantage of these to promote trustworthy channels for distributing content to phones, the more unusual it will be for the user to get security warning dialogs appearing on their phones, with the desired result that mobile phone users will pay much more attention to such dialogs when they do appear.

Enterprise IT administrators and network operators also need to be contributing to mobile phone security; they can provide infrastructure for managing security on the devices, particularly for application lifecycle management: provisioning, updates, revocation, patching and so on.

Lastly, end users also have a part to play. Whilst the industry should resist the temptation to assign responsibility to the end user as a 'cop out', it does need to educate mobile phone users to take reasonable precautions in their own interest. They should be very careful when they receive software they weren't expecting (it is instructive to note that the advice regarding the original Trojan horse, 'beware of Greeks bearing gifts' [Virgil 19BCE], still applies 2000 years later to software trojan horses – be suspicious of unexpected deliveries). Users should also recognize that regular backups are prudent in anticipation of physical harm to their phone. It seems that there have been more mobile phones dropped down toilets [Miller 2005] than have been disabled by malware!

1.4.1 Security as a Holistic Property

We can also look at the shared responsibilities for providing security in another, more theoretical, way (see Figure 1.5).

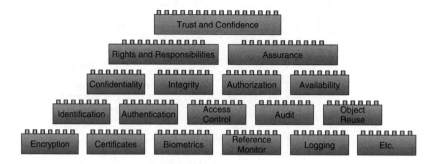

Figure 1.5 Security Building Blocks

The ultimate aim of a secure system is to give rise to trust and confidence on the part of the system's owners and users that clear security policies are being enforced. A common mistake is to look at one or more of the foundation blocks in Figure 1.5, and to assume that, if one of those security features is implemented, the system's security is, therefore, improved. This will only be the case if that feature is integrated into the system as a whole in such a way that it supports one or more of the security functions above it; which in turn gives rise to a system security quality above that; which contributes either to the enforcement of defined rights and responsibilities or the assurance that such enforcement is effective; which then, finally, promotes trust and confidence in the system. Put briefly, security is a *holistic* property; it is more than the sum of its parts (or, if done badly, rather less than the sum of its parts).

Let's work through a specific example: we want the mobile phone user to have confidence that their contacts data will not be disclosed to unauthorized parties. We might decide that a good way to do this would be to encrypt the contacts database. However, this in itself doesn't achieve anything because, if the attacker can get the encryption key, then they can still get the data. The encryption key needs to be protected by an access control mechanism that restricts access to it; which, in turn, must be part of an authorization mechanism that decides which entities should be allowed that access. The authorization mechanism needs to enforce defined rights and responsibilities. For example, a network server could have the right to access contact data for synchronization on the understanding that it has the responsibility for protecting that data when it is stored off the phone. Finally, the security policy being followed by the network server should be clearly expressed to the users, so that they have confidence in using the service.

To provide security in this holistic way, all of the components of the system (and for mobile phones this includes after-market software and network services) need to be cooperating.

1.4.2   Security Incident Detection and Response

Much of this chapter has focused on technology and behavior that is intended to prevent or mitigate security problems. As Bruce Schneier eloquently argues in [Schneier 2000], prevention is only the first part of the story; we also need to look at detection and response because prevention is never 100% effective.

The first person to notice that something is going wrong is likely to be the mobile phone user and they will probably refer the problem to the mobile network operator first, as the problem may appear as unexpected behavior of the network services, or, perhaps, a billing anomaly. From this point we need to ensure that the report gets to the correct party as quickly as possible. Security incident-handling processes are well established for server systems: US-CERT was founded in 1988 at the Carnegie Mellon Software Engineering Institute, and does a fine job of coordinating reports of security incidents and the response from various vendors in the server value chain. At the time of writing, the scale of security incidents for mobile phones is much smaller, but the industry would probably benefit in future from a similar body, providing independent coordination of security issues for mobile phones.

There are two aspects to responding to a security problem. The first is repairing the defect (assuming there is one) which led to the problem. This could, potentially, be a very large-scale operation; there could easily be 10 million phones in use that are running a particular system build which needs a software patch. Over-the-air patching of the system image on the phone may well be the most effective way to do this, but we need to make sure that this process itself is secure. There is a danger in introducing such functionality, in that it might actually create more problems than it solves by opening up a way to bypass the security controls implemented on the mobile phone and replace critical parts of the operating system.

The second aspect of response is recovery. Once the cause of the security incident has been addressed, how will the user's data and services be returned to operation? An important part of this is the ability to recover from configuration problems, which could also arise from non-malicious hardware or software failures, or 'user error'. In order to address this, we recommend that mobile phones should be capable of a 'hard reset', or being booted in a 'safe mode'. In the case where user data has been lost, there should be an easy way to recover it; again this is not just an issue for security problems – many mobile phones are lost and many are physically broken. As we've already suggested, the typical mobile phone user won't care where their data is actually stored – on the phone, on a server, or mirrored between the two – as long as they can get a replacement phone and still have their old data on it. Over-the-air synchronization or backup of the user data from the phone, without user intervention, may well be the best way of achieving this, and may be an additional service.

1.5 How Application Developers Benefit from the Security Architecture

There is a risk that the security features we are discussing in this book could be perceived as an inconvenience rather than as a benefit, particularly from the perspective of an application developer, who will have more things to worry about as a consequence of them. As we have discussed, the primary beneficiary of these security improvements is intended to be the mobile phone user, but it is important to highlight several benefits that they bring specifically to the application developer.

Firstly, by increasing the users' trust and confidence in open OS mobile phones the entire value chain should benefit. Users will be more willing to install after-market software when they have some assurance that they are protected from the worst effects of malware. They will be inclined to buy more after-market software and will appreciate the benefits of open OS mobile phones more. Thus they will buy more of these phones in preference to closed-platform phones or those with layered execution environments, creating a bigger market for after-market software – a 'virtuous circle'.

Secondly, the 'least privilege' aspects of the platform security architecture (see Section 2.4) mean that any unintentional defects in add-on applications (such as a buffer overflow) are less likely to result in serious security vulnerabilities, thus protecting the reputation of the application developer.

Thirdly, the platform security architecture means that security services can be provided in an open way, avoiding 'security by obscurity'. Symbian hopes that this will promote 'best of breed' security services to be provided by the platform and by specialist security vendors to add-on applications, thus avoiding duplication of effort and allowing developers to concentrate on their own areas of expertise.

2

Platform Security Concepts

by Simon Higginson

2.1 Background Security Principles

There's nothing new under the sun

Symbian has a long history of reuse – Symbian OS came from Psion, along with core staff. In addition, the object-oriented software in the operating system encourages reuse – so it should be no surprise that, when Symbian set about improving the security of its platform, the project team included people with a great deal of security experience and drew heavily on design principles firmly established in the field of computer science and already implemented in other systems. This background section outlines those tried-and-tested design principles, before we go on to describe in detail the main concepts in the Symbian OS platform security model. If you prefer to skip the background, you can turn to Section 2.3 where we begin describing how the platform security model is actually implemented.

2.1.1 Reference Monitor

The concept of 'a **reference monitor** which enforces the authorized access relationships between subjects and objects of a system' was first introduced by [Anderson 1972], who wrote that a reference monitor must have three features:

- The reference validation mechanism must be tamper-proof.

- The reference validation mechanism must always be invoked.

- The reference validation mechanism must be small enough to be subject to analysis and tests, the completeness of which can be assured.

Symbian OS has a micro-kernel that undertakes the role of the reference monitor. The combination of the computer hardware, the security kernel, and other highly-privileged OS components together make up the Trusted Computing Base (TCB) – the portion of the system responsible for enforcing security restrictions.

2.1.2   Protection Mechanism Design Principles

According to [Saltzer and Schroeder 1975], there are eight design principles that apply to protection mechanisms:

1. **Economy of mechanism:** keep the design small and simple, enabling easier verification, such as line-by-line examination, of software that implements the protection mechanism. Symbian has adopted this by only fully trusting a subset of Symbian OS (the TCB) which is small enough to be effectively code-reviewed. The TCB is described in detail in Section 2.3.2.

2. **Fail-safe defaults:** decisions are based on permission and, by default, software has no permission. The permissions to carry out particular services can be called privileges – software built for Symbian OS by default has no privileges; procedures are in place to ensure that privileges can be granted to suitably trustworthy software. These procedures, including 'Symbian Signed', are described in Chapter 9.

3. **Complete mediation:** access permission to a protected object must always be checked, and any temptation to cache decisions for performance reasons must be examined skeptically. Symbian OS provides this architecture in the client–server framework, described in Chapter 5.

4. **Open design:** security should not depend on keeping the mechanisms secret – such secrets are difficult to keep, and forego the benefits of others reviewing the design. This principle was first stated by Auguste Kerckhoffs [1883]. Symbian's design is open – you're reading about it!

5. **Separation of privilege:** a protection mechanism that requires two keys to unlock it is better than one requiring only one key. This is not universally applicable, but there are cases where requiring two competent authorities to approve something is beneficial. The ability to require software to have more than one signature in order to be granted privileges is described in Chapter 8.

6. **Least privilege:** a program should operate with the smallest set of privileges that it requires to do the job for which it has permission. This reduces the risk of damage through accident or error. This is similar to a military 'need to know' rule, which provides the best chance

of keeping a secret by disclosing it to as few parties as possible. Least privilege is achieved in Symbian OS by controlling privileges using several distinct 'capabilities' (introduced in Section 2.1.3). The different tiers of trust this enables are outlined in Section 2.3.1 and the rules for assigning capabilities are covered in Section 2.4.5.

7. **Least common mechanism:** the amount of common services, used by multiple programs, should be kept to a minimum because each provides the potential for a leak of information between programs. In Symbian OS, the best example of 'common services' may be shared libraries (DLLs, or Dynamically-Linked Libraries). The rules for the loading of DLLs, covered in Section 2.4.5, ensure that a privileged process cannot use a shared library which is less trustworthy than itself.

8. **Psychological acceptability:** the user interface must be easy to use and fit in with what the user might expect to be reasonable security concerns. Symbian OS provides for security-related prompts at the point when software is installed and tries to minimize security prompts when a service is actually being used, to avoid the user dropping into a routine that could lead to an ill-advised choice. The choices presented, determined by the privileges that may be granted, have been designed to be readily understood, e.g. whether the user wants to let the program make a phone call. Those privileges designed to be understood by users are covered in Section 2.4.4.

2.1.3 Capability-Based Security Model

[Dennis and Van Horn 1966], in a paper discussing the challenges of multi-tasking and multi-user computer systems, proposed a mechanism for 'protection of computing entities from unauthorized access'. They introduced the notion of each process in the system having a '**capability list**' determining which protected resources it can access, and what are its access rights. In their example (protected memory segments) each capability includes both a reference (or pointer), allowing the segment to be addressed, and the respective access rights granted to the process.

Following that influential paper, the concept of a capability-based security model has been somewhat broadened (the original model is sometimes referred to as the 'object capability model' for clarity). We consider the essential characteristics of a capability to be that it is something which is a persistent attribute of a process, that it is pre-determined when that process is created and that it completely defines the access rights of that process to a protected resource (no other rules need to be consulted at the point at which the resource is accessed).

The role in Symbian OS of a capability permitting a process privileged access to a protected system operation is described in Section 2.4.

2.2   Architectural Goals

Symbian set a number of architectural goals for the platform security project. This section explains each of these goals.

2.2.1   Ensure Understandability

When exposed to the security model, the phone user should be able to understand it.

It is well understood by security professionals that the most vulnerable parts of a security system are its human users. A security system that baffles the user is likely to lead to unintentional security vulnerabilities – if a user is confused or just doesn't understand, then that user is going to do a risky thing at some point. To minimize this problem, Symbian's goal was to identify a small number of things that the user could clearly understand and make simple choices about, and to hide the rest.

This has been quite a challenge, as it is a strong temptation for a system designer to leave difficult questions to the user, on the basis that the users will be the ones facing the risk, and therefore they should make the decision. Although from a strictly logical viewpoint this is reasonable, it neglects the inevitable fact that most users won't understand, and don't want to learn about, security terminology.

Consider the sorts of prompts that users of PC web browsers see. 'This page contains both secure and non-secure items. Do you want to download the non-secure items?' Is there a right answer to that? When would a user want to say 'Yes' or 'No'? What does 'non-secure' mean? Is this prompt coming up simply because the web-browser designer couldn't decide what to do, or is it allowing the user to make a meaningful choice? The characteristics of mobile phones, such as limited screen size and limited input methods, only make such complicated dialogs an even worse user experience.

2.2.2   Support Open Phones

Enhanced platform security should not prevent third parties from producing exciting software for Symbian OS.

Symbian firmly believes that the mobile phone market will flourish when software for the phones flourishes, just as in the 1980s the PC market flourished because of the wide range of software that many developers wrote for it. PCs were open devices – third parties could write and sell software for them. Symbian wants the phone market to grow and believes that the key to this is innovation through an open software development environment.

During the design and implementation of this platform security architecture, Symbian has constantly kept in mind the goal to minimize the impact on third-party developers. There are some inevitable effects, often resulting from the difficulty of distinguishing between legitimate, well-intentioned developers and authors of malware. We hope you will agree that Symbian has introduced mechanisms and infrastructure which allow legitimate developers to continue to produce compelling add-on software while helping to avoid 'bad apples' spoiling things for everyone.

2.2.3 Protect the Network

The network infrastructure should not be at risk from open phones.

Many network operators have taken an understandably cautious approach to promoting mobile phones on their networks that are open to third-party software developers, due to the risks of malware and so on. Symbian's goal is to provide mechanisms that ensure untrustworthy software is not able to affect adversely the network itself or other devices on that network, so that network operators can realize the benefits of open-OS mobile phones, such as easy deployment of new services to mobile phones in the field, without being exposed to undesirable risks as a consequence.

2.2.4 Provide a Lightweight Security Model

The model should be secure, but be so in a lightweight way.

This means that run-time performance should not be noticeably worsened and software should not be much more demanding of scarce silicon resources. Similarly, the new features should not overly affect the end-user's interaction with their mobile phone, or adversely impact on developers.

Naturally there is extra software, some APIs have had to be changed and various parts of the system architecture have been redesigned. There is an impact on developers and Symbian OS v9 is not binary- or source-compatible with earlier versions. However, changes that need to be made to add-on software are not extensive.

To minimize the impact on performance, Symbian OS only makes security checks where necessary to ensure the integrity of the system and protect sensitive services (this encompasses approximately 40% of all Symbian OS APIs) and the use of capabilities means that the access rights of processes are computed in advance, rather than every time a decision needs to be made.

2.2.5   Provide a Basis for Trust

Replace a trusting relationship with a trustworthy one.

In Chapter 1, we mentioned trust and confidence as separate but related concepts. Trust is about relationships – someone trusts someone else to do (or not do) something. The act of trusting someone is separate from having confidence that they will do as you expect, but such confidence would make you more likely to be willing to trust them. Confidence means they are trustworthy. The following example illustrates this.

If you give a stranger in the street some money to go and buy a loaf of bread for you, you trust them to do so and to bring you back the bread and the change. What's to stop them taking your money and never being seen again? This might make you think twice about giving them the money in the first place.

If, instead, the person is well known to you, is of good character, and has reliably carried out this service for you before, then you've no problem with asking them to do this. There is an established basis – you know the person is worthy of your trust.

The same concepts apply to computer systems in general and mobile phones in particular. The industry hopes that users will trust the phone and the network services to spend their money and to look after their private information. Symbian's goal is to provide mechanisms and infrastructure which increase mobile phone users' confidence in a Symbian OS phone's ability to do reliably just that.

2.3   Concept 1: The Process is the Unit of Trust

There are three concepts, which are the foundation of Symbian OS platform security architecture. This section looks at the first: what is the unit of trust? In other words, what is the smallest thing about which Symbian OS can make a decision regarding its trustworthiness?

2.3.1   Tiers of Trust

A mobile phone tends to be used by one person only – this is particularly true of 'smart' phones which hold personal information such as contact details and calendar entries. The design of Symbian OS assumes this – for example there's only one contacts book; there is no second contacts book for the owner's spouse for when they borrow the phone. If you've got a phone that's shared between members of a team at work, it's not likely to be used for much other than phoning the boss.

Because Symbian OS has been designed as a single-user operating system, there's no concept of logging on to the phone with a username and password. You can (and probably should) use a PIN to lock the phone when it's not being used, but once that's entered you're in control of everything. Given that there is only one user, this simplifies the security model. There is no need for access control lists, which specify which of a number of users may access a particular file stored on the phone. This helps towards the architectural goal of a lightweight security model.

The security system does not need to concern itself with whether the phone's user is trustworthy – if they're able to use the phone, they're implicitly authorized to do so. It does, however, need to concern itself with the trustworthiness of the processes that are running on the phone on behalf of the user, which may include various programs downloaded to, or otherwise installed on, the phone after it has left the shop. Such programs might perform operations that spend money or affect the way the phone or network operates.

Symbian's platform security architecture has been designed to control what a process can do. A process is only able to carry out activities for which it has the appropriate privileges. How these privileges are assigned will be covered shortly. But the important point to note here is that, without a specific privilege, Symbian OS will not let a process carry out a requested service which requires that particular privilege (on the grounds that it is not considered trustworthy enough).

Let's consider what a process is. In Symbian OS, a process has at least one thread of execution and it has resources, particularly physical blocks of memory controlled by a Memory Management Unit (MMU) in the hardware. The process is the unit of memory protection; the hardware raises a processor fault if access is made to an address not in the virtual address space of the process. This hardware-assisted protection is what provides the basis of the software security model. Symbian OS can trust a process not to access directly any other virtual address space – the hardware won't let it. For the same reason, the process's own virtual address space is private to it – no other process can access it because the hardware won't let it. The part of the operating system that controls the MMU hardware directly, therefore, has ultimate control. Naturally, there also have to be mechanisms for somehow sharing data between processes and inter-process communications – these operations are managed by the operating system kernel, and we will cover how security is provided for them later in this book (see Chapter 7).

The trusted computing platform that is Symbian OS consists of the Trusted Computing Base (TCB), the Trusted Computing Environment (TCE), other signed software and the rest of the platform. In broad terms there are four corresponding tiers of trust that apply to processes running on a Symbian OS phone, ranging from completely trustworthy to completely untrustworthy. This is shown in Figure 2.1.

What does it mean for Symbian OS to decide the trustworthiness of a process? As we mentioned in Chapter 1, the user and the network service provider trust the mobile phone manufacturer to provide a phone, that

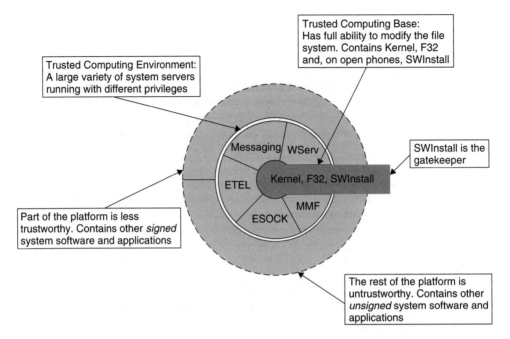

Figure 2.1   Tiers of Trust

preserves privacy, reliability and defensibility. The user will be judging the trustworthiness of the manufacturer (or perhaps the network operator, if it's an operator-branded model) at the time they buy the phone, probably based mainly on the brand reputation, or perhaps their previous experience with phones from the same manufacturer. The manufacturer, in turn, will judge the trustworthiness of software installed on the phone based primarily on where it comes from, but also potentially on testing or other evaluation of the software. For software that is supplied in the phone's read-only media (typically flash ROM), this trustworthiness is recorded directly, based on internal quality assurance processes. For add-on software, this trustworthiness is indicated by a digital signature. The mechanisms for checking this signature and assigning appropriate privileges are covered in Chapter 8. The phone manufacturer determines which authorities they will trust to determine the trustworthiness of add-on software for them, and configures the phone appropriately. Such authorities will typically include the manufacturer themselves, potentially the network operator, and probably also a common signing program for third parties, such as Symbian Signed, covered in Chapter 9.

In Symbian OS, there are now two new identifiers associated with each executable binary file (EXE) – the 'secure identifier' (SID) and the 'vendor identifier' (VID). SIDs are required to be present and unique for each EXE on the device (this is similar in intention to the existing UID3 identifier, which is in fact the default value for the SID if one is not explicitly specified). There is a protected range of SIDs, which may be used to make security decisions; EXEs are only permitted to use SIDs in this range if they are signed by a trusted authority. VIDs are not required to be unique (the intention is that multiple EXEs from a single source would share the same value); they also may only be used if the EXE is signed by a trusted authority. More practical details on these special identifiers are given in Chapter 3.

The unit of protection remains the process; Symbian rejected allowing a program to link to a DLL whose code ran with different capabilities, or indeed allowing one thread to run with different capabilities from another in the same process. The principle of least privilege may have suggested permitting these; however a protection system not built on top of the fundamental hardware-assisted OS mechanism would have been very cumbersome and expensive. Malicious code could in such cases modify any data including function pointers, thereby perverting the path of execution and services accessed. Consequently many plug-in architectures have changed, including applications which, as described in Chapter 3, are now built as stand-alone programs.

2.3.2   The Trusted Computing Base (TCB)

The Trusted Computing Base, or TCB, is the most trusted part of Symbian OS, as it controls the lowest level of the security mechanisms and has the responsibility for maintaining the integrity of the system. The first protection mechanism design principle in Section 2.1.2 states the design should be small and simple, and therefore our TCB is as small as possible, in order to support this level of trust.

The TCB includes the operating system kernel, which looks after the details of each process, including the set of privileges assigned to it. The file server (F32) is also included in this tier because it is used to load program code to make a process. The process's privilege information is established in the kernel during this loading activity. Some Symbian OS phones are 'closed', that is they do not support installation of native add-on software; on such a closed phone, the kernel, including the kernel-side device drivers, and the file server are the only fully-trusted components. On an 'open' phone, the software installer (SWInstall) is also part of the most-trusted group. This is the program that runs when you install files from a Symbian OS Software Install Script (SIS) file package. It extracts the files from the package (for example, program binaries) and it has the important role of validating the privileges requested for the program binaries against a digital signature on the installation package. Note that most user libraries are not included in the TCB – only those few which need to be used by the file server or software installer are given the highest level of trust.

The kernel, the file server process and the software installer have been carefully checked to ensure they behave properly and are considered completely trustworthy. They therefore run with the highest level of privilege of any processes on the phone. We should note here that strictly speaking the TCB also includes the phone hardware, including the MMU and other security-related hardware features; however, we will not be dwelling on that in this book as the hardware is not supplied by Symbian.

Figure 2.1 deliberately does not show the TCB as the center of a set of onion rings. First, although the kernel might normally be thought of as occupying this position, some of its services are available to all processes; secondly, the file server, rather like other servers, is both a client of the kernel and available to other processes; and thirdly, the software installer is shown stretching to the outer perimeter because it acts as the gatekeeper for the phone.

2.3.3   The Trusted Computing Environment (TCE)

The Trusted Computing Environment, or TCE, consists of further trusted software provided in the mobile phone by Symbian and others such as the UI platform provider and the phone manufacturer. This code is still judged to be *trustworthy*, but need not run with the highest level of privilege in order to get its job done, so it can be less *trusted* than TCB code. TCE code usually implements a system server process – failure of one server should not threaten the integrity of the operating system itself: the kernel can restart the server and maintain that integrity. Each server has limited privileges to carry out a defined set of services. By not granting all privileges to all servers, Symbian OS limits the threat exposed by any flaw in, or corruption of, a server. By requiring servers to have certain privileges, it is possible to limit access to sensitive low-level operations to selected servers and, thereby, prevent misuse of these operations by other processes.

For example, the window server has privileged access to the screen hardware but has no need to access the phone network; the telephony server (ETEL) has privileged access to the communications device driver but does not need access to the screen. The TCB controls access to the low-level operations (such as access to the screen hardware or to the communications device driver) and ensures that only the appropriately-privileged TCE components are able to perform them. The TCE components (such as the window server or the telephony server) then provide services to software outside the TCE, which is unable to perform directly the low-level operations.

2.3.4   Signed Software

It is possible to install software that adds to or modifies components in the TCB or TCE, but only if that software is signed by a trusted authority and that authority is permitted to grant the necessary privileges. Most add-on software will, however, be outside the TCE.

Even though such software is not part of the TCE, it may still need certain privileges in order to use services provided by the TCE. One example of this is access to network services, such as opening a network socket. The socket server (ESOCK) is part of the TCE, and handles the low-level operations on the network interface. A program that wishes to open a network socket requests the socket server to do so on its behalf (the program is not able to control the network interface directly). The socket server will only honor that request if the program has been granted the appropriate privilege – we don't want to provide free access to network sockets to software that is completely untrustworthy; it might, for example, be malware trying to attack the network or other devices.

Signed software outside the TCE can be less trustworthy than software within it. When an authority is deciding whether to sign a program to allow it, for example, to open network sockets, the assurance (testing the program, checking the *bona fides* of the developer, and so on) does not need to be as strict as it would be for software that is inside the TCB or TCE. This is because such software is less trusted – it is not allowed to affect the integrity of the system or to access sensitive low-level operations.

2.3.5 Unsigned Software

With unsigned software, or indeed signed software if it has not been signed by one of the trusted authorities (as configured in the mobile phone), the system has no basis for determining its trustworthiness and so it is therefore *untrusted*. This does not necessarily mean that the software is evil or worthless – there are many useful operations that can be performed on a mobile phone that do not require privileges, because they do not have any security consequences. A solitaire game, for example, would not need to perform any actions that access user-sensitive data or system-critical data and services. Such software can be installed and run on the phone without needing a signature (at least not for security purposes – a signature may still be useful to give users confidence in the quality of the signed software). In effect, unsigned software is 'sandboxed' – it can run, but it is not trusted and thus can't perform any security-relevant operations.

2.4 Concept 2: Capabilities Determine Privilege

The second concept underpinning the Symbian OS platform security architecture is the privilege model – each process carries along with it capabilities which determine what sensitive operations it can perform.

2.4.1   Capability Definition

> *A token [is] usually an unforgeable data value (sometimes called a 'ticket')*
> *that gives the bearer or holder the right to access a system resource.*
> *Possession of the token is accepted by a system as proof that the holder has*
> *been authorized to access the resource named or indicated by the token.*
> [Shirey 2000]

A capability is a token that needs to be presented in order to gain access
to a system resource. In Symbian OS, these system resources take the
form of services provided via an API – different APIs may require different
capabilities to gain access to restricted services, for example, functions
provided by a server or device driver, or data such as system settings.
Possessing a capability indicates that the process is trusted not to abuse
resources protected by that capability.

In the earlier parts of this chapter we have used the term 'privileged' to
describe software that has authority to carry out a restricted operation that
provides access to sensitive system resources. Symbian OS platform security is built around using capabilities to represent these access privileges.
Executable code can have no capabilities or it can have a collection
of capabilities. The kernel holds a list of capabilities for every running
process. A process can ask the kernel to check the capabilities of another
process before deciding whether to carry out a service on its behalf.

Symbian OS defines 20 capabilities, aligned with specific privileges.
This number is a balance between reducing the number of capabilities
and hence reducing complexity ('economy of mechanism', 'psychological
acceptability') and increasing the number of capabilities giving a fine
degree of control ('least privilege'). One extreme would be having just one
capability to authorize everything (similar in scope to the UNIX 'superuser'
model) whereas the other extreme would be a different capability for
every protected API (over 1000!) As we have identified four tiers of trust
(see Section 2.3.1), we need at least three different capabilities in order
to distinguish between them. In fact Symbian has chosen to define a few
more than that, to provide some separation between the privileges of
different TCE components and to subdivide privileges granted either by
the user or by a signing authority.

Symbian OS supports three broad categories of capabilities: one capability only possessed by the TCB itself, other system capabilities and,
finally, user capabilities. This is illustrated in Figure 2.2. For add-on
software, the software installer, acting as gatekeeper, validates that the
program is authorized to use the capabilities with which the executable
code was built, and will refuse to install software that does not have the
correct authorization (digital signature).

Capabilities are *discrete* and *orthogonal*. This means they are not
a hierarchical set of access tokens, with each one adding more and
more privileges until reaching the level of the TCB. Instead, any protected

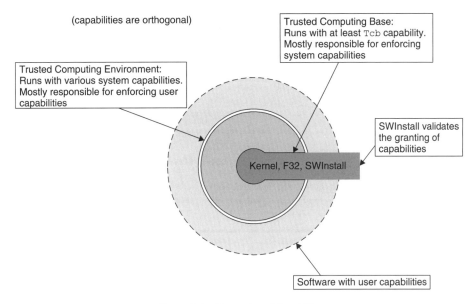

Figure 2.2 Categories of Capability

resource will be controlled by just one specific capability, and any process accessing that resource, even including TCB processes, must possess that specific capability in order for the access to succeed; in other words, capabilities do not overlap. It is also worth noting here that different operations may require different capabilities even if those operations are implemented using APIs within the same Symbian OS component – for example, different capabilities may be required depending on whether the data being accessed is considered to be user data or system data, even if it is stored using the same mechanism.

2.4.2 TCB Capability

The TCB runs with maximum privilege, in that it is granted all capabilities. As there are some things that TCB code must be able to do that nothing else can (such as creating new executables), there is one capability which is only given to TCB code: this capability is called 'Tcb', logically enough. Processes with this capability can create new executables and set the capabilities which will be assigned to them. As this could be used by malware to create and then run another executable with any capability it wanted, Tcb capability is very much the 'keys to the castle', and therefore it should only be granted to add-on software in strictly controlled circumstances.

2.4.3 System Capabilities

The largest group of capabilities is the system capabilities. The granting of a system capability allows a process to access sensitive operations,

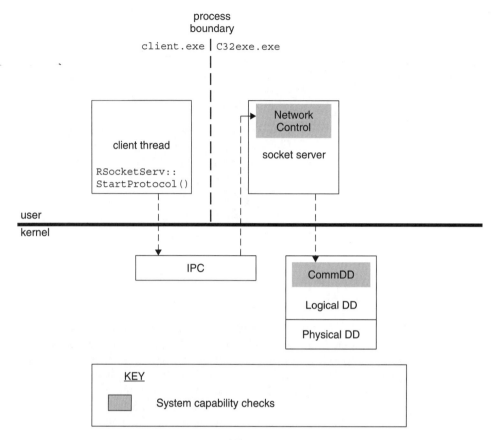

Figure 2.3   System Server Enforcing System Capabilities

misuse of which could threaten the integrity of the mobile phone. System capabilities are not particularly meaningful to the mobile phone user, and are not intended to be referenced in user dialogs. Software which needs system capabilities should be granted them either by building them into the phone ROM, or by being signed by a trusted authority.

The TCB is responsible for enforcing most of the system capabilities (for example AllFiles, which is enforced by the file server). Some device drivers, also part of the TCB, require a system capability to access them (for example CommDD). Other system capabilities are enforced by the TCE (see Figure 2.3), where the capability controls access to higher-level services (for example NetworkControl, which is enforced by the socket server, among others, which itself has CommDD so that it can access the necessary lower-level services).

Table 2.1 summarizes the available system capabilities. More detail on the use of each capability is provided in Appendix A, Section A.1.

Table 2.1 System Capabilities

Capability	Privilege Granted
AllFiles	Read access to the entire file system and write access to other processes' private directories.
CommDD	Direct access to all communications equipment device drivers.
DiskAdmin	Access to file system administration operations that affect more than one file or directory (or overall file-system integrity/behavior, etc.).
Drm	Access to DRM-protected content.
MultimediaDD	Access to critical multimedia functions, such as direct access to associated device drivers and priority access to multimedia APIs.
NetworkControl	The ability to modify or access network protocol controls.
PowerMgmt	The ability to kill any process, to power-off unused peripherals and to cause the mobile phone to go into stand-by, to wake up, or to power down completely.
ProtServ	Allows a server process to register with a protected name.
ReadDeviceData	Read access to confidential network operator, mobile phone manufacturer and device settings.
SurroundingsDD	Access to logical device drivers that provide input information about the surroundings of the mobile phone.
SwEvent	The ability to simulate key presses and pen input and to capture such events from any program.
TrustedUI	The ability to create a trusted UI session, and therefore to display dialogs in a secure UI environment.
WriteDeviceData	Write access to settings that control the behavior of the device.

2.4.4 User Capabilities

User capabilities are a smaller group of capabilities deliberately designed to be meaningful to mobile phone users, relating to security concepts that should be easy for users to understand and about which to make choices. As a general principle, assigning a user capability to a process should not allow that process to be able to threaten the integrity of the mobile phone – user choices when installing add-on software should never prevent the phone from working. It may however be appropriate for mobile phone users to make decisions about whether add-on software can spend their money on phone calls (NetworkServices capability) or have access to their personal data (ReadUserData capability, for example).

User capabilities will typically be granted to add-on software that is making use of services provided by the TCE. The TCE is responsible for checking and enforcing user capabilities, and then performing the requested services on behalf of the add-on software. Those services will typically be performed using system capabilities granted to the TCE, as shown in Figure 2.4:

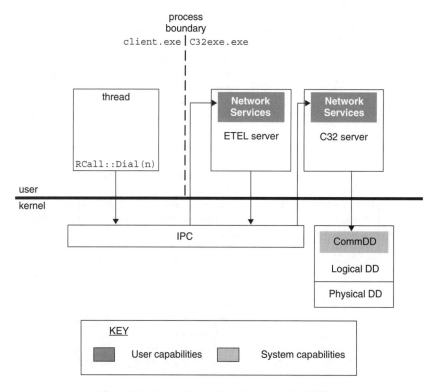

Figure 2.4 System Server Enforcing User Capabilities

Table 2.2 User Capabilities

Capability	Privilege Granted
LocalServices	Access to services over 'short-link' connections (such as Bluetooth or Infra-red). Such services will not normally incur cost for the user.
Location	Access to data giving the location of the mobile phone.
NetworkServices	Access to remote services (such as over-the-air data services or Wi-Fi network access). Such services may incur cost for the user.
ReadUserData	Read access to confidential user data.
UserEnvironment	Access to live data about the user and their immediate environment.
WriteUserData	Write access to confidential user data.

The available user capabilities are summarized in Table 2.2. More detail on the use of each capability is provided in Appendix A, Section A.2.

Although user capabilities are designed to be understandable by the mobile phone user, it may, nevertheless, not be appropriate to offer some of these choices to the user, depending on the environment in which the phone is being used. The platform security model is deliberately flexible and it is not realistic to expect a 'one size fits all' security policy. Mobile phone manufacturers therefore have some discretion in exactly how they configure platform security on their phones. These configuration options are discussed in detail in Chapter 3. Where the security policy permits, it is possible for a mobile phone user to choose to authorize the use of certain user capabilities by unsigned software at the time that software is installed.

We also note here that some actions, which are protected by user capabilities, can still be performed by unsigned and untrusted software. One example of this is sending an SMS message; there are three ways in which software can be permitted to do this:

- The software is signed by a trusted authority and granted Network-Services capability.

- The software is granted NetworkServices capability at install time by the user (if the phone's security policy permits).

- The software uses the 'SendAs' API, which invokes a system server, which, if the software does not have `NetworkServices` capability, asks the user for a 'one-shot' permission to send the message.

2.4.5 Capability Rules

When a developer builds a binary (an EXE or a DLL) for Symbian OS v9, that binary has a set of capabilities (possibly just an empty set) declared within it (see Chapter 3). A binary will then be put onto a mobile phone, either by a phone manufacturer building it into ROM or by it being installed as add-on software. In either case, a decision will be whether that binary is sufficiently trustworthy to be assigned the capabilities that have been declared. In the first (ROM) case, this will be a manual process of checking the declared capabilities. In the second (add-on) case, it is an automatic process handled by the software installer (see Chapter 8).

Thus, after a binary is built into ROM or an add-on binary is installed, Symbian OS can assume that the binary is sufficiently trustworthy to be granted the capabilities declared within it. For an EXE, this means that a process created from that EXE will run with that declared authority to carry out certain privileged operations. In contrast, the capabilities declared within a DLL indicate the degree to which it is trusted, but that DLL may be loaded into a process that is running with less privilege. The code within a DLL cannot assume that it will necessarily be running with the capabilities declared within it, whereas the code within an EXE can (it is still prudent to check for run-time errors due to insufficient privilege in case the EXE was installed with incorrect capabilities declared).

Rule 1: Every process has a set of capabilities (as defined by the EXE) and its capabilities never change during its lifetime.

At run-time the loader, which is part of the TCB (it runs as a thread in the file server process), creates a new process, reading the executable code from the filing system and determining the set of capabilities for the process. The kernel maintains a convenient list of capabilities for all processes to save frequent re-reading of the relevant part of an EXE whenever one process wants to check the capabilities of another.

Once the set of capabilities is determined for a process, it never changes – it remains the same until that process terminates. This is in contrast with some systems that allow privileges to be voluntarily dropped or given up by running processes. Symbian has chosen not to allow this, for simplicity and security – security vulnerabilities have resulted from the careless use of such features in other systems.

Rule 2: A process can only load a DLL if that DLL has been trusted with at least the capabilities that the process has.

When a process loads a DLL it does not enlarge or reduce the capability set of the process; it remains the same, as required by Rule 1. The DLL load will fail if the DLL does not have a superset of (that is, at least the same set as) the capabilities of the process loading it. This prevents untrusted (and thus potentially malicious) code being loaded into sensitive processes, for example a plug-in into a system server. The loader provides this security mechanism for all processes; relieving them of the burden of identifying which DLLs they can safely load. This is illustrated in Figure 2.5 – capabilities declared in the binaries are shown as 'C*n*':

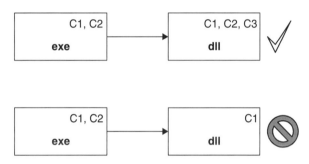

Figure 2.5   Direct Loading of DLLs

Rule 2 has some interesting consequences for *statically-linked* DLLs. Most programs using DLLs will be built using static linking – dynamic loading of DLLs is primarily used when a program has plug-ins that may or may not be present at run time. Static linking resolves references to symbols in the linked DLL at build time so that the run-time loading is more efficient. The most interesting case with regard to capabilities is when one DLL statically links to another – this means that when the first DLL is loaded by a process, the second DLL is also loaded into that process at the same time. Consider the case where the first DLL has a capability that the second DLL does not have, as in Figure 2.6.

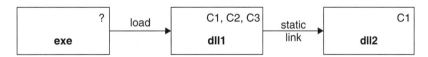

Figure 2.6   Static Linking of DLLs

In this case, because DLL1 is statically linked to DLL2, DLL1 can never be loaded into a process that has capability C2, because that process cannot load DLL2 (which is not trusted with C2). There is therefore no point in declaring capability C2 for DLL1, because it can never be used. In fact,

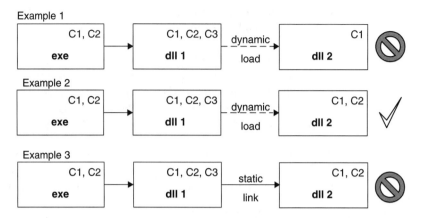

Figure 2.7   Indirect Loading of DLLs

because other processes often reuse loaded DLLs, Symbian has made an optimization to Rule 2 (see also Figure 2.7):

Rule 2b: The loader will only load a DLL that statically links to a second DLL if that second DLL is trusted with at least the same capabilities as the first DLL.

If a DLL that has already been loaded for another process is being reused, the loader only needs to check the capabilities of the first DLL, and not those of any of the other DLLs to which the first DLL may be statically-linked. To avoid being impacted by this rule, developers should not statically link any DLL to another DLL with a subset of capabilities.

2.4.6   Run-time Capabilities for DLLs

There is a consequence of these rules that developers should be aware of. There is a clear difference between capabilities that a DLL is trusted with (declared at build-time) and the subset of capabilities that it relies on having (determined at run-time) to perform its functions. Whilst the former is recorded in a third-party DLL binary's header, there is no similar information about the latter.

You may ask 'Which capabilities do I assign to my executable, because I don't know which capabilities are used by the DLLs to which it links?'. To answer this you need to look at the documentation for each DLL function you use. That documentation should list the capabilities required for the function, and hence the capabilities that you should assign to your executable (in addition to any other capabilities used by system functions that your executable calls directly).

To support this, all DLL authors are strongly encouraged to adopt the Symbian practice of documenting their DLL functions, indicating which capabilities a function (or the ones it calls) *uses*. Symbian uses an in-source comment tag '@capability'. They also need to indicate whether these capability checks will always occur, or under which run-time conditions they apply (for example, when certain options are specified as a parameter). This is much like having to document any function's behavior, parameter input values, output values, return values, leave codes or panic codes.

2.5   Concept 3: Data Caging for File Access

The third and final concept of Symbian OS platform security architecture is the file access control model. This section explains how the integrity and confidentiality of stored files is preserved.

2.5.1   Data Caging Basics

Data caging is used to protect important files (the term 'data caging' applies to files regardless of whether the content is code or data, so perhaps Symbian should really have called it file caging). These can be either system files or user files. Many system files are critical to the functioning of the system – securing the mobile phone means protecting the integrity of these files. Many user files are personal to the user; securing the mobile phone also means protecting the confidentiality of this user data. The system needs to protect program code from corruption and to prevent undesirable access to system-critical or confidential data.

Not all files are protected – data caging is only applied where necessary. In Symbian OS data caging is achieved by providing special directories that 'lock away' files in private areas; these directories are in addition to the public parts of the filing system. There are three special top level paths: \sys, \resource and \private; access restrictions apply to these directories and, also, to all subdirectories within them. Other paths remain public, this provides compatibility for existing software, which does not need its data to be protected, and allows free access to existing files, which may be on removable media.

The access controls on a file are entirely determined by its directory path, regardless of the drive. This is a simple, lightweight mechanism – the directory in which a file resides determines the level of access protection. It is not necessary to have explicit access control lists for each file to determine which processes may access it. Therefore no precious storage space is taken up with recording information for each file, and the impact on performance and battery life is minimized as there is no list to walk through and process each time.

The consequence of the access rules being implied by the full path to a file is that, should the developer want to limit access, the file only

Table 2.3 Data Caging Access Rules

Directory Path	Capability Required To:	
	Read	Write
\sys	AllFiles	Tcb
\resource	none	Tcb
\private\<ownSID>	none	none
\private\<otherSID>	AllFiles	AllFiles
\<other>	none	none

needs be moved to another directory. The access rules are summarized in Table 2.3.

2.5.2   Caged File Paths

sys

Only TCB code can access the directory \sys and its subdirectories. There are two subdirectories of particular interest: \sys\bin and \sys\hash.

The \sys\bin directory is where all program binaries (executables) reside. Executables built into the mobile phone ROM run from z:\sys\bin; add-on software is written into c:\sys\bin (or \sys\bin on some other writeable drive). This ensures that only TCB software, the most trustworthy, can create new executables (via SWInstall) or load executables into memory (via F32). Executables stored elsewhere will not be runnable, which protects against malware creating new, or modifying existing, binaries in order to get the system to execute malicious code. If your program code attempts to load executable or library code from a different directory, the loader ignores the path and only looks in \sys\bin.

The \sys\hash directory is used to check for tampering with executables which are stored on removable media. It could be possible to make changes to files on removable media by putting that media in another, non-Symbian OS device. This directory is managed by the software installer, which we will cover in more detail in Chapter 8.

resource

This is a directory tree that is intended for resource files that are strictly read-only. Examples are bitmaps, fonts and help files as well as other resource files that are not expected to change after installation. Only the TCB can write into this directory; this provides software with assurance that its resource data cannot be corrupted. As with \sys, files here are either built into the mobile phone ROM or are installed on writeable media as add-ons by the software installer.

\private

Each EXE has its own caged file-system area as a subdirectory under \private. This subdirectory is identified by the SID of the EXE, thus it is private to that process. If there are two processes loaded from the same EXE they share the same private subdirectory.

It is up to the developer to choose in which directory a program should store its data, for example, \resource, its private subdirectory or a public directory. By default it will be its private subdirectory, though the path will still need to be created the first time the executable runs. There is an API to discover the name of the private path, and also to restore the current path to this setting. Note that data files on removable media, even those under the private path, can still be subject to tampering; protecting data from tampering is covered in detail in Chapter 7.

2.5.3   Data Caging and Capabilities

The concepts of capabilities and data caging work together in providing flexible options for controlling access to a program's data. The various options are covered in detail in Chapter 7, but we will discuss here the two capabilities which allow processes to bypass the normal data caging access controls, as shown in Table 2.3:

- Tcb – allows write access to executables and shared read-only re-sources.

- AllFiles – allows read access to the entire file system and write access to other processes' private directories.

The enforcement of these capabilities is the responsibility of the TCB (specifically the file server) and, once granted, they apply to all files on the mobile phone. In general, software should not be given these capabilities if it just needs to read or write one specific sort of data – it would be like giving out a master key to someone who just needs to open one particular safety deposit box in a bank. System services and applications should offer APIs that allow data to be shared with more limited privileges, for example by checking the ReadUserData, WriteUserData, ReadDeviceData and WriteDeviceData capabilities, or by checking the requesting process's SID or VID.

2.6   Summary

This chapter sets out the main concepts in Symbian's implementation
of its secure platform. Implementation of these concepts, while new to
Symbian OS, is not new to the industry.

In the first section we pointed out that in 1966 Dennis and Van
Horn came up with the idea of a capability-based security model, then
Anderson described a TCB/Reference model in 1972 and in 1973 Saltzer
established a set of protection-mechanism design principles.

Symbian's platform security project had a number of architectural
goals that strongly influenced the implementation. The mobile phone user
should understand the exposed parts of the security model, the model
should be a lightweight one, it should replace a trusting relationship with
a trustworthy one, and, finally, network operators should confidently
provide open mobile phones supporting after-market software.

The next three sections outlined the main concepts around which
Symbian based the development, drawing on those set by Saltzer *et al*.

The first was that the 'sphere of protection', the unit of trust for
privileged operations, is a Symbian OS process, which the underlying
memory-protection hardware supports. The unit of trust gives rise to four
tiers of software in Symbian OS. The TCB is the smallest part of the
system that processes can fully trust. Many system servers are part of
the TCE and therefore can be highly trusted by other processes to carry
out particular, privileged operations. Network operators, mobile phone
manufacturers and users are able to put appropriate trust in other signed
software because of the systems put in place and agreed with industry
stake-holders by Symbian Signed prior to signing that software. Lastly,
unsigned software is completely untrustworthy (i.e. there is no basis for
trusting it beyond safe operations) but large parts of the system API are
available to it to carry out unprivileged operations.

The second concept is that of capabilities as a means of restricting
access to privileged operations (and data) in the secured system. There
are system capabilities that are there to protect the integrity of the phone
operating system, and user capabilities that are there to protect access
to user sensitive operations and data. Capabilities apply to a process.
They are assigned to executables as a statement of intent as to which
capabilities a process should have, subject to the loader rules. The rules
on DLL loading mean that the capabilities of a process do not change
after a DLL is loaded; thus they remain the same as the ones assigned
to the EXE at build time. A process is prevented from loading DLLs that
should not be trusted with the capabilities it possesses.

The third concept is that of data caging as a means of protecting
code and data from processes that should not have access to it. This
is an example of the least privilege principle cited by Saltzer, whereby
processes do not have access to things unless they are authorized to do

so. Data caging is restricted to three special directory trees under \sys, \resource and \private. The TCB processes have full read/write access to these directories, whereas other processes have limited access. The mechanism for policing access is a combination of the directory path itself and the privileges of the process that wants to make the access.

In the rest of this book we consider and introduce some of the implications of the above concepts on how to organize and secure the design of software.

PART 2

Application Development for Platform Security

3

The Platform Security Environment

by Michael Bruce and Phil Spencer

3.1   Building Your Application

Platform security introduces a number of new features for building applications on Symbian OS. These are relatively straightforward to implement and in many cases will not result in significant changes.

The features covered in this chapter are changes that have been made to the build tools to support the specification of platform security attributes in binaries – the scheme for allocating UIDs has changed and the project specification (MMP) file syntax has been extended to include new platform security keywords. For general guidance on building binaries for Symbian OS please refer to your software development kit documentation or to [Harrison 2003].

3.1.1   Application Binary Format

The binary format used for EXEs and DLLs in Symbian OS v9 is the same as that introduced in Symbian OS v8.1b, the ARM Embedded Applications Binary Interface (EABI) format. With the introduction of platform security in Symbian OS v9, the main application binary is now built as an EXE rather than a DLL. This is because, as described in Chapter 2, the capabilities of a process are determined by its EXE and each application therefore has its own EXE so that its capabilities can be individually set.

3.1.2   UID Allocation, SIDs and VIDs

A UID is a 32-bit number allocated by Symbian, which may be used for several purposes in Symbian OS. You may already be familiar with the three UIDs used in the binary header in previous versions of Symbian OS. UID1 identifies the file type (EXE or DLL) and is automatically generated by the build tools. UID2 and UID3 are defined in the project's MMP file – UID2 represents the interface definition that the binary conforms to, and UID3 is a unique identifier used for file associations and so on. Another existing use of UIDs is the package UID (pUID) of a SIS file, as specified in the PKG file (we will return to PKG files in Section 3.3).

Platform security brings with it two new uses of UIDs in binaries: the SID and the VID. These concepts were introduced in Chapter 2, here we will deal with the practicalities. Because these new uses of UIDs have security implications, the method of allocating UIDs has changed. Previously UIDs were issued by email to *uid@symbiandevnet.com*, but for Symbian OS v9 and later, UIDs are issued from the web site *www.symbiansigned.com*. Registration is required, but it is simple and provided your application does not need signing, registration is free.

SID

The SID of an EXE is a 'Secure Identifier' which uniquely identifies a process when it is running, and is used to control access to protected resources such as the private directory of the process. The SID value is not relevant for DLLs as a process's SID will always be that of its EXE. As UID3 is already intended as a unique (but unenforced) identifier, we recommend that the same UID be used for both UID3 and SID, simply to avoid confusion. Every EXE on a particular mobile phone is required to have a different SID from all other EXEs on that phone.

SIDs are divided into two ranges: $0x00000000 - 0x7FFFFFFF$ is the 'protected range', and the installer (see Chapter 8) will only allow EXEs to be installed with SIDs in this range if the package is signed by a trusted authority (such as Symbian Signed (see Chapter 9)). The range $0x80000000 - 0xFFFFFFFF$ may be used by unsigned applications – there are no controls on the use of SIDs in this range, so avoiding collisions relies on voluntary cooperation, and thus the security of these SIDs should not be relied on.

If you have previously been allocated UIDs under the old scheme, they will be in the range $0x10000000 - 0x1FFFFFFF$. If you do not require a SID in the protected range, you are welcome to reuse your existing UIDs by adding $0xE0000000$ to them (resulting in the range $0xF0000000 - 0xFFFFFFFF$).

VID

The Vendor Identifier (VID) of an EXE is another attribute that can be used to control access to protected resources for a process. Unlike the SID, the VID is not unique to a particular EXE (all EXEs provided by a particular vendor can share the same VID), and an EXE is not required to have a VID. (In fact there are no services in the underlying Symbian OS which use the VID – it is intended for use by the UI software and add-on packages.) The VID of a DLL is not relevant – similarly to the SID, the VID for a process will always be that of its EXE.

There is no unprotected range for VIDs – if you wish to use a VID, the installation package must be signed by a trusted authority.

Allocation Ranges

Table 3.1 summarizes the use of UIDs allocated under the new scheme.

Table 3.1 UID Allocation Ranges

UID Range	Intended Use
0x00000000	KNullUID
0x00000001-0x0FFFFFFF	Reserved for future use
0x01000000-0x0FFFFFFF	Legacy testing range, not used in v9
0x10000000-0x1FFFFFFF	Legacy allocated UIDs, not used in v9
0x20000000-0x2FFFFFFF	Protected range UID/SID for v9 onwards
0x30000000-0x6FFFFFFF	Reserved for future use
0x70000000-0x7FFFFFFF	Vendor Ids (VIDs)
0x80000000-0x9FFFFFFF	Reserved for future use
0xA0000000-0xAFFFFFFF	Unprotected UID/SID allocated for v9 on
0xB0000000-0xE0FFFFFF	Reserved for future use
0xE1000000-0xEFFFFFFF	New testing range for v9 onwards
0xF0000000-0xFFFFFFFF	Legacy UID compatibility range

Note that the testing range should not be used when shipping products, but these ranges are guaranteed not to be officially allocated so that they are safe to use for testing purposes without clashing with other legitimate applications.

3.1.3   MMP File Format

Here is an example MMP file for an application that will be signed, using a capability, a protected-range SID, and a VID. The new MMP file syntax is shown in **bold**:

```
TARGET          project.exe
CAPABILITY      ReadUserData
TARGETTYPE      EXE
```

```
UID              0x100039CE 0x2911003A
VENDORID         0x70B3237D // optional
SECUREID         0x2911003A // optional, defaults to UID3

SOURCEPATH       ..\source\project
SOURCE           component1_source1.cpp
SOURCE           component1_source2.cpp
SOURCE           component1_source3.cpp

USERINCLUDE      ..\inc
USERINCLUDE      ..\source\project

SYSTEMINCLUDE    \epoc32\include
SYSTEMINCLUDE    \epoc32\include\project

LIBRARY          euser.lib
LIBRARY          estor.lib
```

The CAPABILITY parameters can be specified in an inclusive list, as shown above, or an exclusive one through the use of the All keyword. Highly-trusted system DLLs would commonly use a specification such as:

```
CAPABILITY       All -Tcb
```

Note that Tcb capability is not the same as All, although All does include Tcb. As several system capabilities (which are implicitly included in All) are likely to be reserved by the mobile phone manufacturer, it is safest for add-on software to specify the particular capabilities required, for example:

```
CAPABILITY       LocalServices NetworkServices
```

You can also use the keyword None, although this is the default.

3.2 Developing on the Emulator

Symbian OS v9, like previous versions of the operating system, is supplied with an emulator. The emulator is an invaluable tool for the development and debugging of applications as it simulates mobile phone operation on a Windows-based PC.

With the introduction of platform security in Symbian OS v9 it is no longer possible to deploy an application which performs sensitive operations to a mobile phone without it being signed by a trusted authority. Using the emulator is, therefore, a distinct advantage because you don't need your application to be signed before testing it. The emulator also has the flexibility to allow platform security to be turned off, which can be useful during development although, for security reasons, this won't be possible on a mobile phone.

To use the emulator for development you need to ensure that you have established a suitable environment. For more information on setting up the emulator please refer to Chapter 1 of 'Getting Started' in [Harrison 2003].

3.2.1 Emulator Configuration

When porting an application from a previous version of Symbian OS it can be useful to temporarily disable platform security. This can be done by modifying the settings in the file \epoc32\data\epoc.ini. In the example below, enforcement of the capabilities ReadUserData and WriteUserData has been disabled for testing purposes.

```
PlatSecEnforcement ON
PlatSecDiagnostics ON
PlatSecProcessIsolation ON
PlatSecEnforceSysBin ON
PlatSecDisabledCaps ReadUserData+WriteUserData
```

The following list describes each of these parameters in more detail:

- PlatSecEnforcement – this parameter determines the action that is taken when a capability or other platform security policy check failure occurs. If platform security enforcement is enabled, the appropriate action for the failure is taken, otherwise the system continues as if the check had passed.

- PlatSecDiagnostics – when a capability or other platform security policy check failure occurs, this keyword causes the failure to be logged to the epocwind.out file, located in the temporary directory defined by the Windows %TEMP% environment variable. If PlatSecEnforcement is OFF a warning will be logged instead of an error.

- PlatSecProcessIsolation – this parameter disables insecure APIs inherited from EKA1.

- PlatSecEnforceSysBin – this parameter forces the loader to look for and load binary executables from the \sys\bin directory alone, ignoring any other paths that are specified.

- PlatSecDisabledCaps – this parameter prevents any platform security errors from occurring for each of the listed capabilities by instructing the loader to grant them to all processes. This also means no error or warning is logged to epocwind.out even when PlatSecEnforcement is ON.

3.2.2 Run-time Platform Security Errors

When a process encounters an error due to a platform security issue, this will usually result in a method leaving with the error KErrPermissionDenied(-46). There are two main causes for this – a process loading something that is insufficiently trustworthy, or a process attempting an operation for which is has insufficient capabilities.

Insufficient Trust

When a DLL is loaded into a process (EXE), it must be trusted to use at least the same capabilities as the process. For instance, if an EXE has the capabilities `ReadUserData` and `WriteUserData`, it will only be able to load a DLL that has been assigned these capabilities, as shown in Table 3.2.

Table 3.2 Capability Mismatches Between a DLL and an EXE

DLL Capabilities	Result
ReadUserData	KErrPermissionDenied (-46)
ReadUserData WriteUserData	KErrNone (0)
Location ReadUserData WriteUserData NetworkServices	KErrNone (0)

If you are writing an EXE that uses a third-party DLL with insufficient capabilities you can either review your own capability settings and try to align them with the DLL or contact the DLL vendor. Another alternative is to split the functionality you require by creating a supporting server process (EXE) with capabilities that match the DLL. You should police the APIs on this server to ensure that only your client's SID or a process with sufficient capabilities has access. Policing of server APIs is described in detail in Chapter 5.

Insufficient Capabilities

Platform security requires all servers to police their APIs to ensure that the calling client has the required capabilities. When a client is found to have insufficient capabilities a `KErrPermissionDenied(-46)` error is returned. This is illustrated in the following example code:

```
void SomeClass::WriteFileL(const TDesC& aFileName)
  {
  // open a file server session
```

```
RFs fs;
User::LeaveIfError(fs.connect());
CleanupClosePushL(fs);

// open the output file
RFile outputFile;
User::LeaveIfError(outputFile.Open(aFileName, EFileWrite));
CleanupClosePushL(outputFile);

// function body omitted for clarity

// cleanup
CleanupStack::PopAndDestroy(2, &fs);
}

void SomeClass::WritePrivateL()
  {
  // set filename to a file in my private directory
  _LIT(KPrivateFile, "c:\\private\\2911003A\\mySettings.ini");
  WriteFileL(KPrivateFile());
  }

void SomeClass::WriteSystemL()
  {
  // set filename to file in the \sys\bin\ directory
  _LIT(KSysBinFile, "c:\\sys\\bin\\myDLL.dll");
  WriteFileL(KSysBinFile());
  }
```

Function `WriteSystemL()` will leave with `KErrPermissionDenied` unless the application has `Tcb` capability, whereas function `WritePrivateL()` will succeed regardless of what capabilities the application has. For clarity, the private directory path has been hardcoded; normally you would use `RFs::PrivatePath()` to avoid specifying the SID directly.

Debugging Platform Security Errors

If a platform security error does occur, one of the best methods of resolving it is to view the `epocwind.out` file, located in your Windows `temp` directory. Also present in previous versions of Symbian OS, this file now provides detailed information on why platform security errors occur. The file is overwritten each time the emulator is started. Searching the file for '`*PlatSec*` ERROR' will show which process caused a platform-security-related error and, often, details of which API was being called at the time the error occurred:

```
  55.130         *PlatSec* ERROR - Secure Id Check failed -
Process X.exe[10208c4e]0001 attempted an operation requiring the
secure id: 01234567. Additional diagnostic message:
RProperty::Define with invalid category
```

You may want to disable platform security either partially or completely to get past such problems during testing, as described in Section 3.2.1.

3.2.3   Assigning and Testing Capabilities

Predicting Required Capabilities

The enhancements introduced with platform security mean that early in the design phase you need to determine what capabilities your application is likely to use. Depending upon the capabilities required it might be necessary for an application to be certified through a program such as Symbian Signed (see Chapter 9).

There are several methods you can use to determine the capabilities an application will need:

- Consider what general operations the application will be performing and select appropriate capabilities. This is usually quite easy to do since the capabilities are coarse-grained and thus there are relatively few to choose from. For instance an instant messaging application might require `NetworkServices` to access the Internet and `ReadUserData` for reading from the user's address book.

- Review each API that you plan to use and record the capabilities required. Note that it may be possible to find a higher-level API which can perform the operation required with fewer capabilities (for example, the Send As server can be used to send SMS messages without requiring the full access to telephony APIs granted by the `NetworkServices` capability).

- Trial and error, adding capabilities as they are required.

A mixture of the first and second approaches is recommended, examining APIs in detail when it is not clear from inspection alone. Trial and error is strongly discouraged; it is important to plan ahead in a project when the application may need to be approved by a third party (e.g. Symbian Signed, a network operator, or the mobile phone manufacturer) in order to be granted certain capabilities.

Testing Capabilities

When testing your application you may wish to try calling APIs both with and without sufficient capabilities to confirm that the application behaves as expected in both scenarios. This is particularly important when you are testing a server that exposes APIs to clients that may have very different sets of capabilities. The best way to do this is by creating multiple copies of your test harness, each with a different capability set. The `petran` tool can be used to modify the binary's E32 header parameters, including its UID, SID, VID and capabilities. This tool can also be used to determine which capabilities are declared in a particular EXE or DLL, using the command:

```
petran -dump s e32imagefile
```

This command only works for EABI binaries and does not detail which capability polices each API. For detailed information consult the Symbian OS Library at **www.symbian.com/developer/techlib** or, for a third-party DLL, consult the vendor. Note that the capabilities declared in a DLL indicate those it is *trusted* with, not necessarily those it will use.

As there are no capability warnings generated at build time, you will only discover mismatches by run-time testing. This is because many of the capability checks that are made are conditional. For example, calls to file system APIs may or may not require a capability, depending upon the path supplied as an argument (as illustrated in the example code above).

3.3 Packaging Your Application

The software installer (covered in detail in Chapter 8) is the 'pinch point' for getting an application correctly installed on to a Symbian OS v9 mobile phone. Unlike the emulator, where binaries can simply be copied for testing, on a real mobile phone it is the installer that places files in the correct locations and verifies that binaries have capabilities that do not exceed what is allowed based on the signature. Once a binary's capabilities have been checked by the installer, the installer's requirements are satisfied and there is no further action – the binaries are then resident on the mobile phone. The *only* legitimate method for running an application on a real mobile phone is to pass it through software install first, where it will be subject to these checks. In this section we cover the new platform security features in the tools used to create an installable software package.

3.3.1 Package File Changes

Developers use a Symbian OS *package* file to give the package creation tool (MakeSIS) the information necessary to build the final SIS file.

The package file (PKG) options are numerous, non-trivial and won't be covered here. Instead we recommend you refer to the Symbian OS Library documentation under *Tools and Utilities*, then *Installation Reference*. Looking at the examples provided in that documentation may also help you understand the large number of software deployment options that can be provided by a single SIS file.

The only significant recent addition to the package file is the inclusion of a field called *Non-Localized Vendor Name* (which is specified in PKG syntax by the colon ':' directive). The reason for this being a *non-localized* field is simply that we don't want signing bodies to have to store and track all the possible names belonging to an international vendor.

Prior to Symbian OS v9, only localized vendor names existed – that is a 'vendor name' provided for each of the languages supported by the package. In Symbian OS v9 a single consistent non-localized name is required *in addition* to the localized names. This field remains consistent the world over and may be used by signing authorities to further identify a package vendor prior to signing (more on that later).

Note that, although this field may not be employed by all signing authorities, the MakeSIS tool and the software installer will check that it is present. Here is an example of the use of this new field in the PKG file:

```
&EN,FR                    ; Languages

; Package Header
#{"App Name","Nom d'App"}, (0xE1234567), 1, 0, 0, TYPE=SA
; Localized Vendor Names
%{"Joe's Software", "Logiciels de Joe"}
; Unique Vendor Name
:"Joe Bloggs PLC, London"
```

Some changes have been made to the tools for signing packages; as a consequence, signing certificate information is no longer specified in the PKG file. If you wish to reuse existing PKG files from earlier versions of Symbian OS, including any certificate data, the certificate information should be removed or commented out, as follows:

```
;
; No longer used in Symbian OS v9 PKG file
; * "MyACSPublisherID.key","MyACSPublisherID.cer"
;
```

3.3.2   Package Creation Tools

Prior to Symbian OS v9, developers would have used two PC-based tools from the developer kit: `makekeys.exe` and `makesis.exe`. In Symbian OS v9, however, the signing features of `makesis.exe` are split out into a new tool called `signsis.exe`. There is also a wrapper tool for certain environments. A summary of these features is given below.

MakeSIS

`makesis.exe` generates package archives using the new SIS file format covered in Chapter 8. These archives contain all the information necessary to achieve the installation of the package on a mobile phone – except the digital signing material. If you want to be sure you have the new version of `makesis.exe` then invoke `makesis -v` and it should report a version of 4 or above.

MakeSIS is primarily driven by supplying it with the PKG file that specifies all the files, rules, options, and dependencies that you require. The package file format is fully specified in the Symbian OS Library, but as a quick reminder you can always invoke makesis -h to view some help information.

MakeSIS can also be used to create upgrades for packages that are already deployed, and to create the necessary controller files, which are required to deploy packages on removable media cards so that they become available to the mobile phone simply by inserting the media card.

3.3.3 Package Signing Tools

Chapter 2 introduced the concept of capabilities. By no means all of the Symbian OS APIs require capabilities in order to use them – we estimate that around 40% now do. Also keep in mind some of these are so specialized and low-level that only a handful of applications ever have good reason to use them. Some of these capabilities may be granted by the user at the time the application is installed (depending on how the manufacturer or operator has configured the mobile phone – see Section 3.4.1). Other capabilities may require the application package to be digitally signed by a trusted authority (such as Symbian Signed, covered in Chapter 9).

Makekeys

makekeys.exe is unchanged from previous Symbian OS releases, and can still be used by the developer to create digital certificates or PKCS#10 certificate requests.

If you wish to create your own signing certificate to sign your package, then use makekeys.exe to generate a self-signed certificate and private key (although note that packages you sign yourself will not be granted capabilities automatically). Alternatively, if you are planning to have an authority sign your digital certificate, then you can generate a certificate request, which can be sent off to a certificate authority via the web or email.

Note, in some cases, you may receive a signing certificate without using makekeys.exe – this is the case, for example, with developer certificates (covered in Section 3.4.2) issued by Symbian Signed (see Chapter 9).

SignSIS

Package files can now be signed more than once. Symbian considered that making packages and signing packages were two separate activities, so the signing activity was split out into a separate tool called signsis.exe rather than have one very complex makesis.exe with multiple roles and yet more command-line switches.

SignSIS takes a SIS file as input, along with a certificate (or list of certificates) and a private key, and then produces a signed SIS file as output. `signsis -h` will remind you of the parameter ordering. You'll notice there is a switch to provide you with some useful information about the output file.

Finally, note that signings are performed in such a way that they encapsulate previous signings. For example, if you sign your SIS file and send it to an authority for signature, their signing will encapsulate both the SIS file *and* your signature. SignSIS also allows the removal of a signature, but because of this encapsulation only the outer signature can be removed each time – it is not possible to remove an inner signature while leaving outer signatures present.

CreateSIS

For convenience, Symbian also provided a script called CreateSIS (`createsis -h` for help on the syntax) which will execute Makekeys, MakeSIS and SignSIS in the right order and with the right options for straightforward signing operations. CreateSIS can automate the generation and use of a self-signed certificate and private key when the need is simply to have a signed package rather than to have it signed by a trusted authority.

3.4   Testing on Mobile Phone Hardware

The emulator uses binaries compiled for a different target from a real mobile phone and, although most applications can be fully tested on the emulator, it's imperative that you test your applications on real mobile phone hardware before release. Although the emulator tries to be as close to a 'real' phone as possible, there will always be differences in behavior due to the fact that your PC is a much more powerful device, with more memory and storage space at its disposal, and it is based on a different processor architecture to the mobile phone. Only by testing on real hardware can you combat real-world performance problems or design flaws.

3.4.1   The Mobile Phone's Security Policy

When building a Symbian OS-based phone, the mobile phone manufacturer can make many choices that affect the look and behavior of various features. The security policy settings are among these choices. We, therefore, cannot be definitive regarding the security policy that the manufacturer of your targeted mobile phone will have chosen. Symbian is, however, encouraging mobile phone manufacturers to base their security policies on a common reference point, which is described in a series of documents entitled *Symbian Recommended Practices*. The latest version of these documents can be found on ***www.symbian.com***, in the 'Technology' section.

Be aware, however, that each mobile phone manufacturer may configure the software install certificate store as they please, to determine who is entitled to grant which capabilities. This will in turn determine what authorization is required. Some particularly sensitive capabilities such as Tcb and Drm may be reserved for the mobile phone manufacturer's own use.

3.4.2   Developer Certificates

The use of trusted authorities to sign packages and to approve the granting of capabilities presents us with an interesting 'catch 22' situation. If the installer will only install SIS files that use some of the more sensitive capabilities when they are signed, but, in order to get a SIS file signed to allow access to those sensitive capabilities you must submit it through an industry-agreed test procedure which it must pass, how does a developer test such an application during development? A few options were considered:

- Special hardware could attach to mobile phones and 'unlock' the installer. This would not only be a risk in general (for example, users disabling the security model on their mobile phones), but it would also be costly.

- Special software builds could be supplied from licensees for use by developers only, which would disable the security model just for them. Again this would be costly and unworkable

- An interim certification process could enable capabilities, but would not allow reuse of the application by anyone other than the developer.

It was the latter option that was decided upon because it was easy, cheap and elegant, with none of the drawbacks listed for the other options. These temporary, interim certificates, which allow testing on your own mobile phone, are called 'developer certificates'.

The basic concept of a developer certificate is simple. It is:

- a certificate issued to you (or your organization) by a trusted signing authority (for example, Symbian Signed, or perhaps a mobile phone manufacturer or network operator)

- locked to a specific mobile phone or phones (in the case of GSM phones this is, typically, done by specifying the unique IMEI numbers)

- limited to granting a chosen subset of capabilities for software running on those phones
- valid for a limited period from the date of issue.

You will need to check the availability of developer certificates for the particular mobile phone model you are targeting. However, we expect that in most cases developer certificates will be available from Symbian Signed (see Chapter 9).

Anyone with a copy of SignSIS and a valid developer certificate can sign an existing SIS file. This will aid you, as a developer, during your testing process if, for example, you wish to make your SIS file available to a limited group of external beta testers. Your beta testers will be able to obtain developer certificates for their own handsets and resign any 'raw' SIS files you send them to test, thus ensuring they can test your application with the appropriate capabilities. The syntax for SignSIS is as follows:

```
>signsis "SISFileToBeSigned.sis" "NewSignedSISFile.sis"
    "DevCert.cer" "DevCert.key"
```

It is worth noting at this stage that the 'user experience' of SIS files signed using a developer certificate is not a pretty one – neither is it intended to be! When installing such SIS files, several 'health warnings' will be displayed to notify the user that the application is test software, not a shipping product and that there are risks involved in continuing. Such warnings are no problem for developers or experienced testers – but they are in place to ensure developer certificates are not accidentally misused or deliberately abused to distribute software to 'real' end users.

3.4.3   Packaging the Completed Application

The final stage of your development process is, of course, the release of your application to your target end-users. Once you have completed thorough testing and debugging on both the emulator and target phone as described in this chapter, you should rebuild a new SIS file with MakeSIS (see Section 3.3.2) containing your final release build binaries. You will then be guaranteed a 'clean' SIS file with the correct binaries inside it and without any developer certificates attached.

Once you have this SIS file you can complete the final steps of the release process. If you are not using any capabilities which require a digital signature for access, your SIS file can be released directly to users (although note that they will still see a warning that the SIS file is from an 'untrusted' source). If you are using capabilities, or wish to build user confidence and remove the standard installation warnings, you should complete your release process by submitting your application to an appropriate testing and certification program, in order to have it countersigned officially against the appropriate root certificate in your target device.

3.5 Summary

This chapter examines some subtle changes to the development lifecycle in Symbian OS v9, concerning how applications are built, tested and packaged.

In the first section, we covered how to build an application as an EXE and assign its capabilities, SID and VID. This determines the security attributes of the application that will be used at run time.

In the next section, we considered use of the emulator when initially developing an application, how to determine which capabilities are needed and how to test the use of capabilities. The emulator provides diagnostics which are helpful in determining the cause of problems due to incorrect assignment of capabilities.

In the third section, we explained how to use MakeSIS and the new SignSIS tool to create a signed application package. A signature from a trusted authority is required for some capabilities to be used by an application. The SIS file also now includes a new 'non-localized vendor name' field.

In the final section, we discussed how to test an application using capabilities on an actual mobile phone, including the new concept of developer certificates which enable you to freely and easily develop and test your applications on your own hardware.

4

How to Write Secure Applications

by Matthew Allen

4.1   What Is a Secure Application?

Before considering how to write secure applications, it is worth examining what we mean by a secure application and why you would want your application to be secure.

There are many definitions of a secure application involving concepts such as mutual authentication, remote attestation and provable behavior but, although these concepts are useful in their specialist domains, most application writers are looking for a more general definition.

> A secure application is one that its audience can trust without being disappointed. Conversely, an insecure application is one that either its audience does not trust or that disappoints those who trust in it.

Clearly there may be several categories of interested parties in the audience and they may trust your application in different ways. They may also be disappointed in varying degrees and at varying times, and they may respond in different ways, but, as an application writer, you will need to take this variety into account.

In particular, trust may be based on reasonable or unreasonable expectations. By being aware of the security of your own application you can minimize unreasonable expectations by not overselling it, and maximize sales by not underselling it.

As with most forms of security, application security has two strands to it, the first being an analysis of the potential threats and their impacts and the second being the deployment of appropriate countermeasures.

4.2   Analyzing the Threats

4.2.1   Who Is Interested in my Application's Security?

If you examine the groups of people that trust your application, you can consider what is important to them. This can then guide you in determining what should be protected and how well it should be protected. We will list those people typically involved in an application and what their concerns usually are, but you need to think about which groups are interested in *your* application, what their concerns will be and whether you want to take their concerns into account when producing your application.

There are several categories of people that are involved with the lifecycle of an application and so have an interest in its security. They have differing but overlapping concerns and need to be considered individually.

The first, of course, is you, the application writer. There are four areas that commonly need to be secured:

- anti-piracy information such as registration codes, expiry dates and trial-mode flags. There may be a significant financial impact if this information is compromised

- intellectual property such as pictures and artwork. You may have expended considerable effort in developing these and wish to prevent unauthorized copies, or you may have licensed them from a supplier under terms that require you to protect them

- information that may devalue your product if it became widely known, such as a map of all of the high-value items in a game

- methods of bypassing parts of your product without your consent, such as using your game engine with a different client or reskinning your media renderer.

Some of these may be of particular interest to developers of software products that compete with yours, and we will see later that this should also guide your security strategy.

The next category of people to consider is the end-users. Their concerns are usually straightforward and are three-fold:

- incurring unauthorized financial cost. This is often caused by messages that are sent, or voice or data calls that are made, without the user's consent, particularly to high-charging end-points. Less commonly, malware may attempt to use financial information on the mobile phone, such as using account details to make unauthorized transactions

- disclosure of personal information. This is a particularly sensitive area as different users have different concepts of what information is personal and what is a reasonable disclosure

- inability to access valuable data. There are three common cases of this: loss (deletion) of data, corruption of data and data being held in a proprietary format that can no longer be accessed.

Another group with a vested interest in the security of your application is the retailers. Although not usually concerned with specific security issues, other than anti-piracy protection, they will not want to sell products that generate end-user complaints or damage the market for their other products. Network operators will also be concerned about unhappy end-users, particularly if your application gives rise to disputed call charges. In an extreme case an application that could be provoked to flood the network with call set-up attempts, or other messages, would also arouse the interest of the operator.

The owners of other content on the mobile phone, whether data or applications, will also be concerned with the integrity of your application, even though you do not intend your application to access their content. In particular, they will expect that your application does not cause the following problems:

- the ability to read data that another application protects. A file browser that allowed the viewing of another application's DRM decryption keys would undermine the integrity of that application

- the ability to subvert data on which another application depends (such as resetting the timestamp on an evaluation copy of an application)

- the ability to use your application as a stepping-stone to increase privileges in an uncontrolled fashion. This, typically, occurs when your application is trusted by another application with more capabilities. Subverting your application may persuade the higher capability application to misbehave. This is classically known as an 'escalation of privilege' attack.

Lastly, the organization that signs your application will usually need assurance that it is secure, especially if your application requests one of the more sensitive capabilities. Their concerns will encompass many of the concerns of the other parties, including those of the owners of other content and applications. They may restrict you from writing a file browser that obtains other applications decryption keys, but they also stop other applications from having the capability to read your registration codes, and so they provide a safe but fair playing field for all developers. They can do this by signing applications but also by revoking the signatures on badly behaved applications.

Writing your application in a secure way is a winning strategy for a developer, as signing increases your application's visibility and the security increases the end-user's confidence and happiness with your product. An insecure application may lead to poor distribution and, in an extreme case, could lead to the application being blocked, and, possibly most significantly, damage the developer's reputation.

4.2.2 What Do They Expect to be Secured?

Having decided who the stakeholders in your application's security are, what their concerns are and which ones are of concern to you, you should produce a list of those areas that you need to protect in your application. The list for a typical application, considering the stakeholders listed above, might be:

- data that is not to be disclosed outside the application. This might include registration codes, etc.

- data that is not to be disclosed except to the user or other trusted software. The user's contact list may be displayed to the user or sent to a printer but should not be left where an untrusted application could access it. The software that you trust will depend on the data – for example, you may wish to have your artwork displayed but not printed

- data that requires high integrity. This is data that should be protected against inappropriate modification, such as a certificate that identifies the bank to which the user is willing to send their account number and password

- normal behavior that can be used in abnormal ways. For example, an image renderer that is trusted to print DRM-protected content, used in conjunction with a printing module that will print to file, could easily be used to obtain an unprotected electronic copy

- securing the environment against unexpected modification by specific attacks designed to cause abnormal behavior.

4.2.3 Who Is Interested in my Application's Insecurity?

Now that you have decided what you want to protect, you can consider who might want to attack your application, and why and how they might go about it. This will guide you in deciding the level of risk, and, therefore, the level of security that you need to protect your application. Attacks come in various guises but usually fall into one of four categories:

- attempts to cause damage or inconvenience to the user of the mobile phone, without regard for specific applications

- attempts to trawl the mobile phone for data deemed useful to the attacker. This might include names, addresses, financial account details, passwords and PINs

- attacks specifically on your application for the data it holds or can access

- attacks that specifically use your application as a means of replication, or of elevating the attacker's capabilities.

Attacks on your application can come from one of several routes. These are:

- other installed software that includes malicious behavior that is either unknown to or condoned by the user

- specific messages sent to the phone using mechanisms such as SMS, MMS, Bluetooth or infrared

- your own user interface. This could be because the authorized user of the mobile phone is attempting to exploit your application (e.g. to avoid registration) or it might be an attempt by an unauthorized user to obtain information from a stolen phone.

4.3   What Countermeasures Can Be Taken?

4.3.1   Know What your Application Does

Moving on to the means to protect your application, it may seem strange that the first topic is ensuring that you know what your application does. However, most applications start small and grow in functionality with each release. At the beginning it is clear to the developer what the purpose of the application is, but, as more features and options get added, the breadth of functionality often clouds clarity of purpose. Eventually, some applications reach the point where there are so many combinations of behavior that it is impractical to remember all of the possible internal interactions. This increases the chances that an attacker can cause unexpected behavior or data disclosure. A simple word processor that is enhanced to display DRM-protected embedded images and is further enhanced to support macro directives in the text might suddenly be used to save an image in an unsecured form.

Modularity

A large piece of code, potentially with many capabilities and with considerable functionality, is not only more difficult to secure but more dangerous when exploited. If your application is reaching this stage, and you have not already done so, you should consider partitioning it into more manageable (and easier to secure) modules. The degree of partitioning will depend on the protection that you require. At the most extreme, using multiple processes gives you the full protection of the operating system, with each process having its own platform security capabilities, so that no piece of code need have more capabilities than it really needs. Processes can only interact through defined APIs, have their own data-caged private filestore and cannot modify each other's memory, giving you rigid security. The disadvantages of this approach are extra code, more complex MakeSIS package files and a potential impact on performance. Less extreme forms of partitioning include using multiple threads within a process and, of course, the traditional C++ object class structure. Each thread may have a separate memory allocation but this is not protected against corruption from other threads. Likewise classes in the same thread, and threads within a process, all share a common filestore and capability set.

Whatever form of modularity you choose, you should concentrate on the APIs between each component. Good object-oriented design will have taught you encapsulation; this skill can be reused for protection. A secure API will expose only the information that needs to be exposed, ensure that modifications to its data retain consistency and is at a sufficiently high level that it is not vulnerable to having a series of requests disordered. For example, if a database expected the following sequence of calls:

```
TRecordId recordId = database.FindRecord(key);
database.Lock();
database.DeleteRecord(recordId);
database.Unlock();
```

providing instead the single call:

```
database.FindAndDeleteRecord (key);
```

will protect against attempts to delete an arbitrary record, to lock the database and never unlock it, or to delete without locking. Even if you haven't partitioned your application into separate processes, this approach will reduce exploitable programming bugs.

Plug-ins

When you consider what your application does (or what you think it does) you should give plug-ins special treatment. If your application allows plug-in code to execute (typically using ECOM), then you may need to limit which plug-ins can be loaded. Fortunately, platform security will not permit DLLs with a lower capability set than your process to be loaded by ECOM, but you may wish to provide further restrictions if you don't want other developers providing plug-ins for your application. Plug-ins are covered in more detail in Chapter 6.

4.3.2   Mind your Capabilities

Most platform security capabilities have particular associated risks, either individually or in combination. If your application has capabilities, it should be designed to ensure that they cannot be maliciously exploited. The following are some examples of common risks associated with particular capabilities.

NetworkServices

Network connections can incur charges and may affect other users. A destination number used for telephone calls or messaging should be protected against malicious modification. Consider limiting the number of messages sent, or the amount of data transferred before confirming with the user. This will minimize unexpected costs and reduce the chances of being used as a conduit to broadcast malware.

ReadUserData, ReadDeviceData, Location, UserEnvironment

Applications with these capabilities have access to information that the user may not want others to see. Be wary of where you store this information (log files are sometimes a source of leaks of information) and be particularly stringent if your application has `NetworkServices` or `LocalServices` capabilities (or communicates with other processes that do) as this gives an opportunity for remote snooping.

AllFiles, Tcb

Applications with these capabilities have unrestricted access to the file system (`AllFiles` can read everything and write all but `\sys` and `\resource`; `Tcb` can write to `\sys` and `\resource`). It is imperative that they take the highest level of precautions against race conditions with creation, deletion and rollback, and are allowed minimal run-time variations in behavior. It is well worth partitioning the trusted code into a separate process and ensuring that it rigorously identifies which processes it communicates with.

PowerMgmt

Applications with this capability can kill other processes, switch off the power or switch it on again. These operations should not be performed purely at the behest of other applications – user authorization should be sought. Any code that repeats such operations should limit the recurrence rate (or count) so that the user does not lose control of the mobile phone.

ProtServ

This capability is specifically relevant to servers rather than normal applications. However, you may have partitioned your application to include such a server. It is essential that a server using this capability does not usurp the name of any other protected server and so you should choose the most specific name that is reasonable. More details on secure servers can be found in Chapter 5.

4.3.3   Keep your Data Protected

Keep your Data Files Private

The introduction of platform security in Symbian OS has included the ability to place an application's data in a secure data 'cage' where nothing else can access it. This alone is probably your most powerful tool in protecting your application so make sure that you use it to the full! Each application has a directory under \private in which only that application can create, read and write files.

> You should always plan to use your application's private directory to store all of your files unless there is a specific reason to the contrary.

When you install your SIS file, you can arrange for files to be put into your private directory, which the installer will create for you automatically. If you haven't done so, your application can create the directory itself when it runs.

```
RFs fs;
User::LeaveIfError(fs.Connect());
CleanupClosePushL(fs);
TInt err = fs.CreatePrivatePath(EDriveC);
if (err != KErrAlreadyExists && err != KErrNone)
  {
  User::Leave(err);
  }
User::LeaveIfError(fs.SetSessionToPrivate(EDriveC));
```

One common reason for placing a file outside a private directory is to allow many different processes to access it. However, it is rare to have a file that you want to share with all processes; you usually wish to share with a particular group. In this case, you should consider writing a server to provide and police access to the data, so that you can still keep the file in a private area. A simple way to do this is for a handle to the file to be passed by the server to any other process that you are willing to grant access to (see Chapter 5). This may not give a sufficient level of interlocking or granularity for many applications but, if it is appropriate for you, it is easy to implement. If you have small quantities of data to share then you also have the options of using either the central repository or the secure DBMS server to store the data (see Chapter 7 for more detail on the various options available for sharing data securely).

Do make sure that data that you intend to keep in your private directory remains there at all times. A common error is to create temporary files in public directories where they can be read or modified by other processes. Even exclusive access won't protect your applications if the mobile phone reboots at the wrong time.

Expect External Access to your Files

Earlier we said that no other application could access your application's private directory. Strictly speaking this isn't true as an application with `AllFiles` capability has full access to all private directories. It is unlikely that any application would be signed to give it an `AllFiles` capability unless the signing authority was confident that the capability would not be misused. Of the few components that actually have this capability, examples are the native software installer itself (which needs to access private directories to allow applications to be installed and uninstalled) and the secure backup and restore engine (which needs to access private directories to read their backup configuration files and to backup and restore the selected files). You need to consider your application's interaction with these two components, together with the possibility of direct access to the file system by bypassing the Symbian OS; these cases are described below.

Don't Trust Removable Media

If your private directory is on a drive that is on a removable medium, for example, a Memory Stick or MMC, then there is nothing to stop the user from removing the card, placing it in a PC and reading it there.

> Data on removable media can be accessed without going through the Symbian OS protection mechanisms when it has been removed from the mobile phone.

Whether this is an issue for your specific application is for you to decide but you should consider two points:

- Could your application use the card to store data that you've identified in the category that you don't want the user to access?

- Could your application store data on the card that the user wouldn't want to be retrieved from a stolen card?

If the user has all their account details stored in your banking application, it doesn't matter how many passwords your application needs from the user if a thief can bypass it entirely by taking the card out of the mobile phone! Some phones support password-protected cards but you shouldn't assume that all cards on all mobile phones have this protection.

You can force particular files to be installed on particular drives by explicitly specifying the drive letter in the target path in the PKG file, instead of using the '!' character that lets the user select the drive at installation time. You should use this sparingly however as it stops the user from making the most of their total storage space and may even prevent them from installing your application at all. Obviously your choices will be guided by the size and sensitivity of your files and the space on the mobile phone but some options to consider are:

- Only store sensitive data on an internal drive.

- If you are protecting access to the data with a user-supplied password or PIN, your application could encrypt the stored data with that password or PIN and the user could select the drive of their choice at install time.

- If you have no user-supplied encryption key, your application could create one and store it on an internal drive, using it to encrypt any sensitive data stored on a removable drive.

You can tell if a particular drive is removable by calling RFs::Drive and examining the iDriveAtt member of the returned TDriveInfo for the KDriveAttRemovable attribute.

```
RFs fs;
TDriveInfo driveInfo;
User::LeaveIfError(fs.Connect());
CleanupClosePushL(fs);
User::LeaveIfError(fs.Drive(driveInfo, KDefaultDrive));
if(driveInfo.iDriveAtt&KDriveAttRemovable)
   {
   // Removable
   }
else
   {
   // Not removable
   }
```

The encryption methods available to you depend on the particular SDK that you are using.

Of course, even an internal drive is vulnerable to someone willing to take the mobile phone's circuit boards to pieces and pull the data out of the storage chips. As you've already considered what might be of value and who might conduct an attack, you'll be able to tell if that's a risk that you're willing to take.

The second problem that you may have with removable drives is that the user may modify the contents of the card on a PC and then reinsert it on the mobile phone. You may not care if the user fakes their high score in your game, but you might be more concerned if the expiry date for a trial version of your application is changed. You cannot prevent tampering when the card is out of the mobile phone, so any data that must be tamper-proof should be stored on an internal drive. However, it is often more efficient to use tamper-detection, where the user can change the data but the application can detect this and deal with the situation appropriately. For example, if a user did change their high-score table, the application could reset it to zero. If a change was made to the expiry date of an evaluation copy of an application it could simply refuse to run. The simplest form of tamper-detection is to store a cryptographic hash of the vulnerable data on an internal drive. A hash is similar to a checksum but has the property that it is particularly difficult to change data while keeping the same hash, whereas that is relatively easy to do with a checksum. Symbian OS uses this technique itself when program binaries are installed on removable media, to ensure that their capabilities and other properties of the binaries (as well as the code itself) are not modified after installation. Just in case someone wires up a removable card so that they can modify it without removing it from the mobile phone, Symbian OS checks the hash each time the binary is loaded. You may wish to use a similar level of security, or you may decide only to check when the card is changed while your application is running e.g. by using the RFs::NotifyDismount API.

Symbian OS provides a range of hash functions (also known as message digests or one-way functions) – such as SHA-1 and MD5, which are implemented by the CSHA1 and CMD5 classes – that you can use to do this.

```
sha=CSHA1::NewL();
CleanupStack::PushL(sha);
TPtrC8 data(_L8("The quick brown fox jumped over the lazy dog"));
TBuf8<128> hash = sha->Hash(data);
```

Don't Trust Backup and Restore

Backups are things that we all know should be done regularly and we see them as something that reduces risks rather than creating them. Although they do indeed reduce the risks of data loss or corruption, they add some security risks in return.

The basic purpose of a backup is to copy your data and code from the mobile phone and put it on the user's PC; however, once it is there it can be examined outside of the normal security constraints. This gives rise to the same sort of risks that removable media presents, but with the added risk that the contents of an internal drive may also be present in the backup.

> Data in a backup can be accessed without going through the Symbian OS protection mechanisms while the data is away from the mobile phone.

For backup, there are six different categories into which application data may fit (although not all are likely to apply to a single application):

- There may be some data that it doesn't make sense to backup or restore under any circumstances:

  - It can be easily recreated (e.g. a cache of downloaded web pages).

  - It is dependent on the particular mobile phone (e.g. the IMEI).

  - It is not meaningful to backup and restore the data (e.g. the total duration of all voice calls made so far).

  - It is dangerous to do so (e.g. the usage credits for your application).

- Some data cannot be safely backed up because it is inherently transient (e.g. a temporary file used for spooling) and may be changing while the backup is in progress. As active applications are usually terminated before a backup starts (and restarted after), this will only apply in unusual cases.

- Some data is never backed up because you don't want it disclosed under any circumstances. For example, if the user had provided a PIN to allow your financial software package to access their bank account over the Internet, you may decide that it is better to force the user to re-enter it if needed rather than risk its accidental disclosure.

- Some data needs protecting against unauthorized access (e.g. from malware on a PC holding the backup) but does not need protection from the authorized user. Such data might include contacts, call records etc. This data can be protected by encrypting it with a user-provided key and, depending on the particular models of mobile phones that your application is aimed at, this encryption may be done automatically for you by the backup software. Do bear in mind that users are usually not good at choosing good passwords or PINs if you rely on this.

- Some data is only safe to have backed up provided that it cannot be extracted from the backup. The classic example for this would be an authorization or decryption key. This can be done by protecting it with a key that remains on the mobile phone and again, depending on the model, this may be done for you by the backup software. Of course, this means that the data can only be restored to the same mobile phone it was backed up from. It isn't possible to have data that can be restored on any arbitrary new mobile phone but cannot be decoded on a PC – if you're not convinced, remember that the PC can run an emulator of the phone!

- Lastly, and probably most frequently, you may have data that can be backed up for which you need no protection. As an example, you may decide that web bookmarks are not confidential. Others might think that they are which is why you have to choose carefully – security almost always has a cost, in terms of implementation effort, performance penalty, or user inconvenience which should be weighed against the benefit.

The easiest approach is to ensure that all the data in a given file is to be backed up with the same constraints (this is usually the case anyway).

The backup process 'fails safe' in that it protects your application if you do nothing to handle backups. Unfortunately, it does this by backing up none of your application's program binaries or private files. You can ensure that your files are backed up by creating a `backup_registration.xml` file in your private directory. The most straightforward form of this that will backup all of your files is:

```xml
<?xml version="1.0" standalone="yes"?>
<backup_registration>
  <passive_backup>
    <include_directory name = "\" />
  </passive_backup>
  <system_backup/>
  <restore requires_reboot = "no"/>
</backup_registration>
```

The directory name '\' specifies the whole private directory of the application; however, you are more likely to want to be selective about the files that get backed up so that you can pick specific files and directories:

```xml
<?xml version="1.0" standalone="yes"?>
<backup_registration>
  <passive_backup>
    <include_directory name = "save" />
    <include_directory name = "data" />
    <exclude_file name = "data\count" />
    <exclude_file name = "pid" />
  </passive_backup>
  <system_backup/>
  <restore requires_reboot = "no"/>
</backup_registration>
```

Note that the `<system_backup/>` directive causes your program binary files to be backed up as well. Your binaries were in the original SIS file that was installed, so you will not usually want to keep them secret.

However, if you do (for example, if they were DRM-protected), remove the directive from the file. If you do this, remember that, if the user loses their mobile phone, the binaries won't be in the backup when they restore to its replacement, and they will need to keep the original SIS file in order to reinstall the application.

If your data protection requirements are stronger, or you want to back up selected parts of files rather than whole files, you can use an active backup, where your application passes data of your choosing, packaged with whatever protection you decide to implement. You can do this by providing an implementation of `MActiveBackupData-Client` and using it to create a `CActiveBackupClient` and specifying `<active_backup>` in your registration file.

A useful way of getting the benefits of an active backup without having to write too much code is to register for both an active and a passive backup. When the backup engine starts, your application will be asked to provide an active backup. Instead, your application can use the opportunity to extract the particular data that you want backed up into a suitably protected file, and return no data for the active backup. The passive backup can then back up the specially created file.

The problems with restore are similar to those of writable removable media. However, you do have one extra pair of defenses. If you have an active backup you can filter the data on restore and if you have a passive backup only the directories (or files) listed in your backup registration file will be restored, so you can check these before, perhaps, moving the contents to a different location. Remember that if you use a more generic registration file (as in the first example above) rather than a more specific file (as in the second example), you should be alert for the appearance of extra files from a modified backup.

Lastly, when deciding your backup and restore policy, don't forget any data that you may have in the central repository or the DBMS server.

Don't Trust Import Directories

Although other processes cannot write to your application's private directory (with the exception of processes with `AllFiles` as noted above), if you have a private directory with a sub-directory called `import` (e.g. `\private\13579BDF\import`) then the native software installer will allow other SIS files to deliver files into that directory. If you expect to make use of this, then you should bear in mind that the files could come from any unverified, untrusted source and may arrive at any time (for example while your application is in the middle of checking the directory). You may wish to move such files to a separate directory before checking them but remember that the copies won't be deleted if the other SIS file is subsequently uninstalled.

4.4   Implementation Considerations

4.4.1   Be Careful Who You Talk to

No useful application runs without communicating with other processes, even if these are just the file server or the window server. You should ensure that any process with which you are communicating is the one that you expect before sending it confidential data or trusting data from it.

Connecting to Standard Servers

How can you be sure, when you write your data to a file, that you are talking directly to the file server and not another server that is making a copy of the data before passing it on?

Usually you will access the servers provided by Symbian OS through a client library, which is responsible for creating the link with the correct process. The client code will connect to the desired server (using `RSessionBase::CreateSession`) by specifying the server's name. This has been the traditional means of identifying servers in Symbian OS but has always had an associated risk – a server with a name such as `RandomServer` only meant that that particular server had its name registered first when the system started up, not that it was *the* random number server. The standard Symbian OS servers now have their names beginning with '!' to guarantee their identity. The random number server is now securely named `!RandomServer` and you can be reassured that you are connecting to what you expect. (If you're using a random number to generate an encryption key, you want to be confident about your source!) What stops another server from also calling itself `!RandomServer`? If you try it you'll find that you need the `ProtServ` capability to have '!' in the name.

Communicating with Other Processes

Earlier we suggested sharing file handles with processes that you trust. Each process has a unique Secure ID or SID but, if your application has several processes or you are developing a suite of interoperating applications, you may find it easier to use the Vendor ID or VID. Each process has a VID, which is taken from the VID of the EXE from which it was created. You can set this using the `VENDORID` keyword in the MMP file that you use to compile your application. Any non-zero value requires your application to be signed, and the signing authority will check that no one else uses your VID and that you use no one else's VID. This means that you can be confident that other applications that communicate with your application are part of your application suite by checking that their VIDs match yours. You can determine the VID of a process using the

`RProcess::VendorID` API and its SID using `RProcess::SecureID`. Servers can use similar methods on an `RMessage2` which is described in Chapter 5.

Know your Creator

Some applications allow the process that creates them to pass in options or data, at the point that the process is created, using `RProcess::SetParameter` in the parent process and `User::GetTIntParameter` or `User::GetDesParameter` in the child process. If you have a helper application that does this (for example, to exercise capabilities that you don't want to give to the creator process), it should be suspicious of any of the data that is passed in until it has identified the creating process as one that it trusts. One way to do this is using `User::CreatorSecureId` or `User::CreatorVendorID`. However, a more complete solution is to use the `TSecurityPolicy` class. Although this class is more commonly used in servers, the `CheckPolicyCreator` method is ideal for applications to check out their creating processes.

4.4.2   Be Careful in your Error Messages

No-one is going to be so foolish as to generate an error such as 'the third character of your password was entered incorrectly' (although there have been successful attacks on passwords by timing the error response to determine how many characters were correct.) Nonetheless, some error messages can be too informative. For example, if your application provides a search function on a database of people's names, some of which are only revealed when a PIN is entered, displaying the message 'This entry is PIN protected' rather than 'Not found' allows someone with access to the mobile phone to tell if a particular person's name is in the database without needing to know the PIN. Consider the trade-offs that you wish to make between being helpful and disclosing too much.

4.4.3   Be Careful with your Log Files

Log files can be useful when developing an application and also help to diagnose problems after your application has been delivered. They are also a common cause of accidental exposure of information. Before you finish your application you should consider:

- whether you still need any logs
- where logs should be stored (and how you expect them to be accessed)
- what information needs to be logged.

For example, it may be useful for an email client to log messages of the form 'Connected to server at date/time, downloaded 3 messages'. It may be less desirable to record the server name, still less any user name and password, or the sender and recipient email addresses.

4.4.4 Check your Inputs

As well as being cautious about where your input data comes from, it's important to check the actual data provided. Failure to check input data is the single biggest cause of technical security weaknesses in computing. Symbian OS is less prone to attacks such as buffer overflow than many other systems through its use of descriptors, but care is still needed.

Decide When to Check

The golden rule with input (particularly user input) is 'always check before use'. For efficiency it is best to check only once and this usually means placing the checks at the point of input. It is all too easy to assume that a later check is unnecessary because it was performed earlier and vice versa, so try to have all your checks in one place, where possible, and make sure that any exceptions to this are documented in all the places where the checks are done.

The main exception to the 'check once at input' guideline is when the checks that you are performing are against things that might change. For example, a file that might not exist when you perform the check may have appeared by the time that you come to use the filename, or a future time for an appointment may be in the past by the time that the user has provided the appointment details. Of course, your application should be robust against such things anyway but it is worth minimizing the window of risk.

It is also important to ensure that your checks cannot be bypassed. If you cross a process or DLL boundary, consider whether something may subvert the data on the way. You should ensure that there is no way that the subsequent pieces of your code can be reached without going through the checking code.

Decide What to Check

Few applications need to check all of their data and few need to check none of it. Most applications are in the dangerous middle ground where you, the application author, must decide what needs checking and what is safe to ignore. A financial application may filter the numeric values that it reads, but should it also check the length of a filename? If the file contains a graphical image, might it be corrupt?

Decide How to Check

The checks that you make depend on the semantics of the data of your particular application. However, the following list may help:

- Are unbounded pointers used when descriptors should be used instead?

- Are any data items allocated to be 'big enough'? Is this maximum designed to be big enough for the largest non-malicious use and might it be possible to overflow using maliciously constructed input?

- Might the assumptions for size requirements change in the future? Will the code fail securely if these change?

- Are limits checks done against all directions? For example, an integer count may be zero as well as too large or an absolute filename may be too short as well as too long.

- Are you making assumptions about which values the user will use, such as assuming that only the ASCII subset of UNICODE will be used?

If you have the opportunity, letting the user select from a set of values that are known to be valid removes the risk. For example, letting the user pick a date from a displayed calendar ensures that only displayable dates can be selected. Do be cautious that subsequent selections or input may make the original input invalid (for example, selecting 'January' from a list of months followed by '31' from a list of days followed by a reselection of 'February').

Take Special Care with Filenames

With the advent of platform security you may have noticed that many of the Symbian OS APIs now expect to be passed file handles rather than filenames. This means that the client of the API has to open the file itself and confirms to the API provider that the client has legitimate access to the file. Where possible, you should follow the same approach when accepting files across process boundaries; this is particularly important if your process has more sensitive capabilities. Incidentally, remember that the receiver of a file handle can discover the name of the file (using RFile::FullName) so don't put information in the filenames that you don't want to leak out.

Usually you will be in the unfortunate position of having to handle filenames and these require special consideration for two reasons.

The first problem is in determining the canonical name of a file. Depending on the circumstances, a filename may be relative to a current directory, may contain special sequences such as '.', '. .' or '*' and may be on a substituted drive. Selection from a list (e.g. a file browser) is the easiest way of avoiding this problem but be aware of filenames that are read from files that may have been tampered with (simply rejecting any unexpected sequences may suffice in this case).

The second problem with filenames is that many applications need to discriminate between files that exist to help the application work (e.g. a license key for an image editor) and files that exist for the application to work on (e.g. an image for an image editor). The names of the first group of files are often hard-coded into your application; the names of the second group are frequently user selected. Allowing that selection to encompass a file from the first group may well be dangerous (as an extreme example, consider a word processor that allowed the reading and modification of a file containing a license expiry date). You may choose to protect against this by using a naming convention such as file extensions or by putting all of the files that support your application in a sub-directory with a name that you filter out.

4.4.5   Abnormal Circumstances

Why Abnormal Situations are Often Exploited

There are many error conditions and unusual events that could occur during the execution of an application. For an application to be secure, it not only needs to handle such events but also needs to handle them securely.

Code is frequently designed, written, reviewed and tested assuming normal, successful execution, with abnormal conditions and error handling frequently added as an afterthought or even omitted altogether. When present, such handling is often little more than ensuring that all allocated data is on the `CleanupStack` if an out-of-memory `Leave` occurs. This means that the behavior of the application in unusual conditions has often not been considered and, because of this, creating unusual circumstances is a popular attack from a malicious user or malicious code. Although you may have thought of some combinations of events as being sufficiently improbable that they can be disregarded, once a successful attack has been discovered, many minds will be ensuring that that particular combination happens on demand.

What Events may Occur?

Symbian OS is designed for limited resource devices and as such it is normal practice for code to be written with an expectation that memory allocations might fail. Code is less often written assuming that power may fail at any time or that the mobile phone may be rebooted. Even though the battery may have a full charge, a user might remove it at the least convenient time, for example to put it in a charger, giving your application little or no time to clean up.

Other events may happen during run-time and are usually indicated by error codes being returned from the system APIs. Ignoring error codes is a common practice among programmers but it implies that the programmer knows that the call can never fail (which may be true but only rarely) or that they don't care if it fails (which again is rarely the case) or that they are hoping to be lucky. If you are that confident in your luck, you should consider a career trading stocks rather than writing software! If you're not that confident, check your error values.

Some errors are easily produced by an untrained user, such as removing a media card at the wrong point (for example, when your application is about to update the 'remaining credits' file). Some may need specific software to exploit them (for example, grabbing a semaphore at the wrong time, crashing your server or deleting or creating public files). Remember that it may take a skilled programmer to produce software to create such problems for your application but if it allows attackers to break into your application there will be many copies made.

Handling Unusual Events

Some errors may be handled by terminating the application. If you take this option, you should ensure that before terminating, your application always leaves a secure, consistent environment. A secure environment means that all sensitive data is caged and any resources are tidied up. In particular you should look out for any resources such as network connections that may be reused by other processes, particularly if your application has already provided the authentication or authorization to use them. A consistent environment means that your application can be run successfully when restarted without being confused by the state it finds.

Always leave your external state (especially filestore) in a form that is safe if your application suddenly terminates.

If your application implements some form of roll-forward or rollback on restart, be particularly careful that the list of operations to be rolled forward or back is secured!

For most errors, your application will continue to execute. The chief risk here is that subsequent code may assume that the previous code has executed successfully. For example, code that loops, prompting the user for a password, but exits the loop during an 'out of memory' error does not mean that the password was correctly entered.

4.5   Summary

This chapter explains how to build up a clear view of what you want to protect, why you want to protect it, how you are going to protect it and who you are protecting it from.

First we covered how to analyze the security threats your application may face, based on consideration of who will need your application to be trustworthy, what they expect to be protected (including the need to avoid disclosing inadvertently the data of other applications), and who might want to attack your application's security.

Then we discussed what steps can be taken to address the threats, including structuring your application with security in mind, the need to use capabilities responsibly, and protecting data. This includes consideration of the risks of removable media, of backup and restore operations, and other ways that your data may be inadvertently exposed.

Finally, we covered some tips on secure implementation, including the importance of verifying both input data and its source, and consideration of unexpected situations that your application might have to deal with.

Ultimately, you're the person who knows your application best. When designing, think what to protect. When coding, always think 'what if . . . ?' And when you think that you've finished, always ask yourself 'How would I exploit this?'

5

How to Write Secure Servers

by Jonathan Dixon

5.1 What Is a Secure Server?

In this chapter we look in detail at writing server software. Servers demand special attention as they are, in many ways, a cornerstone of the whole platform security architecture, as we described in Chapter 2. A typical server will have one or more capabilities to enable it to perform its functions, and, in the same way as any other application software, it has a duty to moderate and protect its use of these capabilities, so that it is not unduly influenced in its usage of them by other, less trusted processes. However, servers seem to have a dichotomy here, as the very purpose of a server is to provide services to other processes, which will often have no particular trust level. Resolving this apparent dichotomy is a key part of good server design.

5.1.1 Symbian OS Servers

Before diving into the details of secure servers, we should recap the basics of what we mean by a 'server'.

Symbian OS is built around a micro kernel, with system services such as the file server and communication protocol stack implemented in 'user space' processes. Application processes gain access to these services via a robust inter-process communication (IPC) mechanism modeled around a client–server architecture.

The primary purpose of a server is to mediate and arbitrate for multiple clients who share access to a resource. The server code executes within one process, but clients of its services may execute in multiple processes in the system.

As described in Chapter 2, the process is the unit of trust in the platform security architecture. This means that the process boundary is also the trust boundary. As client–server is by far the most commonly used generic IPC mechanism within Symbian OS, it is the most natural point at which to enforce policies regarding this crossing of the trust boundary. The fact that the client–server IPC is designed for robustness, as are the servers themselves to a large extent, is an additional benefit that helps in this task. The kernel is responsible for mediating this communication between client and server, and so must be mutually and universally trusted by these processes to carry out this role in the secure environment.

There are, however, other places where the process and trust boundaries can be crossed. Examples range from the use of shared memory chunks or global semaphores, through to message queues, properties, settings or even the file system itself. Some of these are discussed here or in subsequent chapters, however, client–server is the primary mechanism and we recommend this is what you use as your primary interface to such services. It is what we concentrate on in this chapter.

One exception to the use of client–server is device drivers. The kernel provides the means for user code to communicate with hardware device drivers via channels into the kernel executive. However, both conceptually and in practical terms there are many similarities and equivalencies between a channel to a logical device driver (LDD), and a client–server connection to a server. For this reason, a great many of the principles and procedures presented here are quite relevant to producers of LDDs. (In this context a physical device driver (PDD) is analogous to a plug-in to a server. See Chapter 6 for more on this.)

Writing Symbian OS servers was once considered something of a 'black art', however, recently several books, such as *Symbian OS C++ for Mobile Phones* [Harrison 2003] and *Symbian OS Explained* [Stichbury 2005], have gone a long way to demystify this process. Rather than repeat what is covered in those volumes we will build upon them, highlighting points where interface methods or development methodology may differ when working in the platform security world.

5.1.2   An Example Secure Server

Before getting started on the process of designing security measures for your servers, it is useful to have a look at how the key concepts work in practice. For this reason, we will walk you through a simple example of securing your first server.

As already mentioned, the role of a server is to mediate access to a shared resource, to enable one or more clients to access that resource, sequentially or concurrently – much in the same way that the server at the front of a school dinner queue mediates access to the pot of stew, and acts as a proxy to accessing it on behalf of each hungry pupil standing in line!

To keep life simple for server developers, whilst also being frugal with system resources, servers are typically implemented within a single thread of execution in a dedicated process, ensuring the server's exclusive access to the underlying resource being shared.

Multiple clients can then access the server, via the kernel's IPC mechanism, by establishing a session with the server. The clients can then pass messages to the server to request that certain actions be performed. The messages are delivered to the server in order, and processed by the server as appropriate. The command protocol used in these messages is defined by the server. For this reason, virtually all servers supply a dedicated client-side library (DLL) that encapsulates this protocol, and generally serves to make the application developer's life easier.

Let's see what this all means in practice, with this example implementation of a client-side DLL:

```
class RSimpleServer : public RSessionBase
    {
public:
    IMPORT_C TInt Connect();
    IMPORT_C TInt GetInformation() const;
    };

_LIT(KSimpleServerName, "com_symbian_press_testserver1");
        static _LIT_SECURITY_POLICY_S0(KSimpleServerPolicy,
        0xE1234567); // a test UID used as the server's SID

EXPORT_C TInt RSimpleServer::Connect()
    {
    return CreateSession(KSimpleServerName, TVersion(), -1,
        EIpcSession_Unsharable, &KSimpleServerPolicy());
    }

EXPORT_C TInt RSimpleServer::GetUserInformation(TInt aInfoRequired,
                                                TDes8& aResult) const
    {
    return SendReceive(ESimpleServFnGetUserInfo, TIpcArgs(aRequest,
                                                &aResult));
    }
```

If you are familiar with client–server development for previous versions of Symbian OS, there should be little surprise here.

The base class for the client side of a client–server connection is `RSessionBase`; creating a connection to a server is achieved through the call `RSessionBase::CreateSession()`. The version used here is the new overload added in Symbian OS 9.x, and is of the form:

```
IMPORT_C TInt CreateSession(const TDesC& aServer, const TVersion& aVersion,
        const TInt aAsyncMessageSlots, TIpcSessionType aType,
        const TSecurityPolicy* aPolicy=0, TRequestStatus* aStatus=0);
```

The parameter we are most interested in is the pointer to an object of type `TSecurityPolicy`. This allows the client code to stipulate criteria for the server to which it will connect. In the example, we state that the server must be running in a process with a SID of `0xE1234567` (a test UID, see

Chapter 3 for more information), to guard against server spoofing. You will see other uses of these policy objects throughout this book. Other than this, establishing the session is essentially the same as before.

Having established the session, requests can be sent to the server using `RSessionBase::SendReceive()`. In the example the `GetUserInformation` method does exactly this. This has not changed significantly, although small improvements have been made to allow more robust marshalling of arguments. Specifically, you can see the `TIpcArgs` class being used to provide a typed container for the arguments to the message; `TIpcArgs` carries flags to allow the kernel to differentiate the various argument types, and thereby ensure that the server respects them correctly. This mechanism is described in more detail in *Symbian OS Internals* [Sales 2005].

Now let's see how this message is handled on the server side: `simpleserver.mmp`:

```
TARGET simpleserver.exe
TARGETTYPE exe
UID 0 0xE1234567     // test UID as UID3 / SID
SOURCE simpleserver.cpp
```

`simpleserver.cpp`:

```
class CSimpleServer : public CServer2
  {
protected:
  CSession2* NewSessionL(const TVersion& aVersion,
                  const RMessage2& aMessage);
  //...
  };

static _LIT_SECURITY_POLICY_C1(KSimpleServerConnectPolicy,
                               ECapabilityReadUserData);

CSession2* CSimpleServer::NewSessionL(const TVersion&
                aVersion,const RMessage2& aMessage)
  {
  if(!KSimpleServerConnectPolicy().CheckPolicy(aMessage,
      __PLATSEC_DIAGNOSTIC("CSimpleServer::NewSessionL
                       KSimpleServerConnectPolicy")))
    User::Leave(KErrPermissionDenied);

  // proceed with handling the connect request
  }
```

Here you see a server-side implementation of a security policy test. A simple way to protect an IPC interface is by restricting who can establish sessions with the server. After a connect message has been processed by the kernel, it reappears in user space in the server process, and is handled by the framework code – specifically the `CServer2` base class. This then calls the NewSessionL() method that is implemented by the derived concrete class, in our example, CSimpleServer. Here we perform this simple policy check: a security policy object is defined that requires the client to hold the ReadUserData capability. The connect message, as indicated by the RMessage2 parameter to NewSessionL(), is tested against this policy, and if it fails, the method throws a leave exception, with the new error code KErrPermissionDenied.

If the server has a more complex security policy, it may not be appropriate to restrict access to clients at the point that the connection is established, but instead individual IPC operations might be restricted.

```
class CSimpleSession : public CServer2
  {
protected:
  void ServiceL(const RMessage2 &aMessage);
  void GetUserInfoL(TInt aInfoRequired, TDes8& aResult);

  //...
  };

static _LIT_SECURITY_POLICY_C1(KSimpleServerUserInfoPolicy,
                                    ECapabilityReadUserData);

CSession2* CSimpleSession::ServiceL (const RMessage2& aMessage)
  {
  switch(aMessage.Function())
    {
  case ESimpleServFn1:
    // ... handle function
    break;

  case ESimpleServFnGetUserInfo:
    if(!KSimpleServerUserInfoPolicy().CheckPolicy(aMessage,
            __PLATSEC_DIAGNOSTIC("CSimpleSession::ServiceL
                        KSimpleServerUserInfoPolicy"))
    User::Leave(KErrPermissionDenied);
    // Process the request as normal
    RBuf8 result;
    result.CreateLC(aMessage.GetDesLengthL(1));
    result.CleanupClosePushL();
    GetUserInfoL(aMessage.Int0(), result);
    aMessage.WriteL(1, result);
    CleanupStack::PopAndDestroy();
    break;

  default:
    User::Leave(KErrNotSupported);
    }
  aMessage.Complete(KErrNone);
  }
```

Here we see that the server session code performs a very similar security policy check to the last example, but this time it is conditional on the value of aMessage.Function(). Here we are just picking out IPC messages that have a function value of `ESimple-ServFnGetUserInfo`, which corresponds to the call to `RSimple-Server::GetUserInformation()` in the client library that we started off with. We could also take this down to the next level, the security policy might depend on the value of `aInfoRequired` that was passed into the client call. This is represented on the server side in the `aMessage.Int0()` message parameter. An additional level of switch would be required in order to achieve this.

From this quite simple example, we can pick out some important points which we will explore further in the remainder of this chapter:

- Both the client and the server can make use of the platform security architecture to protect their IPC boundaries.

- The client will typically have a simple security policy, and the changes to client-side code are minimal.

- The server can have as simple or as complex a policy as its IPC protocol demands, thus the changes to the server code may be simple or complex.

- A complex server security policy could result in a great deal of repetitive security check code in a standard form. `CPolicyServer`, described in Sections 5.3.2 and 5.4.2, is a framework provided to help manage this complexity and minimize copy and paste bugs.

- Security policies are tested at the process boundary: the server does not rely on code in its client library to protect its interface.

- At any point where a trust boundary may be crossed, a check may be required.

5.2 Server Threat Modeling

Having now seen a simple example of how a server can protect its interface in practice, let's take a step back and look at how to design security into a server. As the old adage goes, always design security in, rather than bolt it on as an after-thought.

As we recommend throughout this book, a good place to start is through a threat model.

5.2.1 Step 1 – Identify the Assets you Wish to Protect

In most cases, a server provides a layer of abstraction over a lower level resource, and provides access to this resource for its clients. For example, the file server provides a file system layer over the raw disk device driver interface to the hardware, and arbitrates access to this resource on behalf of all file-using clients.

The primary assets to be protected are the underlying resources and the means by which the server allows direct or indirect access to those resources. The file server must protect the raw disk driver interface in order to avoid physical disk corruption, but it must also protect assets that are derived from this underlying physical resource, the individual files themselves. The file server and the file-system drivers it hosts must work together to ensure that, whatever a client does to one file, the contents of none of the other files are altered. Additionally, in the new platform security data caging architecture (see Chapter 2), clients must only be able to read or write files to which they are permitted access. Finally, the server must ensure it does not compromise one client through the actions of another. For example, a malicious client should not be able to use the file server to write data into another client's memory space – a duty of care, if you like.

To summarize, the assets for a typical server will consist of:

- the access to any 'physical' resources it owns (including its memory, data-caged files, and even its server name)

- any services it provides derived from or built on top of these resources

- the client sessions, which are assets to be protected from any other sessions.

Note that the order here is intended only to aid logical and comprehensive analysis; it is not intended to indicate any prioritization of risk levels.

5.2.2   Step 2 – Identify the Architecture and its Interfaces

As already stated, a server provides a layer of abstraction in a generic system model. It sits on top of lower layer (physical) services, and provides access to higher layer (application) clients. The most obvious interfaces a server exposes are:

1.   The IPC interface it opens to its client, via the client–server framework.

2.   The interface to underlying services or resources it needs in order to function.

3.   Any other interfaces into the server's process.

A server runs in a normal OS process – there may be occasions where one process would expose several server interfaces (such as ESOCK and ETEL, for instance) but often a server interface will have a dedicated process behind it. All the means of interfacing to a simple application process, as described in Chapter 4, should also be considered here – item numbers 2 and 3 in the above list are really just a reiteration of that. In this sense, a server process is the same as any other process, but with an increased attack surface due to its server interface.

Bear in mind the principle from Chapter 2, that the unit of trust in the platform security architecture is actually the operating system process, not the server. In many cases there is a one-to-one relationship between servers and processes, and this can help simplify one's reasoning. Note that it is a practical impossibility for one Symbian OS server (that is, the `RServer` or `RServer2` instance) to span multiple processes. However, when analyzing possible interfaces to a server, be aware that other code might execute within the same process as that server. Any interface opened by that code is also a potential interface to your server, so all interfaces into the *process* must be analyzed. It follows that all server interfaces into the process in question should be considered as a whole.

It may well be that you perform threat model analysis across a number of servers that co-operate to perform some common goal. Here you must look at both the external interfaces to the functional subsystem, and also analyze each internal interface, to ensure no 'back doors' into the subsystem are overlooked.

As with all processes, files used by the process should be identified because they form an interface with the process. In particular, do not overlook temporary files and log files, if they might be generated in a production (non-debug) build of your server.

As well as identifying the attack surface, this architectural analysis achieves an additional goal. By identifying the responsibilities of the server in question, and the interfaces that it depends on, the capability set of the server can be determined (if this is not already known).

5.2.3   Step 3 – Identify Threats to the Server

Using the information obtained from the previous steps, specific threats to the server can be identified and documented.

Detailed knowledge of the functionality provided by the server, and the way in which it is presented through its client API, is, naturally, very useful in driving this analysis. If the API is already well established, then working through it item by item, brainstorming on each of them, and on all other identified interfaces, is a methodical approach.

This is a good point to consider the capabilities held by the server. In many cases these might well be more numerous or more sensitive than those held by a typical application process. As such they provide a greater incentive for attack, and require a greater duty of care in identifying and addressing such threats. Threats can be brainstormed on a per-capability basis. For example, a server possessing the `ReadUserData` capability would need to consider if there is any way it could be manipulated or tricked into unknowingly revealing the user's private data or leaking confidential information. Processes that do not possess this capability would have fewer threats to consider here. There is a strong practical argument for striving to limit the set of capabilities held by any one server!

5.3 Designing Server Security Measures

We will now review how a server can implement countermeasures in order to minimize the risk posed by the threats identified. Measures are targeted to address specific threats. If you find yourself getting involved in developing a complex security policy or mechanism for your server, it is often worth checking what the threats are that the mechanism is addressing, whether the threat justifies the cost, and whether there isn't a more appropriate simpler measure. Don't forget hidden costs, such as maintaining the solution and reduced utility to the intended audience if the security policy is impractical.

The countermeasures are split into three broad types:

- platform security architecture – features provided 'for free' by the OS architecture

- server design and implementation – aspects of good server development that can work to mitigate security threats

- platform security mechanism – security mechanisms provided by the platform for use by the code, but which the code must be designed to utilize.

5.3.1 Platform Security Architecture

Loader Rules (prevent untrusted code execution in a trusted environment)

The platform security loader's rules provide a strong level of protection against rogue or malicious code executing within servers and gaining access to server-owned resources. However, this is no protection against well-meaning but bug-infested code within your server!

Process Isolation (prevents tampering with server execution environment)

From its inception, Symbian OS was designed to support a strong model of process isolation, using the processor's MMU to segregate physical memory address space. Indeed, the client–server architecture itself is a key part of this design, providing a robust means for processes to interact while minimizing the coupling between these processes. However, a number of the original APIs did provide means by which one process could interfere with another. These APIs had mainly been provided for the efficient implementation of specific use-cases on now outdated hardware. One example of this is the IPC v1 client–server APIs – hence the reason these are now superseded by the strongly-typed IPC v2 framework.

The above are generic features, afforded to all processes under the platform security architecture. However, they are worthy of repetition in this chapter on servers, as the server has an implicit responsibility not to undermine these mechanisms, if it wishes to receive the benefit of them! For instance, a server should be particularly careful not to accidentally execute untrusted code, which could be reached via a pointer passed by its client (or indeed any other process). One particularly insidious way that this could happen is by calling virtual functions of C++ objects supplied by the client. If the client were able to tamper with the object, it could change pointers in the `vtable` to cause arbitrary code to be executed. C++ objects, which may have virtual functions, must not be byte-copied from an IPC message – instead, objects should be externalized and internalized with rigorous bounds checking.

5.3.2   Platform Security Mechanisms

Session Connect Policy Check (detects server name spoofing)

As we illustrated in the example earlier in this chapter, when the client library code connects to a server it can specify a security policy, which the server must satisfy before the connection will be allowed to go ahead. This does not prevent a spoof server from taking the name of your server, but does provide a means through which the client library can detect this.

ProtServ for System Servers

In order to stop spoof servers from taking the names of critical system servers, the name space is partitioned into 'normal' and 'protected' parts. The protected name space is defined by all server names beginning with the '!' character. Registering server objects that have names beginning with this character with the kernel is only permitted for processes possessing the `ProtServ` capability, all others will receive an error return code from their call to `CServer2::Start()`. In this way, only processes trusted with this capability are permitted to provide system services. (As a rule of thumb, a system service can be considered to be one that would cause mobile phone instability if it were to have a fatal error and terminate abnormally.)

A convenient side-effect of this is that all such system servers are going to hold at least one capability – and a system capability at that – meaning that the loader rules prevent such system servers from loading any lesser trusted DLLs (i.e. any DLL lacking the `ProtServ` capability).

IPC Security Policy Check

This is the most significant new security measure available to servers within the platform security architecture. Servers can specify security policies defining which clients are allowed access to which parts of their IPC interfaces.

As we saw in the opening example, servers can make policy checks against clients at any time that it is appropriate, in order to determine whether a client is authorized to perform a given operation. This check can be against the identity of the client – i.e. against its SID – or, more generally, against the capability set held by the client, or a combination of both. In addition, it is possible for servers to derive their own security framework, built upon these building blocks, should it be necessary.

CPolicyServer Framework

As we touched upon in Section 5.1.2, correctly coding, verifying and maintaining a large or complex set of security policy checks within a server is a potentially error-prone activity. For this reason, the user library provides base-classes to make life easier for the server writer; this framework is called `CPolicyServer`, and allows for the definition of a static policy table based on the opcode number of the function being invoked over IPC. Once mastered, this can reduce the repetition involved in setting up a server's security policy. This is an important framework, and we will cover it in more detail in Section 5.4.2.

Data Caging

A server has the use of the private data-cage owned by the process it is running in. Once again assuming a one-to-one process–server relationship, this implies one private data-cage per server.

This is one mechanism through which the server can store non-volatile information it needs for its operation. Storing and sharing data is discussed further in Chapter 7.

There are numerous examples of servers making use of their data-caged area for storing private or confidential files – for example, the messaging server holds messages such as emails and text messages within its data-caged area.

Anonymous Objects and Secure Handle Transfer

The EKA2 kernel provides a powerful mechanism through which handles to kernel objects can be securely passed between processes, to allow secure sharing of the underlying resource. For example, a handle to an `RMsgQueue` may be passed from a producer process to a consumer process, and no other process will be permitted access to the kernel queue object.

There are two primary means for transferring such handles: at process start up in so-called process environment slots, and over the client–server interface.

Only handles to global objects can be transferred between processes using this mechanism. However, traditionally global objects were always accessible to any process, through an open by name operation. For this reason, unnamed (or anonymous) global objects have been introduced. To create an anonymous global object, `KNullDesC` should be passed as the name parameter in the appropriate `Create()` method.

5.3.3   Secure Server Design and Implementation

The following are design and implementation best practices, which, if followed, can also be considered as security measures employed by the server.

Constrain Server Responsibilities and Dependencies

A server that performs many different roles is harder to develop securely, and more of a liability should there be a security vulnerability within it. A server that has run-time dependencies on many other parts of the system, will be more fragile than one that has a constrained set of dependencies.

Architecturally, it is far simpler to consider and validate the behavior of a server that has clearly identified responsibilities, and constrained and identified dependencies, than one that performs many roles with dependency on many disparate subsystems. The simpler the design and validation of a server the better, as there will be fewer opportunities for introducing errors that could result in security vulnerabilities. Conversely, the more services a given server depends on, the more variables there are, and so the more complex the validation of its behavior will be. And the more security sensitive a server is, the more consideration should be given to this issue.

Parameter Validation

Whenever a client passes data to a server, the server must carefully validate the data before acting upon it – just as it must for any data coming in to the mobile phone, via a file or communication socket, for instance. This does not just apply to parameters supplied by the client application to the client library, but to all parameters received via the IPC message. So, even if a particular parameter is only ever provided by the client library itself in normal operation, it must still be validated in the server in case of an inept or malicious application creating its own messages to send to the server.

Particular problems are seen with asynchronous methods, as there is increased potential for the client data to go out of scope (for example, if a function with locally-scoped data terminates) between it being referenced in the message and the message being processed by the server. This is true even if the server runs at a higher priority than the client, as it may be blocked on some other operation at the moment the client thread issues the request. If a careless client releases and reuses the parameter's memory space before the server has processed the request, then it's probable that the server will receive an error in its attempt to read, write, or validate the data. A multi-threaded client, or one using shared memory, may exhibit similar bugs on synchronous calls too. One thread may modify the parameter's memory contents or allocation state while the client thread is blocked, even on a synchronous request.

To combat this, the server must expect to handle errors arising during client memory access, i.e. the `Read()`, `Write()` and `Get-DesLength()` members of `RMessagePtr2`; wherever possible, use the leaving overloads. Useful additions to particularly note are the new `RMessagePtr2::GetDesLengthL()` leaving overloads – these allow the server to safely discover the length of a client buffer, and have the standard exception framework take the burden on handling a descriptor error, without having to remember to manually check for negative error results, as is the case with the older non-leaving version.

Also, a server should never accept or use a pointer received over IPC. We have already noted that you must never call code via a pointer received in such a way, but security problems can also result from data that is pointed to being changed in unexpected ways or at unexpected times. In particular watch out for global or shared chunks – using them in a useful yet secure fashion is tricky enough not to be worth the effort except in the most bandwidth-critical applications.

Robust Error-handling Framework

Continuing from the previous point, the server-side error-handling framework should not be overlooked, as it is a very significant part of the security design of the server interface. The server error framework is built upon the standard `CActive` implementation of the leave/trap Symbian OS primitives. Unlike the IPC v1 `CServer` class, both `CServer2` and `CPolicyServer` provide an implementation of the `CActive::RunError()` interface, and, if relevant, they pass the trapped error onto the specific `CSession2` instance that was handling execution at the point the leave was encountered, providing it with the message that was being processed at that time via the `CSession2::ServiceError()` method. This means that concrete implementations of `CSession2` are able and encouraged to make maximum use of the leave framework. If required, the concrete session class can override `ServiceError()` with a custom implementation, although the default implementation, which simply completes the message with the leave code that was thrown, will suffice in many instances.

This means that if, during the initial (synchronous) processing of a client request, any error occurs – for example, low memory or disk resources, an invalid parameter in a deeply nested structure provided by the client, or a security policy failure – the same error handling framework will tidy up any partially allocated resources and complete the request, signaling the error condition back to the client.

Robust API Design

Getting the API design right can greatly ease the design and implementation of the security policy for that API. Here are a few points to consider:

- Functions with a specific purpose are easier to provide a policy for than multipurpose, generic or ambiguous methods, where the context must be taken into consideration in order to decide on the appropriate policy. For example, contrast `RDisk::Format()` with `RDisk::PerformAdministrativeOperation(TOperation)` or `RDisk::Extension(TExtId)`.

- Having a specific purpose also helps the user of the API to create secure code, as it is clearer what the consequences of calling the method might be.

- The primary outcome of a security policy failure in an API is an error code result, for example, `KErrPermissionDenied`. The error modes of APIs should be considered in general.

- Error codes should be returned to the client application at every point where an error can legitimately arise, but not in a place where the client would not be able to handle the error (such as when canceling or closing down). Generally the error should be indicated at the point at which failure has become inevitable, but no sooner.

Server Name

We saw how a client can use a security policy to ensure they only connect to the intended server. However, it is useful to ensure that the server chooses a sensible name in the first place. Longer names reduce the chance of conflict, and, as you can see in the opening example of this chapter, using the unique part of a DNS name owned by yourself can further improve matters.

It is also worth pointing out that the server name is quite distinct from the process name. Both are stored by the kernel, the server name in a

`DServer` object, the process name in a `DProcess` object. As already mentioned, one process can have many servers running in it. By default the process name is equal to the name of the EXE that was used to launch it, however, a process can rename itself to any name it wishes, as long as the new name is unique at that time. The only real value in a process name is for debugging and diagnostics. Specifically, no security check should be made based on a process's name – use the SID instead – and it should not be displayed to the user, as it is meaningless at best and potentially downright misleading at worst.

5.3.4 Determining the Security Policy

We now turn to one of the most common questions in the design of secured APIs: what capability should I use to protect access to my sensitive resources?

Here are the questions you should ask yourself in order to determine the answer:

Does it need protection at all?

Use threat analysis to drive this.

Is this the right point to make a policy check?

The aim is to make the security policy test at the point where the client has requested a security sensitive operation, and repeat the check on every such operation. Making a policy check early, and caching the results for future use, can lead to so-called 'TOCTOU' (time of check; time of use) errors in the code. Do not rely on the client following a preferred order of function calls to the server to implement the correct policy – every security-sensitive action should consider its own policy check requirements. The one exception to this rule is where *every* operation on a server has the same security policy requirements. In this case, the policy check can be made once at session establishment, and need not be repeated on each subsequent operation in that session.

Another point to remember is that security policy checks against a client must only be made within the context of the server, and not within the client-side code. You cannot trust the client not to skip over or corrupt such a client-side check – this is why we refer to the process boundary as the trust boundary.

Can the API be made secure without restricting it with a capability or caller identity?

Careful API design can often reduce the threat presented by an API. For example, by designing fair brokering of access to a shared resource such as display screen or speaker, a server might let all clients have some degree of access regardless of capability. When detection and response are possible this may be preferable to prevention – for example, if the user can detect undesired sound being output, and can respond by muting the device, sound output can be left unrestricted.

What aspects of the API need restricting?

Arrange the API so that sensitive operations are separated from non-sensitive ones – for example, under different methods and server op-codes – where possible.

Do you know the identity of a single process that is, architecturally, the only client of this method?

If so, its SID may be checked instead of a capability.

Is it acceptable to use a list of known clients as the policy?

Generally this is undesirable – the capability model was created specifically to avoid the need to manage large access control lists – but in some application domains it may be acceptable.

What is the asset and what is the threat to it, which you are protecting against?

Check if there is an existing system API that is sufficiently similar to have set a precedent for how this asset is to be protected.

Is there an external or industry policy or requirement about how this asset must be protected?

There may be some regulatory or commercial circumstances that require separate cryptographic or other mechanisms to be employed to verify the authenticity or permissibility of the requester or the request.

Does this method layer over some other API?

Consider whether the new API fully exposes the lower-level API (and if so, why this duplication?) or if it does so in a limited form. Consider also whether the policy on the lower-level API is appropriate for this higher level method, and whether the threat is reduced by using this method. For example, the Symbian OS Bluetooth stack enforces `LocalServices` at its client API, even though it is revealing functionality that is implemented over APIs protected with the CommDD capability. On the other hand, a CSY offering direct serial port access to the Bluetooth hardware would duplicate the device driver policy of requiring CommDD. One particular aspect to consider here is whether your server might be 'leaking' access to the underlying sensitive API. All processes holding capabilities have a duty to mediate their use of them on behalf of other processes, and not leak access in this way.

What would be the impact of not protecting this method?

Possible consequences could be loss of users' confidential data, unauthorized access to the network, unauthorized phone reconfiguration, and so on. This can give an initial pointer as to which capability should apply.

Will the client application be able to get the necessary capabilities?

Once you have identified a proposed capability (or set of capabilities) under which the API could be protected, you should carefully consider whether this capability is realistically going to be available to the target audience of the API. As a rough indicator, the division of user and system capabilities can give some idea, however more detailed information can be sought from the signing authority, responsible for allocating capabilities for applications on the mobile phone – for Symbian Signed the common criteria are covered in Chapter 9. If the capability is not available, then rethinking of the API might be required, or you might have hit upon an intractable incompatibility between the desired access to a resource and the risk in providing that access.

5.3.5   What to Do on Security Policy Failures

When you reject a client request, it is generally recommended that you do so by completing the relevant message with an appropriate error code. KErrPermissionDenied should only be used in the case where a policy check has failed, as it gives a clear indication to the application developer or user that it is a security policy failure, rather than simply an invalid argument or resource error.

Another option is to modify the behavior of the method in a minor way, but let the request proceed. This might be useful for maintaining compatibility, but it can introduce problems for the application developer in the future. If, at some future point, the circumstances change and the request is now able to pass that policy check (for example, the client acquires additional capability for an unrelated reason), then suddenly the debugged and working client will experience the alternative behavior having unintentional and potentially insecure results.

5.4   Server Implementation Considerations

5.4.1   Client-side Considerations

Many servers provide a client-side library to encapsulate the client–server protocol and expose the API as a set of exported methods. There are two significant things to bear in mind, if you use this architecture:

1. As this code is running within the client process, it is futile to perform any security checks as they can easily be defeated.

2. As this code is running within the client process, it must be sufficiently trusted to be loaded by that process.

Statement 1 is a re-iteration of what we've seen in the previous sections – security policies should only be checked at the point where a process boundary is crossed. Within the client library, no boundary has been crossed, so a security check is unnecessary and ineffective.

We need to consider statement 2 a little further. This asserts that the client needs to trust your code in order to use it. This is to avoid the client process being tricked into doing something unintentional through the use of untrusted code.

If the client library is distributed as a binary DLL, as most are, then the loader's capability rules, as described in Chapter 2, will enforce this trust dependency – the client library must have at least the capability set of each client trying to load it, in order to be loaded by that client. For a general-purpose server, intended for use by a wide range of clients, this means that the client library must have a wide set of capabilities. For this reason, the client libraries on most Symbian provided servers are assigned all capabilities except Tcb. This is accepted as a trade-off between maximizing the utility of the server and constraining the code base trusted to run within the most sensitive part of the system. It is envisaged that any general-purpose third-party server would follow a similar approach, but choosing a set of capabilities for the client library in accordance with the capability set the application is targeted at.

What if the client library cannot be provided with the full set of capabilities that clients might possess? This is, in effect, an architectural 'early warning' indicator for the developer of the application wishing to use the less-trusted library. It means that the application is dependent on a service that is less trusted, and perhaps lower quality, than itself.

However, in some circumstances it may still be necessary to keep to this architecture. In this case, the server's client library could be supplied in either source or static library (LIB) format to the application developer, to be included directly within their own binary. This moves the burden of responsibility for the code to the application developers, who must satisfy themselves that they trust the source and intent of the code at application build time (as opposed to security being enforced at run-time), just as they must be responsible for all instructions in their compiled binary.

Remember that if the client code is distributed in this way, then the IPC protocol is not encapsulated within a binary interface but instead is a public interface. This has consequences for compatibility reasons – for example, any changes to the IPC function numbers or server name might break compatibility with existing clients.

The other important considerations for the client library were illustrated in the opening example. To recap:

- The `RSessionBase::SendReceive()` methods should be re-coded in IPC v2 format – that is, using `TIpcArgs` in place of `TAny*` parameters.

- When creating a session to the server, it is wise to add a policy check that ensures that the server is running with the expected SID.

- For servers that operate in the `ProtServ` domain, the name will need to be changed to start with '!'. Only servers which are system critical – without which the system cannot operate – need to implement this, which is, by definition, rare for an after-market application.

A final point to consider is the documentation for the client interface – this is most importance where the client interface is to be shared with others. As a rule security objectives are met when observed behavior meets expected behavior. Clear client interface documentation is an important means through which those expectations can be established.

5.4.2 Server Considerations

The recommended way of adding security policy checks into a server is to use the `CPolicyServer` framework. This involves deriving the server's main class from the `CPolicyServer` base class, instead of `CServer` or `CServer2`.

If you are migrating a server to this framework, you will see that the following changes need to be made:

- On construction the `CPolicyServer` requires a parameter of type `CPolicyServer::TPolicy` to be supplied to it.

- Two virtual methods, `CPolicyServer::CustomSecurity-CheckL()` and `CPolicyServer::SecurityCheckFailedL()` may need to be overridden, if referenced by the `TPolicy` table provided in the constructor.

Policy Tables

The policy table is designed to allow a very compact representation of large or complex server policies, and to allow fast lookups on that data. In addition, it is designed to allow the table to reside in constant static data, which not only saves on construction time, but also makes it far less likely to be tampered with, as the memory page holding it will usually be marked read-only.

Alas, all these good features come with a slight penalty of legibility. A diagram (see Figure 5.1) is useful for understanding how the `TPolicy` table works.

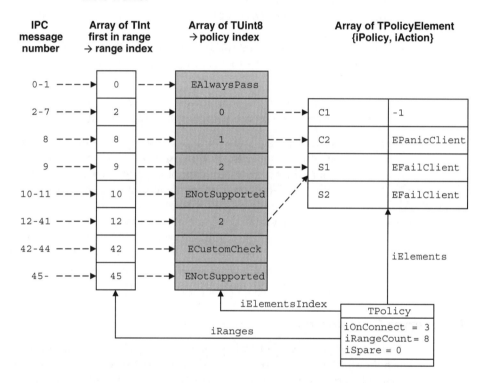

Figure 5.1   TPolicy Structure

Here we see an example `TPolicy` instance, with the three array members – `iRanges`, `iElementsIndex`, and `iElements` – expanded.

The elements of the first array, `iRanges`, correspond to IPC function numbers. When a message is received in a session the value of `RMessage2::Function()` is searched for in this array, in order to determine what action the policy server framework will apply to the message – based on the index of the IPC function in the array. This is called the *range index*. For example, an IPC message with function value 8 will cause the value 8 to be searched for in this first array. Here the

3rd index contains the value 8, but as indexes are counted starting at 0 this yields a range index of 2. If the exact value is not in the array, then the closest value below it is taken. So if IPC function 15 arrives at this table, then a range index of 5 is chosen, as this is the index at which the nearest lower value to 15 – i.e. 12 – is held. To support this the array must be held in sorted numerical order and this also conveniently enables a fast search to be performed. Also note that the table must start with a 0 element – negative entries are not allowed (negative IPC functions are reserved for use by the server framework itself).

The range index is used as an index into the second array, `iEle-mentsIndex`, to determine the *policy index*. So IPC function 9 corresponds to range index 3, which corresponds to a policy index of 2.

Following the same pattern, the policy index is then used as the index into third and final array, `iElements`. This yields the `TPolicyElement` that should be applied to this particular IPC function. Each object of this type contains both the *security policy* that should be applied (encoded in the `iPolicy` member as a `TSecurityPolicy`, seen in our opening example) and the *failure action* to take in the case where the policy check fails (encoded in the `iAction` member).

Using the example of IPC function 8, with policy index of 1, we see the policy that will be applied is labeled C2 – this represents an instance of a security policy demanding that the client hold two specific capabilities. In our example code this is initialized with the `_INIT_SECURITY_POLICY_C2` macro. If a client invoking this IPC function does not hold both specified capabilities, then the failure action `EFailClient` (from the `CPolicyServer::TFailureAction` enumeration) indicates that the message must be completed with the `KErrPermissionDenied` error code.

This policy table is described in code as follows:

```
const TUint myRangeCount = 8;
const TInt myRanges[myRangeCount] =
  {
  0,   //range is 0-1 inclusive
  2,   //range is 2-7 inclusive
  8,   //range is 8 only
  9,   //range is 9 only
  10,  //range is 10-11 inclusive
  12,  //range is 12-41 inclusive
  42,  //range is 42-44 inclusive
  45,  //range is 45-KMaxTInt inclusive
  };

const TUint8 myElementsIndex[myRangeCount] =
  {
  CPolicyServer::EAlwaysPass,    //IPC  0 -
  0,                             //IPC  2 -
  1,                             //IPC  8 -
  2,                             //IPC  9 -
```

```
  CPolicyServer::ENotSupported, //IPC  10 -
  2,                            //IPC  12 -
  CPolicyServer::ECustomCheck,  //IPC  42 -
  CPolicyServer::ENotSupported, //IPC  45 - KMaxTInt
  };

const CPolicyServer::TPolicyElement myElements[] =
  {
  {_INIT_SECURITY_POLICY_C1(KMyCap1), -1},    //IPC 2 - 7
  {_INIT_SECURITY_POLICY_C2(KMyCap2A, KMyCap2B),
            CPolicyServer::EPanicClient},  //IPC 8
  {_INIT_SECURITY_POLICY_S1(KMySID, KMyCap3),
            CPolicyServer::EFailClient},  //IPC 9, 12-41
  {_INIT_SECURITY_POLICY_C1(KMyConnectCap),
            CPolicyServer::EFailClient},  //Connect
  }

const CPolicySErver::TPolicy myPolicy =
  {
  3,             // Connect messages use policy index 3
  myRangeCount,
  myRanges,
  myElementsIndex,
  myElements,
  }
```

If you get confused following these steps, it is useful to remember that the IPC number goes through a *reverse* lookup in iRanges, the result of which (the range index) goes through a *forward* lookup in iElementsIndex, and the result of that (the policy index) goes through a *forward* lookup in iElements.

When a policy check fails, i.e. whenever the CPolicyServer::EFailClient result is encountered, diagnostics can be generated in the emulator to aid debugging, as already mentioned in Chapter 3. Here's an example:

```
*PlatSec* ERROR - Capability check failed - A Message
(function number=0x000000cf) from Thread
helloworld[10008ace]0001::HelloWorld, sent to Server
!CntLockServer, was checked by Thread
CNTSRV.EXE[10003a73]0001::!CntLockServer and was found to
be missing the capabilities: WriteUserData .  Additional
diagnostic message: Checked by CPolicyServer::RunL
```

In this example diagnostic you can see:

- the message function number: 0x000000cf

- the client process and thread that sent the request: helloworld [10008ace]0001::HelloWorld

- the name of the server that received the request: !CntLockServer

- the name of the process and thread in which the server is hosted: `CNTSRV.EXE[10003a73]0001::!CntLockServer` (note the exclamation mark on the thread name here is coincidental, and not enforced by the `ProtServ` capability)

- the reason that the `TSecurityPolicy` check failed: a lack of `WriteUserData`

- the additional diagnostic information, in this case indicating that the security policy check was made from within the `CPolicy-Server::RunL` framework function.

Special Cases

There are some special cases to consider in the framework. Firstly, connect messages do not go through the first two array lookups, as connect messages do not have normal IPC function numbers. Instead, the policy index for a connect request is taken directly from the `iOnConnect` member of `TPolicy` itself. This is then looked up in the third array as normal.

Secondly, if any policy index found by lookup in the `iElementsIndex` array or from `iOnConnect` is a value from the `CPolicyServer::TSpecialCase` enumeration, then no policy element lookup occurs, but instead the policy is inferred as follows:

- `CPolicyServer::EAlwaysPass` – the IPC function is allowed to go ahead with no specific policy check against the client; that is, any client that can establish a session may call this method

- `CPolicyServer::ENotSupported` – the IPC message processing is completed immediately with `KErrNotSupported`. This should be used as the final element in `iElementsIndex`, and also to fill any other 'holes' in the IPC function space – for example, where deprecated functions have been removed, or gaps left for compatibility reasons. If any of these opcodes are used by new API methods in the future, the policy table must be considered and updated to allow the policy check to pass – for this reason having a default position of `CPolicyServer::ENotSupported` is much safer than `CPolicyServer::EAlwaysPass`. Note there is no `CPolicyServer::EAlwaysFail` enumeration – you should instead use `CPolicyServer::ENotSupported` for any opcode that must always fail.

- `CPolicyServer::ECustomCheck` – the security policy is not based on IPC function alone; run-time consideration is required to determine the policy to apply. A call to `CPolicyServer::Custom-SecurityCheckL()`, discussed below, will be made in response to this.

Finally, if the failure action – identified by the `iAction` member of `CPolicyServer::TPolicyElement` – is negative then it means special failure processing should be performed instead of just returning a simple error code to the client (the recommended approach) or a client panic. A call to `CPolicyServer::CustomFailureActionL()` will be made to allow this to occur.

Custom Checks and Failure Actions

If the policy index equals `CPolicyServer::ECustomCheck` then `CustomSecurityCheckL()` is called. If a failure action is negative, the `CustomFailureActionL()` is called. Potentially one IPC message could result in calls to both these methods.

```
TCustomResult CustomSecurityCheckL(const RMessage2 &aMsg,
          TInt &aFailureAction, TSecurityInfo &aMissing);
```

You must override this method if `ECustomCheck` appears in your policy table, as otherwise the base class method will be called which will result in a server panic.

In this method, you can inspect the contents of the `RMessage2` received – passed as the first parameter – in order to determine the correct policy to apply. Use this whenever the policy is based on something other than the IPC function number alone, such as the parameters being passed into the method or the current state of the session or server objects. While you are free to form this code as you wish, we recommend you structure this as two distinct stages:

- Determine the `TSecurityPolicy` object to apply to this request, based on the state of the server, session, or subsession, and the parameters passed in `RMessage2`, and

- Test the message against the policy so determined.

A generalized implementation might look something like this:

```
CPolicyServer::TCustomResult
CMyPolicyServer::CustomSecurityCheckL (const RMessage2 & aMsg,
           TInt & aFailureAction, TSecurityInfo & aMissing)
  {
  TSecurityPolicy policy;
  DeterminePolicyL(aMsg, policy);
  if(policy.CheckPolicy(aMsg, aMissing,
    __PLATSEC_DIAGNOSTIC("example custom check")))
    return EPass;
```

```
    else
      return EFail;
    }
```

`DeterminePolicyL()` can be as simple or complex as required.

Using this structure encourages a more rigorous approach to determining the policy, rather than ad-hoc layers of logic and counter-logic being tested against the message. It also aids debugging, as there is a single place to inspect the policy being applied, in order to determine why it is failing or passing when it shouldn't. Note that using the `TSecurity-Policy` class applied against the `RMessage` object received as shown here is strongly recommended as it maximizes the amount of diagnostics automatically generated by the server framework.

The `aFailureAction` and `aMissing` members passed into this method are primarily of use if you are implementing custom failure actions:

```
TCustomResult CustomFailureActionL(const RMessage2 &aMsg,
        TInt aFailureAction, const TSecurityInfo &aMissing);
```

The `CustomFailureActionL` method is called by the framework whenever a negative failure action is encountered in processing a security check – either in the `iAction` of the resolved `TPolicyElement` for the message, or returned in the second parameter to `CustomSecurityCheckL()`.

It is primarily intended to allow servers to handle security policy failures in a central place. This handling may be for debug logging or tracing, or security audit purposes, or to aid step-through debugging. It may also be used to apply a final override to the outcome of the security check. Such an override is primarily useful for debugging purposes – but do ensure that any such debug-disable is not present in release builds! Also in some limited circumstances this method might be useful for offering the user an opportunity to override the policy failure in a controlled fashion, at run time.

The actual implementation of `CustomFailureActionL()` follows much the same pattern as `CustomSecurityCheckL()` above, so much of the advice expressed there holds here too.

The result of both of these custom methods is indicated in the same form: they should either return one of the three enumerations from `CPolicy-Server::TCustomResult`, or leave with an appropriate error code. A leave will be propagated back to the client in the form of a standard error completion code. The custom result codes are used as follows:

- `CPolicyServer::EPass` – The message is processed as normal; either by passing it to the `ServiceL()` method of a session or, in the case of a connection message, by creating a new session.

- `CPolicyServer::EFail` – The message is considered to have failed its policy check; the `aFailureAction` parameter is used to determine what to do next (on entry this parameter is initialized to `EFailClient`, the common case).

- `CPolicyServer::EAsync` – The derived class is responsible for further processing of the message; the policy server framework will do nothing more with it.

This last case, `EASync`, deserves a little more discussion. If either of the custom methods returns this value, it effectively removes the corresponding message object from the policy server framework's control. It is then up to the specific server implementation to handle the message as and when it sees fit, in the same way as any other message within the 'normal' `ServiceL()` processing path of the server. That is, the same error-handling rules apply here as to any other message that might be completed asynchronously within the server. Most often this method is used where the policy to be applied requires an asynchronous operation to be performed before it can be determined – this might be fetching some data from another server, prompting the user, or whatever. Once this has been done, you can insert the message back into the policy server to continue processing. This is achieved by calling `CPolicyServer::ProcessL()` in the case of a policy pass, or `CPolicyServer::CheckFailedL()` in the case of a policy check fail. You can also complete the message directly, for example, through `RMessagePtr2::Complete(KErrPermissionDenied)`, however this will skip the opportunity for any further custom failure action to be performed on the message.

5.5 Summary

In this chapter we have seen how to go about designing security into your client–server implementation. The simple example at the start gave a taste of the new machinery that is available within the context of a Symbian OS server, as you set about protecting it. It also demonstrated some of the fundamental principles of the security architecture:

- Security checks should only be made when a process boundary (that is, a trust boundary) is crossed.

- Where servers abstract complex underlying resources they may also require a complex security policy for access to those resources, whilst clients typically have a simple connection policy.

- The kernel is the trusted intermediary between client and server, and both client and server rely on it for the implementation of their security policies.

The rest of the chapter then concentrated on the ways in which you can use these basic mechanisms to maximum benefit. First we looked at the threats that are specific to a server, and what you should consider when analyzing the threat model of a server. Next, we saw the various security measures available within the operating system, frameworks that are available for use within servers, and how to design usage of these into your server. Finally, we went though some notes on implementing servers, looking in particular detail at the policy server framework and how to use it.

6

How to Write Secure Plug-ins

by Mark Shackman

6.1 What Is a Secure Plug-In?

Working with Symbian OS means, in many cases, working with plug-ins and frameworks. This applies to all programs that use the Application Architecture or the UIKON GUI framework. It also includes more specialized programming, including printer driver and device driver implementation and implementing new protocols to extend the networking subsystem.

6.1.1 Overview of Frameworks and Plug-ins

Frameworks are a familiar and integral part of Symbian OS which, like other modern object-oriented operating systems, uses them extensively.

A framework is a software system that defines a collection of abstract base classes and ready-made concrete classes, and which is designed for extension. A component will use a framework to broaden its functionality by means of extensions to the framework known as plug-ins. These are classes that derive from interfaces defined by the framework (see Figure 6.1) and which can be loaded by the framework as required at run-time. Further details of frameworks and plug-ins can be found in [Stichbury 2005] and are also touched on in [Harrison 2004].

To extend the framework, a programmer derives a new implementation from its abstract base classes and provides new behavior where required.

Using plug-ins provides a number of benefits:

- The design is architecturally and functionally flexible.

- The client does not need to know about the detailed workings of the plug-in.

- Plug-in dependencies are dynamic rather than static, so don't need to be known at build time.

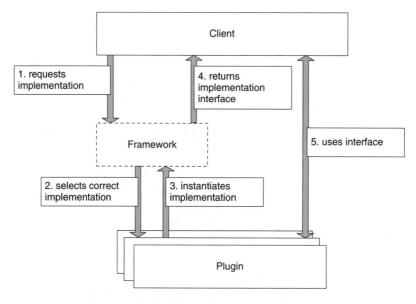

Figure 6.1   Framework Operation

- Richer functionality is possible by enabling integration with third-party add-on software.

6.1.2   Security Considerations for Plug-ins

A number of security issues arise when using a plug-in architecture. For example, consider an application that is authorized to access a bank account. If the application also supports plug-ins, how can it know that the plug-ins can also be trusted with access to your account?

Conversely, consider a case where a plug-in implements some kind of access control to protect content on your mobile phone. How does the plug-in ensure that an application that calls it has the right to access that data? Permitting an untrusted application to gain access to the data could compromise the integrity of the system or the privacy of the mobile phone user.

It is considerations such as these which necessitate plug-ins being carefully designed in order to properly integrate with the platform security architecture. This section discusses the related issues that plug-in developers need to be aware of.

6.1.3   Plug-in Mechanism Considerations

When an application loads a DLL, it does so within the context of its own process. This allows the DLL to run with the same privileges and access rights as the application, and to have full access to its memory space.

Therefore, to maintain security, the capabilities of a DLL are checked by the loader to ensure that it possesses (as a minimum) all the capabilities that the owning application process has. If it does not, the load will be unacceptable and will fail.

This has important consequences for plug-ins that determine whether they should be implemented as DLLs to be loaded by the calling application. If this mechanism is used, it is necessary to ensure that the plug-in possesses at least the same set of capabilities as the process that loads it. A problem arises when the plug-in doesn't know which process might load it and, therefore, cannot know what capabilities it will be required to possess.

Implementers of plug-in frameworks, consequently, have two choices when deciding which capabilities plug-ins should be trusted with.

Application-specific Plug-ins

DLL plug-ins can be designed for a particular application or process. In this case, the plug-in can be given the exact capabilities required by that process, so that it can be guaranteed that the process will be able to successfully load the plug-in.

This works well where the plug-in is dedicated to a specific application and each has complete trust in the other. Within Symbian OS, this technique can be seen in recognizers loaded by AppArc (the application architecture server) and rasterizers loaded by the Font and Bitmap server.

However, application-specific plug-ins have two drawbacks. The obvious one is that tying the plug-in to the application prevents the plug-in from being used by other applications with different capabilities, potentially restricting its marketability and leading to wastage in ROM code if the same plug-in is needed by two applications with different capability requirements. Another drawback occurs when the application is upgraded to use additional capabilities – the plug-in will no longer be loadable as it doesn't possess the new capabilities.

General Purpose Plug-ins

The other approach is to make the plug-in general purpose. This can be achieved by giving a DLL the maximum possible set of capabilities, to ensure that it can be successfully loaded by all applications regardless of their precise set of capabilities. For system plug-ins, which are assumed to be highly trusted, granting them capabilities of All -Tcb achieves this, but this option isn't available to most third-party plug-ins for which the capabilities assigned must be carefully selected and tested. If third-party plug-ins are to be supported in a general-purpose framework, a better choice may be to design the framework to run as a secure server process (as described in Chapter 5) with a fixed set of capabilities that can be assigned to third-party DLL plug-ins.

6.1.4   Plug-in Functionality Restrictions

Capability Restrictions

The introduction of platform security into Symbian OS has meant that plug-ins, previously able to access any API on the mobile phone, now only have access to those APIs which are not protected by capability, plus those capability-protected APIs for which the plug-in has been given the required capability.

An additional restriction that derives from this situation – where a plug-in uses an API restricted by capability – is that not only does the plug-in need the extra capability, but the process that loads it will also need to have the capability, or the call to the capability-protected API will fail.

Data-Caging Restrictions

Data caging restricts the parts of the filing system that are visible to an application or process, ensuring that one process doesn't have access to another's data or memory. These restrictions are inherited by the process's plug-ins, so that a plug-in can see and manipulate only those files owned by the process that loaded it.

For application-specific plug-ins, this is restrictive to the extent that the plug-in may be prevented from doing something that is its primary function (e.g. reading a database owned by another application). In such cases, it is clear that implementing the plug-in as a DLL alone is untenable and that the developer must look for other ways to support plug-ins in their applications.

6.2   Writing Secure Plug-ins

6.2.1   The ECOM Framework

Before Symbian OS v7 was released, the platform contained a number of frameworks, all of which operated independently. Each framework used its own code to identify the plug-ins which were relevant to it, and to load or unload the plug-ins, as required. In Symbian OS v7, in order to gain savings in simplicity, code size and maintenance, a generic extensible framework, ECOM, was introduced.

ECOM is a broad framework for specifying plug-in interfaces, and for calling and writing plug-ins. Most Symbian OS frameworks have been re-designed to use ECOM and now delegate finding and instantiating suitable plug-in objects to ECOM, rather than managing these tasks themselves with their own proprietary code.

For example, in the old scheme, CONE (the graphical interaction framework) searched for available front-end processors (FEPs) and loaded or unloaded them on the basis of their file names. In Symbian OS v7 and later, each FEP is an ECOM plug-in, and CONE queries ECOM to get a list of the FEPs that are available to the system.

ECOM has been further enhanced to be aware of platform security in Symbian OS v9. When a client requests ECOM to find suitable plug-in objects via the `ListImplementations()` method, ECOM filters out any plug-ins that have insufficient capabilities to be loaded by the client. Similarly, calls to `CreateImplementation()`, which instantiates a specified interface implementation, will fail if the requested plug-in has insufficient capabilities.

Details of the ECOM architecture have been published previously. In particular, see Chapter 14 of [Stichbury 2005]. The following sections assume understanding of the basic architecture of an ECOM plug-in, concentrating primarily on the changes required by platform security.

6.2.2 Writing ECOM Plug-ins for Symbian OS v9

This section looks at the differences developers need to be aware of when designing and writing new plug-ins for Symbian OS v9 and later.

Data Caging

Plug-in files are stored in new locations, to comply with data-caging requirements. The DLL plug-in file, in common with other binaries, is now stored in the directory `\sys\bin`, which can only be read or written by processes with special capabilities. Plug-ins in the old location (`\system\libs\plugins`) will no longer be recognized by the security-enabled ECOM.

RSC resource files for the plug-in are both moved and renamed. Their new location is in the `\resource\plugins` directory on each drive. The name of the resource file has also been updated, so that the resource file for a plug-in is renamed to match the DLL plug-in file name. So, for example, in Symbian OS v8.1 and earlier, the JPEG plug-in would have been delivered as:

```
\system\libs\plugins\JPEGCodec.dll
```

```
\system\libs\plugins\101F45D6.rsc
```

In Symbian OS v9 these file paths become:

```
\sys\bin\JPEGCodec.dll
```

```
\resource\plugins\JPEGCodec.rsc
```

Plug-ins Loaded in the Client Process

ECOM now loads the plug-in DLL in the client process that creates the interface implementation, so that the capabilities of the client are used when loading the plug-in.

A consequence of this is that the client process now has the responsibility to release memory and unload plug-ins that are no longer in use (a task managed by the ECOM server in earlier versions of Symbian OS). This is achieved with the client-side API `REComSession::FinalClose()`, which was introduced in Symbian OS v7.0s but had no effect prior to Symbian OS v9. Client code using the call can therefore be used unchanged on all OS versions from v7.0s onwards.

Executables using ECOM (whether servers, applications or test programs) now need to call `FinalClose()` as one of the last statements in `E32Main()` on process shutdown to complete the final cleanup.

MMP Files for ECOM Plug-ins

Some changes have been made to the build tools to remove location-dependent information, due to the need to install files in different locations. This allows developers to maintain a common code base for plug-in projects intended to run on Symbian OS v8.1 and later. The new syntax used in MMP files is discussed in the next section.

6.2.3   Migration of ECOM Plug-ins

Plug-ins written for previous versions of Symbian OS need some minor changes to enable them to conform to the syntax of MMP files which run under platform security, as discussed in Section 6.2.1.

Changes needed to the plug-in project's MMP file are as follows:

- `TARGETTYPE` changes from `ECOMIIC` to `PLUGIN`, to specify that the project is an ECOM plug-in.

- `TARGETPATH` statement is removed (this is now determined by the build tools depending on the `TARGETTYPE`).

- `RESOURCE` statement changes to a `START RESOURCE`, `END` block, to build the ECOM resource file. The `TARGET` statement is used to ensure that the built resource file has the same name (without extension) as the plug-in file name. (Symbian OS v9 requires that the built resource file name matches that of the plug-in file name.)

If there are other resource files generated from the same MMP which use a `TARGETPATH` statement to build to a specific location, it will be necessary

to convert the RESOURCE statements to START RESOURCE, END blocks
each with a TARGETPATH statement inside, to limit the scope.

These changes are illustrated in the example MMP file below:

```
// EComExample.mmp (before)        // EComExample.mmp (after)

TARGET EComExample.dll             TARGET EComExample.dll
TARGETPATH \System\Libs\Plugins
TARGETTYPE ECOMIIC                 TARGETTYPE PLUGIN

UID 0x10009D8D 0x10009DB1          UID 0x10009D8D 0x20000B62
                                   VENDORID 0x70000001

                                   CAPABILITY All -Tcb

SOURCEPATH ..\example              SOURCEPATH ..\example
SOURCE example.cpp main.cpp        SOURCE example.cpp main.cpp

USERINCLUDE    ..\example          USERINCLUDE    ..\example
SYSTEMINCLUDE \epoc32\include      SYSTEMINCLUDE \epoc32\include
SYSTEMINCLUDE \epoc32\include\ecom SYSTEMINCLUDE \epoc32\include\ecom

RESOURCE 10009DB1.rss              START RESOURCE 0x20000B62
                                       TARGET EComExample.rsc
                                   END

LIBRARY euser.lib                  LIBRARY euser.lib
LIBRARY ECom.lib                   LIBRARY ECom.lib
```

Note that the first UID specified (the UID2 value) should be 0x10009D8D,
which is common for all ECOM plug-ins.

Further details for migrating particular types of plug-in are given in
Section 6.3.

6.2.4 ROM-only ECOM Resolver

Applications can differentiate between plug-ins provided on read-only
media and those on read–write media by using the ROM-only resolver.
This allows them to retrieve or create only legitimate 'built-in' plug-in
implementations and ignore plug-ins that either aren't in the ROM, or
are not upgrades to ROM-based plug-ins. Allowing plug-in users to make
the differentiation provides them with some level of protection from
unauthorized implementations of a built-in interface.

To use the ROM-only resolver, the resolver UID KRomOnlyRe-
solverUid (defined in ECom.h) should be specified in the aRe-
solverUid parameter of the ListImplementationsL() and
CreateImplementationL() APIs of REComSession.

6.3   Plug-in Implementation Considerations

6.3.1   Front-End Processors

A front-end processor (FEP) allows users to input characters that aren't
directly available on a mobile phone's keypad. In Symbian OS, different
types of input (such as handwriting recognition, an on-screen virtual
keyboard or predictive text entry) are provided by plug-in DLLs that
implement the FEP interface.

Before Symbian OS v9, CONE searched for available FEPs and loaded
or unloaded them on the basis of their file names. In the secure platform,
each FEP is an ECOM plug-in, and CONE queries ECOM for the system's
available FEPs.

This section outlines how to migrate an existing FEP to work in Symbian
OS v9.

Project File Changes

The MMP file needs to follow the format described in Section 6.2.3,
including the specification of an ECOM resource file.

Resource File

This file specifies the interface UID (identifying the plug-in scheme) and
the implementation UID (identifying the individual plug-in). For FEPs, the
ECOM interface UID 0x1020233F must be used to ensure that the FEP
will be loaded by CONE. An example FEP resource file follows:

```
#include <RegistryInfo.rh>

RESOURCE REGISTRY_INFO r_registry
  {
  dll_uid = 0x20000B63; // UID3 of DLL

  interfaces =
    {
    INTERFACE_INFO
      {
      interface_uid = 0x1020233F; // Same for every FEP
      implementations =
        {
        IMPLEMENTATION_INFO
          {
          implementation_uid = 0x20000B64;
          version_no = 1;
          display_name = "FEPName";
          default_data = "";
          }
        };
      }
    };
  }
```

Source Code Changes

There have been some changes to the FEP classes in Symbian OS v9. Please refer to the Symbian OS Library documentation on the FEPBASE application framework for further information.

6.3.2 Recognizers

A recognizer is a plug-in DLL that examines the data in a file or a buffer and, if it recognizes the specific type it is looking for, returns its data, or MIME, type. Since each recognizer looks for a single MIME type, the Application Architecture (AppArc) server loads a set of recognizer plug-ins, each of which examine the data until one recognizes it and returns its type. Once the data type has been established, the correct application for processing that MIME type can be run.

Prior to Symbian OS v9, AppArc contained its own code to detect and load recognizers; now, however, it uses the ECOM framework to do this. Recognizers are therefore subject to the same capability constraints as other ECOM DLL plug-ins and have to have the correct capabilities in order to be loaded by the AppArc server.

This section outlines how to migrate an existing data recognizer to work in Symbian OS v9.

Project File Changes

The MMP file needs to follow the format described in Section 6.2.3 including the specification of an ECOM resource file.

Resource File

For data recognizers, the ECOM interface UID `0x101F7D87` must be used. For example:

```
#include <RegistryInfo.rh>

RESOURCE REGISTRY_INFO r_registry
  {
  dll_uid = 0x20000B65;  // UID3 of the DLL

  interfaces =
    {
    INTERFACE_INFO
      {
      interface_uid = 0x101F7D87; // For all data recognizers
      implementations =
        {
        IMPLEMENTATION_INFO
          {
          implementation_uid = 0x20000B66;
```

```
        version_no = 1;
        display_name = "DataRecognizerName";
        default_data = "";
        }
      };
    }
  };
}
```

Source Code Changes

This section describes the source code changes needed for a data recognizer.

An example header file would appear as:

```
class CExampleDataRecognizer : public CApaDataRecognizerType
  {
public:
  static CApaDataRecognizerType* CreateRecognizerL();
  };
```

In the CPP file, the previously exported `CreateRecognizerL()` function should be removed and replaced by:

```
#include <ImplementationProxy.h>
const TInt KExampleDataRecognizerImplementationUID = 0x20000B66;
...
CApaDataRecognizerType* CExampleDataRecognizer::CreateRecognizerL()
  {
  return new (ELeave) CExampleDataRecognizer ();
  }

const TImplementationProxy ImplementationTable[] =
  {
  IMPLEMENTATION_PROXY_ENTRY(KExampleDataRecognizerImplementationUID,
                      CExampleDataRecognizer::CreateRecognizerL)
  };

EXPORT_C const TImplementationProxy* ImplementationGroupProxy(TInt&
                                                        aTableCount)
  {
  aTableCount = sizeof(ImplementationTable) /
              sizeof(TImplementationProxy);
  return ImplementationTable;
  }
```

6.3.3   Control Panel Plug-ins

Different control panel plug-ins are likely to need different capabilities in order to change the mobile phone's configuration. Rather than each plug-in running in a parent process with a dangerously large set of capabilities, in Symbian OS v9 each plug-in runs in its own process, so that each can have the minimum set of capabilities that it requires. For this reason, all existing control panel plug-ins, which were implemented as polymorphic DLLs, now become standard applications, but with a special registration file. This registration file is used by the application server to distinguish the plug-in from a normal application.

This section outlines how to migrate an existing control panel plug-in to work in Symbian OS v9.

Prerequisites

- The control panel application should be located in \sys\bin\ <appname.exe>.

- The control panel application's UI resource file should be located in \Resource\apps\<appname.rsc>.

- There should be a registration resource file for each control panel application in \private\10003a3f\apps\ if it is either on the emulator or built into the ROM, or \private\10003a3f\import\apps\ if it is installed via Software Install.

- For control panel applications, a byte in the registration resource file must be explicitly set to indicate that it is a control panel application.

Project File Changes

The MMP file will need changes to build the plug-in as an EXE rather than a DLL. These are the same changes as apply to converting any application from versions prior to Symbian OS v9, as applications were previously themselves DLL plug-ins to the Application Architecture framework.

Source Code Changes

The control panel plug-in will require some source code changes in order to run as a separate application rather than a DLL. There are however no changes needed specifically relating to control panel functionality.

6.3.4 Converting DLL Plug-ins to Servers

Using DLLs can have limitations due to the changes brought in for platform security. Where the default security model offered by the loader may not be appropriate for the intended use of a plug-in, it may be necessary to address it by moving to a client–server model. It is important to note, however, that any security issues causing a mismatch between the capabilities of the client and the plug-in will not have gone away, and will

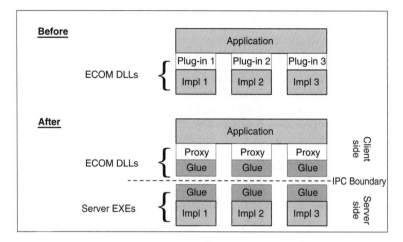

Figure 6.2   Converting Plug-ins to a Client–Server Architecture

have to be addressed by both the client and the server implementations in order to avoid introducing security weaknesses (see Chapter 5 for further details on client–server security).

This section covers how to implement an ECOM plug-in as a server process, with some 'glue' code that all subsequent plug-ins that implement the same interface can reuse. Thus the aim is to effect the transition shown in Figure 6.2.

As shown, the implementation part of the plug-in is replaced with a proxy, which acts as the plug-in. Rather than manufacture the original implementation, the proxy manufactures a client-glue version and a server. The client-glue code then marshals any required parameters and delivers them to the server. The server takes the parameter data and invokes the call on the real implementation.

Any results returned by the server are marshaled by the server-glue code and returned to the client glue which takes them and returns them to the calling application.

Note that the client-glue and server-glue code is the same for each plug-in and is linked into each ECOM plug-in DLL and server implementation.

We must emphasize the importance of addressing the security issues that will arise from introducing a mechanism where the plug-in may be less trustworthy than the client application (in which case the client-glue code must be responsible for ensuring that sensitive data is not provided to the server) or the client application may be running with less capability than the plug-in (in which case the server-glue code must be responsible for ensuring that sensitive data or services are not provided to the client). Chapter 5 presents some mechanisms that can be used to perform such security checks, including the `CPolicyServer` class.

Replacing the Plug-in with a Proxy

All ECOM DLL plug-ins contain a mandatory part, which provides ECOM with a table of implementation UIDs and constructors. Typically, this would look like:

```
const TImplementationProxy ImplementationTable[] =
  {
  IMPLEMENTATION_PROXY_ENTRY(0x2000BAE, CMyPlugIn1Factory::NewL)
  }

/** Lookup method required by ECom.
    Returns the above table to the ECom framework */

EXPORT_C const TImplementationProxy ImplementationGroupProxy(TInt&
                                                       aTableCount)
  {
  aTableCount = sizeof(ImplementationTable) /
                sizeof(TImplementationProxy);
  return ImplementationTable;
  }
```

In the `ImplementationTable` structure, the UID used is unique to this particular implementation and matches the UID specified in the plug-in's resource file.

   The file is changed so that ECOM now returns a proxy object that is of the same type but returns different products. Note that the proxy takes a server name, `MyPlugin1FactoryServer`, which is propagated down into client-glue calls to ensure that calls go to the correct server. These changes are seen below:

```
// The name of the corresponding server of this ECOM plug-in
_LIT(KServerName, "MyPlugin1FactoryServer");

static CMyPlugIn1Factory* CreateProxyL()
  {
  return CreatePlugInFactoryProxyL(KServerName);
  }

const TImplementationProxy ImplementationTable[] =
  {
  IMPLEMENTATIONPROXYENTRY(0x2000BAF, ::CreateProxyL)
  };

EXPORTC const TImplementationProxy* ImplementationGroupProxy(TInt&
                                                       aTableCount)
  {
  aTableCount = sizeof(ImplementationTable) /
                sizeof(TImplementationProxy);
  return ImplementationTable;
  }
```

Client Glue Code

Usually the plug-in objects carry out the required processing, but these have been replaced with a proxy, CPlugInFactoryProxy, which produces proxy objects, such as CPlugInHandlerProxy.

The proxy code in CPlugInHandlerProxy reveals what is going on instead:

```
void CPlugInHandlerProxy::ConstructL(const TDesC& aServerName,
                                     const TDesC& aFileName)
  {
  User::LeaveIfError(iSession.Connect(aServerName));

  // Send the command to construct a handler
  // Param 0: [OUT] TDesC16 - file name
  iSession.SendRequestL(ECreateHandler, TIpcArgs(&aFileName));
  }

void CPlugInHandlerProxy::DataSizeL(TInt &aSize)
  {
  // Client-server parameters
  // Param 0: [IN] TPkg<TInt> - size
  TPckg<TInt> sizePkg(aSize);
  iSession.SendRequestL(EDataSize, TIpcArgs(&sizePkg));
  }

TInt CPlugInHandlerProxy::ProcessData(TInt aResult)
  {
  // Client-server parameters
  // Param 0: [OUT] TInt - result
  return iSession.SendRequest(EProcessData,
        TIpcArgs(static_cast<TInt>(aIntent)));
  }
```

The above code shows that:

- when the CPlugInHandlerProxy was created, a session was established with a server. The first message sent by the new session is one requesting the server to create a corresponding handler on the server side

- the method functions are not performing any real processing, but are simply marshaling parameter data into requests on the session

- data is being copied and cannot be passed by reference.

Only simple data types are used here – complex data types could be handled by storing them in shared buffers. If this is required, the data types must support ExternalizeL and InternalizeL operations if they are to be handled by client–server glue code.

Method functions (e.g. EProcessData) are represented by enumerations, which are common to both client and server). This, along with the methods in the proxies, is why the client and server glue code must be tailored for a particular ECOM interface, but can be reused without change across all plug-ins, except for the specification of the server name.

The proxy object `CPlugInHandlerProxy` would employ an `RSessionBase`-derived object. On `Connect()`, this object handles the transparent start up of the server, if it does not already exist.

Server-Glue Code

The server example implementation code below shows a server being created, and also being given the real (non-proxy) `CMyPlugIn1Factory` constructor that used to be returned by our original client-side ECOM implementation before we replaced it with a proxy.

```
#include "startserver.h"

_LIT(KServerName, "MyPlugin1FactoryServer");

// E32Main calls StartServer with the server
// name and the factory construction function
TInt E32Main()
   {
   return StartServer(KServerName, CMyPlugIn1Factory::NewL);
   }
```

Note that this is also specific to a particular ECOM interface, and that the server name ties in with the name used on the client side.

`StartServer()` creates an implementation of the standard Symbian OS `CServer2` class which will create sessions when required. These sessions provide a standard `ServiceL()` interface, which creates message handlers, based on the method function identifier passed in the `RMessage2` message.

When the session starts, a message handler is created if one doesn't already exist. This server behavior is triggered by the use of the proxy objects on the client side, for example when `CPlugInHandlerProxy::ConstructL()` is invoked, an `ECreateHandler` message is propagated to the server so that the relevant handler can be created.

```
void CPlugInSession::ServiceL(const RMessage2& aMessage)
   {
   if (!iMessageHandler)
      {
      // Create the new message handler based on the message code
      switch(aMessage.Function())
         {
      case ECreateHandler:
         iMessageHandler = CServerHandler::NewL(iServer.Factory(), aMessage);

         break;
```

```
     default:
       // Panic - invalid message
       aMessage.Panic(KServerGluePanic, EServerGlueInvalidMessage);

       break;
       }
     }
  else
     {
     // If the message handler has already been created,
     // then delegate the request
     iMessageHandler->ServiceL(aMessage);
     }
  }
```

The message handler's role is to:

- create a real implementation of the required interface (not a proxy)
- based on the incoming message's 'method' parameter:
    - unmarshal the parameters from the message
    - invoke the 'real' implementation
    - marshal any responses.

6.3.5   Writing New ECOM-based Plug-in Frameworks

Prior to Symbian OS v9, to identify all the polymorphic DLLs that were available for them to load, a framework used to search a directory (or directories) and examine any DLLs it found, checking the UID2 and UID3 for specific values. With platform security, all binaries are located in \sys\bin\, and only processes with the AllFiles capability are able to read from that location. This means that most processes will not be able to scan for binaries themselves.

By ensuring that DLL plug-ins are changed into ECOM plug-ins, developers of new frameworks, or those migrating older ones, can implement them as standard ECOM frameworks and thereby utilize the functionality provided by the ECOM server to discover and load appropriate plug-ins. As discussed previously, the capabilities of any plug-in intended to be loaded in the framework would have to be considered, to ensure that they can be successfully loaded.

Obligations on Framework Developers

As previously discussed, framework developers must ensure that they handle calls to FinalClose() in a graceful fashion as part of their framework termination code.

ECOM Custom Resolvers

A default resolver that selects an implementation to use is provided as part of ECOM. Custom resolvers are commonly provided by large frameworks that define and utilize many ECOM interface classes to provide framework-specific resolution rules for selecting and retrieving implementations. These resolver plug-ins are loaded into the ECOM server process and thus require a high level of trust.

Custom resolvers are themselves interface implementations that implement the ECOM `CResolver` interface. They are instantiated by ECOM as required, in response to `REComSession::CreateImplementation-L()` and `REComSession::ListImplementationsL()` calls that specify a particular custom resolver to use. Custom resolvers must conform to other aspects of interface implementations, including providing registration resource information and publishing their UID and factory functions in an implementation proxy table.

Under platform security, the ECOM server is protected, with the server executable having the `ProtServ` capability. The server can therefore only load resolver DLLs that have been trusted with the `ProtServ` capability, which will normally require a signature from a trusted authority. Custom resolvers developed for earlier releases of Symbian OS will need to be rebuilt and signed to allow them to work with the platform security version of ECOM.

6.4 Summary

This chapter explains the effect that the introduction of platform security has had on plug-ins and frameworks, including security issues relating to the use of plug-in DLLs.

First we covered the definition of a plug-in, including the distinction between a plug-in designed for a specific application, which can have precisely targeted security capabilities, and general purpose plug-ins which potentially need to be trusted with a wide range of capabilities.

Then we examined the use of the ECOM plug-in framework within the platform security architecture, including new locations for plug-in files and security considerations resulting from the plug-in DLL running in the client application's process. We also covered the ability to restrict the selection of ECOM plug-ins to those built-in to the phone ROM.

Finally we discussed some implementation considerations, including how to migrate plug-ins written for previous Symbian OS versions, how to implement a plug-in using a client–server architecture when more sophisticated security controls are needed, and how to implement new plug-in frameworks using ECOM.

7

Sharing Data Safely

by Will Palmer

7.1 Introduction to Sharing Data

This chapter presents the key questions you need to ask – and some possible answers – to share your data in a secure way with Symbian OS platform security. It also shows you techniques you can use to implement data sharing in the Symbian operating system. Files and other resources were previously freely accessible to all running processes; this has led in some cases to bad modeling and design, to shortcuts, and, of course, to the creation of malware. With the advent of platform security this is no longer the case – access to files and other resources is now strictly controlled and managed, so developers need to consider how to share and access data securely.

We will consider all data that is accessed by more than one process. Although sharing data might involve, for example, several messaging applications accessing data from a message server, it also includes participating in a backup operation, or data being remotely provisioned through a device-provisioning server.

You should be sure of your need to share data. If your application's data does not need to be shared, then it is safest to hide it by default. You do this by putting it into your process's private directory, without implementing any accessor methods – and then you'll have no need for this chapter.

7.1.1 Considerations in Sharing Data

When sharing your data with more than one process, there are a number of key questions to consider. These will all be developed in further sections.

Do you need to protect the integrity of your data?

You may need to guard against abnormal behavior of your application or of other applications that are a client of your data. Although you should always make your application robust in the face of unexpected or corrupted data, you may have data whose integrity is relied upon by a client to perform a sensitive action – for example, a certificate or secure URL.

Do you need to protect the confidentiality of your data?

Your data may need to be guarded against 'prying eyes' – for example, if you are storing a password to use for remote access. You might choose never to reveal the plain text of that password, or perhaps to allow the password to be retrieved only if the user supplies a PIN.

What attacks should you care about?

There are several types of attack on data, both on its confidentiality and its integrity. Some of these we have seen exploited in releases of Symbian OS prior to the enhancement of platform security, but new measures are provided to protect against all of them.

When should your data be available?

Do you want to share your data synchronously or asynchronously? You may want your data to be accessible even if your process is not running. You usually do this by making use of Symbian OS system services.

How much data should you share?

You should examine the granularity of your data below the file level. Often data is a collection of information, and you may want to police the elements separately.

There are other important considerations that are more implementation specific, and relate to 'best practice' when developing your application. For example, if you are implementing a server, what are the consequences of allowing concurrency of access to your data and how do you permit this to occur; what are the consequences of too weak or too strong an access policy? We will also cover best practice in more detail in our discussion about levels of trust.

7.2　Categories of Data

7.2.1　What's Out of Scope

Data is a very general term, and encompasses anything from messages (signals, semaphores, datagrams) to settings (persistent configuration, transient property) to files (databases, resources, media 'BLOBs').

We restrict discussion in this chapter to settings and files. The primary mechanism for inter-process message passing is the Symbian OS client–server mechanism, discussed in Chapter 5. Other mechanisms for communicating information between processes, such as shared memory, semaphores and message queues, are also touched on in that chapter. Similarly, getting other processes to undertake tasks on your behalf – for example, the Task Scheduler and SendAs server – is outside the scope of what we discuss here.

7.2.2 What's Out of the Platform's Control

It is worth briefly touching on this topic, in order to clearly understand where the boundaries are. This is important to enable us to look at the 'end-to-end' security of our data. We have already mentioned in Chapter 1 how controls at the network boundary are becoming inadequate because of the trend towards seamless information flow between networks. There is, therefore, a need for a mobile phone to protect the information on it in a robust way, and also to protect any networks that it connects to.

A secure platform allows you to protect your data according to a policy that you choose. Capabilities that allow the use of local and remote network services are carefully assigned to trusted processes to control whether an application can communicate sensitive data across a network, but platform security does not control where a process sends data to or receives data from. We must rely on other technologies to provide end-to-end communications security – for example, a secure data channel protocol such as TLS/SSL, with authentication at each end of the link using digital certificates. By assigning a level of trust to a particular process, we have determined the policy for the type of information it can send from the mobile phone – for example, address book contact information that is synchronized to the PC. The synchronization process has capabilities ReadUserData and LocalServices, and we trust it to send on request only the subset of data that is policed by this capability.

We also cannot control how the data is used once it is received by an external entity. There can be no guarantee that the external entity will respect, or even understand, the security policy applied to the data. Once the data is off the Symbian OS mobile phone, we have no control over the level of privacy applied to the data.

Consider the ramifications of providing a backup mechanism in Symbian OS. Once the backup data is on the remote device – the PC, for example – it is the responsibility of the owner of the device to ensure that the backup data is not tampered with. On restore, Symbian OS can, of course, detect any evidence of tampering using hashing, but cannot prevent it. This is similar to the way it deals with removable media (see Chapter 8). Additionally, the backup architecture provides hooks that mobile phone manufacturers can use, at their discretion, to implement encryption of the backup data to assist with confidentiality. The story remains the same though – once data is off the mobile phone it is out of our control.

7.2.3   Persistency

Persistency of data describes the length of time for which data exists on the mobile phone. Data may either be transient – held in temporary memory and not surviving a reboot – or persistent – written to disk and, therefore, surviving a reboot. As examples of these different types, consider an instant messaging (IM) application. This application might have transient data (friends who are currently online, location information) that exists, at most, for the lifetime of the application, and persistent data (a list of friends, the configuration of the user interface) that is written to disk for use when the application restarts.

Once created, persistent and transient data may have a constant value – for example, mobile phone attributes such as manufacturer and firmware version. Resource files, such as fonts and branding elements (bitmaps, ring tones, wallpapers, etc.), are also in this category. Data may also be dynamic (i.e. changing in value), such as a setting indicating whether the Bluetooth service is available, or indicating the currently active window.

7.2.4   Data Added by the User

Perhaps the most common use of the term 'data' on a mobile phone is when it is applied to persistent information that a user stores. We refine this by defining 'user data' as that which is personal information stored by a user. Address book contacts and calendar entries are examples of user data and Symbian OS defines capabilities for protecting exactly this type of data. Contrast this with data such as downloaded ring tones – this is a type of data that a user might add to the mobile phone, but it is not regarded in platform security terms as user data.

Data added by the user may be considered as two types – public, which the user has no problem with any person reading, and private, which the user does not want any unauthorized person or process reading. Symbian OS platform security does not differentiate between these, since it is content-dependent – data added by the user may be either public or private user data.

As a result of this, it may be necessary to employ other protection techniques in the case of private user data. A piece of text in a notebook application, for example, might be something as innocuous as a scribbled note to oneself or it might be a debit card PIN. In this case it is the responsibility of the application managing this data to enable protection mechanisms such as encryption and password protection. This protection may simply be achieved at the user interface level; an example of this is a calendar entry that might be a public holiday or a medical appointment.

User data capabilities are usually policed symmetrically – that is, both reading and writing the data requires a capability. User data does not *have* to be policed symmetrically though; a media server is an example of this, where the server might be quite happy for anyone to read files in order to play them, but it certainly doesn't want anybody writing to them, potentially corrupting the files. Note also that, in this example, the policing of an application wishing to add files would probably be applied differently too, but this would depend on the content of the data.

7.2.5   Data Resident as Part of the Mobile Phone

We describe this as 'system data' – data that is vital to the integrity of the system, and that, if compromised, could cause a network or device service to fail. Examples of this type of data are network availability (a transient property), network access point (persistent) and IMEI number (persistent and constant value). The hardware abstraction layer (HAL) in the OS kernel contains system data, some of which has a constant value (`ECPUSpeed`), and some of which is variable (`EBacklightState`).

Here though, the type of data does not automatically determine the capabilities it will be policed on – system data capabilities are often non-symmetrical. Write access might be policed by the SID of a system process, in the case where there should only be one process updating the value. (This is generally preferable as it reduces the need for more processes to possess a system capability – this is discussed further in the next section). Read access, in many cases, does not require any capability – anyone can read the data – because confidentiality is not the prime issue, as the description of this type of data shows. An example of this is network signal strength or current call status. In the small number of cases where confidentiality is required in addition to integrity, read access is policed with `ReadDeviceData` and we term this 'device data' since the policy is then symmetrical. An example of this would be an IMAP server address.

Compound data often has both user and system parts – for example, a user account for a SyncML server. The server's address is clearly system data, as changing it would cause the service to fail; however the display name for the account is considered public data.

7.2.6   Capability Summary

Here we summarize the policy that you would apply to the different types of data that we have discussed in this section. The storage mechanism has no bearing on the policy.

Type of Data	Confidentiality Required: access policy	Integrity Required: access policy
User data	`ReadUserData` or none	`WriteUserData`
System data	None	`WriteDeviceData`, SID of process that modifies the value
Device data	`ReadDeviceData`	`WriteDeviceData`

7.3   Deciding the Level of Trust

So you have some data that you want to share – how do you share it safely? You must decide the level of trust to apply. This means undertaking a threat analysis. Analyze the value of your assets (the data), identify the attack surface, consider the threats to those assets, and then decide on an appropriate measure.

Symbian's platform security architecture is designed to empower the developer to decide the level of trust to apply. In practical terms this means the capabilities to assign to the policy for sharing your data. Note that the ability to write data can encompass creating, adding and deleting data as well. It may well be that you need to police access to these differently, depending on the content of your data. For example, a process that wishes to log events may treat adding entries simply as 'noise' but deleting entries as removing an audit trail.

It is sometimes easier to apply an inverse test and ask, 'Who do I *not* want to share my data with?'. This might help you to decide how much you would care if the data was corrupted or deleted, either intentionally or unintentionally, or stolen by an unauthorized entity. If you applied the wrong capability policy, could a phone number be modified to a premium rate number, for example? You must also think about the consequences to subscribers of your data – what is at stake for them? In fact, who are the clients of your data?

Bear in mind that when we asked users what security they expect from a mobile phone, one answer repeatedly made was 'I want my private data to stay private' (as reported in *Symbian OS Internals* [Sales 2005]).

7.3.1   Identification for Authorization

There are sometimes practical requirements for access control based on identity, and so we have chosen to support this as a complement to the authorization model. You may choose to mediate access using the SID or the VID of the process because you are only concerned with identity.

Policing your data using the VID may be considered less secure than using the SID, as the scope of processes with a particular VID is 'open-ended' – new software may be installed that has that VID, which may introduce new security problems. By contrast, only one EXE on the mobile phone can possess a particular SID, so the access control is more precisely defined. When using the VID, it may be useful to combine it with a capability check, in order to constrain further the potential scope of access being granted. The best approach, in this case, is to keep it simple. In many cases policing by the SID or the VID can be considered over-engineering, and by restricting access you could reduce the mass-appeal of your software.

7.3.2   Getting the Right Balance

In defining the policy for your data, you should consider that too strong a policy could be as bad as too weak a policy. The authorization model relies on the correct use of capabilities to be effective.

If you don't protect your data sufficiently you are at greater risk of an attack. If you protect your data too much you may create side effects:

- You limit the number of applications that can use your service, so you decrease its potential market value. Clients will have to pass more stringent tests to obtain this level of trust.

- You weaken the protection of other data policed by this capability by increasing the number of processes requiring it. We call this 'dilution of capabilities'.

Think of it in terms of 'communities' of services and data. The level of trust required to get access to the community protected by a capability is in practice likely to be reduced to that required for the least sensitive service or piece of data.

7.4   Attacks on Data and Countermeasures

Having created a threat model you will have a good idea of the kind of attacks that could occur on your data. We categorize the most common forms of attack below, and focus primarily on *intentional* attacks directed against our data assets. Unintentional compromises, however, can be just as damaging unless we implement robust behavior.

We include some common threats to data storage and management services, since many problems occur as a result of concurrency issues – multiple clients accessing data at the same time [Anderson 2001].

We also discuss specific countermeasures for each type of attack. The platform security architecture gives you the primary countermeasures to threats against your data. In particular, data caging and memory protection, through process isolation, are integral countermeasure tools that you get 'for free'. However there are two things that you must do:

- Implement the countermeasures, made available through the platform security architecture that you have decided on to harden your software against attack.

- Apply 'best practices' as a complement to platform security, to make your software robust in the face of unexpected data. These are critical elements of security engineering in diminishing the threat of attack.

Unfortunately, many instances of compromised data occur as a result of the unintentional behavior of the clients of that data. As a client of shared data, you have responsibilities too. Capability implies trust – trust not to leak data that you have privileged access to. This means that you must ensure that you do not pass this information on to any other process without first checking that it has the appropriate capabilities. In accepting responsibility for privileged access, you must also accept responsibility for policing access.

7.4.1 Data Capture

This is an attack on *confidentiality* and is the most commonly considered attack on data. Here are some ways in which it can occur:

- Malware tricking a process into giving it data – for example, by intentionally passing inappropriate data to glean sensitive information from any output. Alternatively it could use brute force – for example, by cracking a password.

- Snooping on data passed between two legitimate entities (man-in-the-middle). Temporary files and public memory spaces are common attack vectors.

- Unintentionally giving access to files, or data within them, that should not be shared. Often data is part of a collection of information. It may be a set of elements in a table, lines in a file, a typed list of elements, or a set of properties of a class. Sharing more data than you need to leaves that data vulnerable to attack. Log files are an obvious example here, especially if they are recorded to a public location.

Countermeasures

1. Place your sensitive persistent data in the private data cage of your process, and keep your sensitive transient data within its private memory space.

2. Mediate read access to your data by policing APIs exported by your process.

3. Use a system service to mediate read access on your behalf, and register a read policy with it for your data. Your data is hidden within the system service's data cage or process memory space.

4. Share individual files from your data cage with trusted processes using shared handles.

5. Identify and implement different read policies, where necessary, for collections of data. Consider the individual elements of the collection and only share what is necessary.

Best practices

Some best practices to help keep data secure from prying eyes are:

1. Temporary files are often a loophole in security – don't use a public store to temporarily hold sensitive data derived from the original.

2. Don't write data belonging to your own process to a public log.

3. Don't write another application's data to a public log.

4. Protect user-added data with sensitive content with passwords or encrypt the data.

5. When sharing files from your data cage, open only the files you wish to share and no others. Any files that are open may be accessible by the receiving process through the shared file session. Close the session at the first opportunity after the file handle has been received by the process you are sharing with.

6. Where possible, minimize the amount of time for which data is shared.

7.4.2 Tampering

This is an attack on the *integrity* of data and, where system or device data is involved, on the integrity of the mobile phone itself. Here are some ways in which it can occur, some reasons and some effects:

- Most importantly, the attack could be launched to cause instability through corrupted data. This might result in a process crash, or stopping the mobile phone from booting.

- It may be launched to coerce the owner into undertaking an alternative path of action.

- It may lead to service denial – for example, if dialup connection information is altered.

- It may cause the user to unwittingly spend money – for example, by altering a phone number to a premium rate one.

- It may lead to data capture, if connection information is altered.

- Data on removable media is at high risk from this kind of attack – as we have already noted, this is out of our control when the media is removed from the mobile phone.

- Some attacks of this kind are specific to server processes that allow concurrency of access. These occur when inconsistent updates are performed on dependent compound data. There is a risk of being left in an unknown state unless atomic updates are executed.

Countermeasures

1. Place your sensitive persistent data in the private data cage of your process, and keep your sensitive transient data within its private memory space.

2. Mediate write access to your data by policing APIs exported by your process.

3. Use a system service to mediate write access on your behalf, and register a write policy with it for your data. Your data is hidden within the system service's data cage or process memory space.

4. Share individual files from your data cage with trusted processes using shared handles.

5. Take advantage of the static access policy that is applied to the special directory \resource for your resource files. This directory allows you to share your resources publicly but without compromising their integrity. Essentially it is a read-only directory for non-TCB processes. Examples of data you might install here are bitmaps, fonts, RSC and help files.

Best practices

1. Make your process fault tolerant – that is, resistant to corrupted or unexpected data. Create a recovery strategy for all the situations you have identified in your threat model. This may be as simple as resetting the data back to a 'default' configuration for corrupted backup data. Choose a resilience strategy that is both simple and effective for your process, and also right for the type of data in

question. If you are implementing a media player, you are likely to be accepting data from off the mobile phone (OTA or removable media). If such a file were corrupt you would simply not play it.

2. You may refuse unsolicited data but instead only use data that has been installed through the Software Install process. You can do this by not implementing support for a \import directory in your private data cage – see Chapter 8 for more information on import directories.

3. Return errors to clients of your data in a timely fashion, but make sure that a client can process the error. For example, you must not return an error for a method such as CancelTransaction().

4. Threats to server processes associated with inconsistent updates can be mitigated by using a locking transaction model. However, we do not recommend this – instead build this into your recovery strategy. For example, the use of client-side caching of data is advocated in *Symbian OS C++ for Mobile Phones* [Harrison 2003] – this could be used to roll back to a consistent state.

7.4.3   Denial of Service

This is an attack on *availability* of data and is especially important to address for the system services presented next in this chapter. Here are some ways in which it can occur:

- Changing a setting, resulting in the user being deprived of a service, such as a setting on a POP account stopping a user from picking up email.

- Removal of an application's data file resulting in an application not running.

- Sending data too large to be handled by the receiving process – resulting in buffer overflow.

- Causing a priority inversion – an attack on a server process – where a high-priority thread waiting on that service fails to run because a low-priority thread has locked the resource it wishes to access. A resource can be locked for an extended period of time, for example, if a large transaction takes place (or indeed if a locking transaction never completes), or if frequent and extensive searches through the data are made.

Countermeasures

1. Place your sensitive persistent data in the private data cage of your process and keep your sensitive transient data within its private memory space.

2.   Police the transaction APIs correctly on your server process to guard against denial of service through locking.

Best practices

1.   Make your process fault tolerant and create a good recovery strategy.

2.   Implement a 'non-serialized optimistic' transaction model on your server process in order to achieve high concurrency of access. This model allows any number of clients to start a transaction (optimistic) at any time (non-serialized), which eliminates the threat of blocking access to shared data.

7.4.4   Physical Loss and Damage

Lastly, there is, of course, what we might consider as the biggest threat against data by users themselves – data being lost through losing or breaking a mobile phone.

Best practices

Recovery of lost data can be achieved if processes back up their data. You should consider using the Symbian OS secure backup service – being robust in this way will certainly make your application more attractive to the user. Another way of backing up data is through synchronization (for example, SyncML), although this has the added complication of the remote software (server) needing to understand the MIME type of your data.

7.4.5   Threats and Countermeasures Summary

Here we summarize the threats and their countermeasures that we have discussed in this section. Abbreviations used in the table are as follows: data capture (DC), tampering (TA), and denial of service (DoS).

Threat scenario and type	Countermeasure
Tricking of APIs by malware (DC)	Data cage all sensitive data, or keep in private memory space
Snooping (DC)	Data cage and implement API read policy (use system service if practical) Use shared file handles
Unintentionally allowing access (DC)	Implement read policies at the right level of granularity

Threat scenario and type	Countermeasure
Modification of data to cause unintended or unexpected behavior, including failing to execute (TA, DoS)	Data cage and implement API write policy (use system service if practical) Use shared file handles Use \resource directory for your resources
Altering dial-up information (TA, DoS, DC)	Data cage and implement API write policy
Inconsistent update made (TA, DoS)	Police transactional APIs accordingly
Causing a buffer overflow (DoS)	Implement fault tolerance (best practice only)
Causing a priority inversion or locking of a resource (DoS)	Police (transactional) APIs accordingly

7.5   Using System Services

We now look at how you choose the right mechanism for sharing your data. We recommend that you use existing system services where possible, unless:

- your security policy does not fit these services
- your data should only be accessible when your process is running
- your data type is not supported.

In this case you should implement a custom server to tailor the shared service to your needs (see Chapter 5). This may be appropriate for BLOBs, for example, such as media files, for which there is no system service at the time of writing.

System services that are currently available for you to share your data safely are:

- publish and subscribe
- DBMS
- file handles.

We will discuss the security features of these services and show how to use them. Additionally, we will look at security in the central repository – a system service that has restrictions on who can use it, but we will look at how you can make use of it. Lastly, we will touch on a few other mechanisms that are pertinent to this topic, and review the implications of their use.

7.5.1   Publish and Subscribe

Publish and subscribe is a state-oriented service for asynchronous distribution of information where the latest value of a setting is the only one relevant. We term each setting held in this service a *property*. Key functional points are:

- It provides a means to store and broadcast *transient* data at run time.

- It can provide a run-time data cage into which each process can publish its properties, providing protection from spoofing or denial of service.

- Under certain circumstances it provides bounded execution time for critical tasks that require real-time guarantees. Guarantees are made for:

  - publishing a property of up to 512 bytes in length via a handle, if the new data length does not exceed a buffer size that you can pre-allocate

  - reading the value of a property of up to 512 bytes in length using a handle to the property.

The run-time data cage is the point of interest in platform security terms. Here is the prototype for defining a property:

```
IMPORT_C static TInt Define(TUint aKey, TInt aAttr,
            const TSecurityPolicy& aReadPolicy,
            const TSecurityPolicy& aWritePolicy,
                    TInt aPreallocated=0);
```

When a process defines a property it is stored in a category with a value equal to the SID of the process. No other processes can define a property in this keyspace, so the property can't be spoofed – the net effect being a run-time data cage. At the point of definition, the process must also supply a read and write policy, which allows the service to limit access to trusted clients you have specified.

Note that the lifetime of the property defined in the service is not necessarily linked to the lifetime of the defining process. The property will exist until either the mobile phone is switched off or the defining process deletes it. This provides flexibility in how long your shared data is available. It could be:

- for the length of time that your process is running (for example, a state flag during a task execution phase)

- for the lifetime of your process (for example a 'friend online' Instant Message signal)

- or, from the point that it is defined to when the mobile phone is switched off (for example, system properties such as network signal availability and battery strength).

Consider an example from an instant messaging application, whose design is split between a server and a UI application (see [Harrison 2003]) to allow, among other things, different UI applications to be built. A function of this application might be to notify a user when a 'friend' goes online or offline. This could be achieved by the server defining a property 'new friend event':

```
static const TInt32 KIMServerSID = 0x89ABCDEF;
static _LIT_SECURITY_POLICY_S0 (KFriendsListChangePolicy,
                                KIMServerSID);

void CIMServer::ConstructL()
  {
  ...
  User::LeaveIfError(
          RProperty::Define(KKeyFriendsListHasChanged,
                                   RProperty::EInt,
                                   KAlwaysPassPolicy,
                            KFriendsListChangePolicy));
  ...
  }
```

There are a couple of interesting points that come out of this. Firstly, we simply define a property to publish the fact that the friends list has changed, rather than trying to say 'you have a new friend'. If you look back to our definition of 'Publish and Subscribe' you can see why – we state that 'the latest value of a setting is the only one relevant'. This is because it cannot be guaranteed that every event will be received by a subscriber. Consequently your behavior as a subscriber should always be to react based on the current value, not a change in state.

The following code snippet shows how the server publishes to the property when a friend's online status changes:

```
void CIMServer::OnCommunicationEventL(TEvent aEvent,
                      TEventData aBuf, TInt aError)
  {
```

```
switch (aEvent)
  {
  case EFriendOnline:
  case EFriendOffline:
    {
    UpdateFriendsListL(aBuf);
    User::LeaveIfError (RProperty::Set(KIMServerSID,
                         KKeyFriendsListHasChanged,
                              iFriendsList.Count()));
    }
  ...
  }
}
```

Consider the client code for the UI application. First, in its `ConstructL()` the application creates an instance of an active object that tracks 'friends online change' events from the server:

```
void CIMApplicationUI::ConstructL()
  {
  // connect to the server
  User::LeaveIfError(iIMSvr.Connect());
  // create the active object that tracks events
  iWatcher = CFriendEventWatcher::NewL(*this);
  ...
  }
```

The following code shows how the active object handles and acts on these server events:

```
void CFriendEventWatcher::ConstructL()
  {
  // attach to the property
  User::LeaveIfError(iProperty.Attach(KIMServerSID,
                      KKeyFriendsListHasChanged));
  CActiveScheduler::Add(this)
  // initial subscription and process current property value
  RunL();
  }

void CFriendEventWatcher::RunL()
  {
  // re-subscribe to help prevent missing notification of updates
  iProperty.Subscribe(iStatus);
  SetActive();

  // test availability of property
  TInt numfriends;
  TInt err = iProperty.Get(numfriends);
  if (KErrNotFound == err)
    {
    // server is not running
    User::Leave(KErrIMServerNotRunning);
    }
```

```
else if (KErrNone == err)
    {
    if (numfriends)
        {
        // enable friends online icon
        }
    else
        {
        // disable friends online icon
        }
    }
...
}
```

Here we are checking the latest value in order to enable or disable a 'you have friends online' icon. If a friend came online at the same time as another went offline, there would be two published events – however, the UI application might only receive one. This is why the event could not be an increment ('new friend online') in its own right. Imagine a toggle switch property – if a subscriber missed one event and didn't check the value, it would have its logic reversed.

The second interesting point is with regard to the 'friends online' icon. This is a good technique for avoiding polling overhead – an application could ask the server for the complete list of friends each time it is notified, however, if it only does this in response to a 'show friends' command, processing is minimized.

Finally, note that the UI application does not need any capabilities to read this property as we consider it public information – we only protect what needs to be protected – however, only the IM server can write a value to it. This is an example of non-symmetrical policing.

Good practices

Multiple publishers of values to a property are generally discouraged. There are two reasons for this. Firstly, it encourages the, potentially unnecessary, proliferation of 'write policy' capabilities. Secondly, it could give rise to race conditions, especially with respect to Booleans or bit masks. An exception to this might be publishing to properties that represent events where the subsequent processing of subscribers is simply in response to the event.

Client code should not perform substantial processing on each notification for properties that change value frequently. Publishing to a property could potentially lead to multiple clients servicing the notification – if this property's value has a high frequency of change, it can lead to a large amount of processing. It is, therefore, a good idea to document the expected update frequency of your property.

Sometimes data represents the current state of part of a mobile phone. An example might be the current volume level of the speaker, the value of which may be highly volatile while it is being changed through the user interface. The publish and subscribe service should be used for just such transient data. Note that once the target volume is reached (it's *final* state), the property ceases to be volatile. In this case the value is written to disk in order to save the *initial* state of the volume should the mobile phone be rebooted or media application restarted.

7.5.2   Central Repository

The central repository provides a centralized service for safe, secure persistence of shared settings. It is implemented in the OS to enhance ease of programming through a unified settings API, to promote a common policy for platform security, and to allow simpler customization, factory reset and data backup of the mobile phone. Key functional points are:

- It uses simple partitioning of data using a UID-pair to create a two-tier structure: up to 2^{32} top-level 'keyspaces' or repositories, within which up to 2^{32} settings of any simple type, may be defined.

- It provides the ability to define separate read and write access policies to settings within a keyspace at three levels: a default policy for the whole keyspace, a policy for a range of settings and a policy for individual settings.

- It provides the means to change the read and write access policy of a setting at run time.

- It provides non-serialized optimistic transactional support for reading and writing multiple settings – ensuring consistency between multiple values within a keyspace.

Policies are defined in a keyspace initialization file held in the data cage of the central repository server, and these may reside in ROM, or be installed via a SIS package. A new keyspace may only be created through software install; it cannot be created at run time, which prevents the potential problem of unchecked bloat through badly behaved applications not deleting keyspaces that are no longer used.

It is important to note that the central repository is not generally available for use as a storage mechanism at the time of writing. Third parties with sufficient capabilities can find and read from settings, and be notified of any changes, but cannot write their own changes. This restriction is likely to be lifted in the future.

The INI file may also contain settings and default values for that keyspace. Here is a simple example, an instant messaging server's initialization file:

```
# 89ABCDEF.cre
# Instant Messaging Server keyspace

cenrep
version 1

[platsec]
# default capabilities for this keyspace
cap_rd=ReadUserData cap_wr=WriteUserData
# define a range for server private data
0x100 0x200 sid_rd=0x89ABCDEF sid_wr=0x89ABCDEF
# define a range for public data
0x1000 0x1100 cap_rd=AlwaysPass cap_wr=AlwaysPass

[defaultMeta]
0x1000000

[main]
# protected by default capabilities
# autologin: specifies whether to login on startup of application
0x1  int  1
# usesslport: specifies whether to use SSL
0x2 int 0
# anonsearch: specifies whether to undertake anonymous searches
0x3 int

# server private data
# imhostname: host address of server
0x100 string "host1.imserver"
# defport: default port number
0x101 int 5269
# sslport: ssl port number
0x102 int 5223

# account data (device data) - using individual policy
# username
0x200 string "username" cap_rd=ReadDeviceData
cap_wr=WriteDeviceData
# password
0x201 string "password" cap_rd=ReadDeviceData
cap_wr=WriteDeviceData

# public data
# onlineicon: user profile icon
0x1000 string "defUser.gif"
# displayfont
0x1001 string "swissA"
# fontsize
0x1002 int 10
#timeout: timeout value (min) for inactive chat sessions
0x1003 int 10
```

The ability to define access policies at different levels makes this service very flexible. This is particularly important as you can store up to 2^{32}

settings in a single keyspace. Note that the policies are governed by the standard rules applied by the `TSecurityPolicy` class. The policies at successive levels *supersede* any more general policy defined, and these cannot be applied or changed dynamically. This does not prevent the policy applied to the setting being changed at run time, as we stated.

In the previous example we defined a range of keys with a read and write access policy equal to the owning process's SID. The central repository supports the ability to move settings within a keyspace, given that the process that moves the settings has the write capabilities applying to both the source and target keys. In this example, settings could be moved into this key range, effectively hiding them from all but the owning process. This can be used to achieve temporary sharing (or hiding) of data. There is a potential drawback to this mechanism – the potential to 'downgrade' the policy on a setting. So, for instance, a client may have added what was considered as user data, and another client makes it available to anyone. Also, the clients of some shared settings may not be robust enough to deal with data they expect to be available suddenly disappearing. The trust relationship between processes sharing settings is evident here, as well as the need for resilience to unexpected events.

The transaction model implemented in the central repository achieves high concurrency – a number of transactions are allowed to be opened on a keyspace, however, the first to commit causes all others to fail with `KErrLocked`. Consequently, clients are rewarded for keeping their transactions short since they are less likely to fail. Clients that must guarantee success place their transaction in a `do-while KErrLocked` loop. Concurrency is further guarded by checking that the capabilities of the requesting client were at least equal to the default policy for the keyspace – making sure that people without the ability to read and write settings cannot start a transaction.

7.5.3   DBMS

DBMS is a service that provides a general interface for access to relational databases. The service provides two different implementations: a client-side service and a client–server service. The former gives you DBMS functionality to use within your own data cage and you would police access through your own API. The latter is of more interest in this context, and provides you with a way to share your data asynchronously. Key functional points are:

- It provides the ability to define *cumulative* separate read and write access and schema manipulation policies on two levels: a default policy for the database and a policy for individual tables.

- It provides a lightweight client-side implementation, enabling processes to store data in their own data cage, and police it accordingly.

Databases may be manipulated either through a subset of SQL or through a Symbian OS C++ API. This API has been extended to support creation and manipulation of secure, shared databases and also allows a thread to query the policy applied to a database or table. This can be useful for a middleware server, for example, that provides querying functionality on top of DBMS, and which polices this API according to the data it is acting on in DBMS. However, this will not be a very common pattern – most clients would use the DBMS API directly.

Access to secure DBMS databases is controlled through pre-registered policy files, each of which has a UID, and is applied to the database by its creator. The policy file states the read, write and 'modify schema' policies to apply to a database and it can be used to add capabilities for accessing tables. Note that the policies are governed by the standard rules applied by the TSecurityPolicy class and that this table-level security can only *strengthen* the database policy, rather than override it. Here is an example policy file that an instant messaging server might register to be used to police access to an IM 'friends' database:

```
; dbms policy file for Instant Messaging 'friends' database
; 87654321.spd

[database]
; friends are considered to be user data. The tables containing
; contact information will be policed on these default policies
read
capability = ReadUserData
write
capability = WriteUserData
schema
; only the server process can change the schema
SID = 89ABCDEF

[table]
; this is a table relating to friends, and contains data
; private to the server process, for example, local UIDs etc
; the policies below strengthen the default policies
name = metadata
; only server process can read or write metadata
read
SID = 89ABCDEF
write
SID = 89ABCDEF
```

There is no concept of ownership in the context of a policy file, and hence there is no limit to the number of databases that can use one. This is certainly the case for the Contacts Model, which allows a user to create more than one database – for instance, one for personal contacts and a separate corporate directory.

> It is important to note here that access policies are only read from ROM at the time of writing. This restriction is likely to be lifted in the future.

In order to make the creation and manipulation of secure shared databases available to third parties, a mobile phone manufacturer could choose to embed a 'default' policy file in ROM that polices access on user capabilities:

```
; default security policy file for third party use
; 12345678.spd

[database]
read
capability = ReadUserData
write
capability = WriteUserData
schema
capability = WriteUserData
```

Given that the UID for the policy file is published, third parties could then use the DBMS secure shared database extension API to create their own database with a policy based on this file:

```
RDbs dbms;
User::LeaveIfError(dbms.Connect());
CleanupClosePushL(dbms);
RDbNamedDatabase file;
file.Create(dbms, _LIT("c:myDb.db"), _L("secure[12345678]"));
CleanupClosePushL(file);
...
```

Obviously a table-level policy is not possible in this case, since you must write the name of the table in the policy file.

7.5.4   File Handles

Symbian OS supports the means for a process to temporarily share a file with another process under controlled conditions. The kernel provides the basic support for handle-sharing across the process boundary, and the file server builds on this to provide specific support for sharing file handles. Some key points to note:

- The owning process opens a file in a mode that cannot be changed by the receiving process under normal circumstances.

- The receiving process accesses the file through the shared handle it receives, but does not get access to the shared file's private directory.

- The owning process shares a file server session with the receiving process.

- Revocation of sharing a file is not possible.

Note that file handles are not handles in the sense of a reference to a kernel object, but, instead, they are a unique identifier of an open file within a file server session.

Files can be shared in this way using the following family of methods published on the `RFile` API:

```
RFile::TransferToClient() and RFile::AdoptFromClient()
RFile::TransferToServer() and RFile::AdoptFromServer()
RFile::TransferToProcess() and RFile::AdoptFromProcess()
```

These methods allow transfer of a file handle using the client server IPC mechanism, and also from one process to another.

We said that the mode of a file cannot normally be changed. The only change allowed is to toggle between the modes `EFileShareExclusive` and `EFileShareReadersOnly`, and this is only allowed under limited circumstances that would not compromise the use of the file by the other process you are sharing with.

Our example IM server could make good use of file sharing if it receives a file as an attachment during a chat session and needs to hand the file on to an appropriate application or recognizer. The server needs to share that file and no other. The IM server code might look as follows:

```
void CIMServer::HandleNewAttachmentL(const TDesC& aName)
  {
  // create a new session to the file server specifically for
  // sharing just the attachment
  RFs fs;
  User::LeaveIfError(fs.Connect());
  CleanupClosePushL(fs);
  // allow session to be shared by receiving process
  User::LeaveIfError(fs.ShareProtected());

  // open file where data has been previously stored
  RFile attachment;
  User::LeaveIfError(attachment.Open(fs, aName, EFileRead));
  CleanupClosePushL(attachment);
  RProcess handler;
  User::LeaveIfError(handler.Create(_LIT("Handler.exe"),
                                          KNullDesC));
  CleanupClosePushL(handler);

  // transfer file to process
```

```
User::LeaveIfError(attachment.TransferToProcess(handler, 1, 2);
TRequestStatus status;
handler.Rendezvous(status);
if (KRequestPending != status.Int())
    {
    handler.RendezvousCancel(status);
    handler.Kill(0);
    User::Leave(status.Int());
    }
handler.Resume();
User::WaitForRequest(status);
User::LeaveIfError(status.Int());

// safe to close all handles including shared session
CleanupStack::PopAndDestroy(3, fs);
}
```

Notice that the IM server opens the attachment in read-only mode for sharing. Notice also that the file server session is open specifically for sharing, and the only file opened using this shared session is the attachment. This ensures that the handler process only has access to that file and no others in the IM server's private directory. If any other files were opened using this session there is a possibility that the receiving process could also open it – by speculatively incrementing the handle number, for instance. Finally, we see that the session is open only for as long as required for the handler process to receive the handle, and no longer. This is achieved with the Rendezvous code, which allows the IM server to be notified when the handler has received the attachment.

Here is the corresponding code in the handler process:

```
LOCAL_C void MainL()
    {
    // adopt the file
    RFile attachment;
    User::LeaveIfError(attachment.AdoptFromCreator(1, 2));
    CleanupClosePushL(attachment);

    //signal transfer complete
    RProcess::Rendezvous(KErrNone);

    // use the file
    ...
    // close the file
    CleanupStack::PopAndDestroy(&attachment);
    }

GLDEF_C TInt E32Main()
    {
    __UHEAP_MARK;
    CTrapCleanup* cleanup = CTrapCleanup::New();
    CActiveScheduler* scheduler = new CActiveScheduler;
    TInt ret = KErrNoMemory;
    if (cleanup && scheduler)
```

```
    {
    CActiveScheduler::Install(scheduler);
    }
  delete scheduler;
  delete cleanup;
  __UHEAP_MARKEND;
  return ret;
  }
```

The client can use the file through a hidden shared file server session inside the `RFile` object, removing the need for a separate `RFs` object to be maintained. This session is automatically closed when `RFile::Close()` is called on the attachment.

The trust relationship between the two processes is evident here once again; there is no chance of revocation on the part of the sharing process. Similarly, the receiving process has a duty to protect the file it has received (note, though, that there is no technical reason why this process cannot pass the file on to another process).

7.5.5 Services Summary

The table below summarizes the system services and the categories of data with which they are best used. 'Custom server' in the table denotes the implementation of your own dedicated server to manage access to the data.

Characteristic / Service	Persistency	Volatility	Size	Exchange
Publish and subscribe	Transient	Any	Prefer <512 bytes	Asynchronous
Central repository	Persistent	Non-volatile	<2 KB	Asynchronous
DBMS	Persistent	Non-volatile	Any	Asynchronous
File handles	Transient	Non-volatile	Any	Synchronous
Custom server	Any	Any	Any	Synchronous

7.6 Summary

Getting the level of trust correct for your data is essential in order to ensure it is secure enough, and to maintain a strong and balanced capability model on the mobile phone. Creating a threat model is crucial in achieving this outcome.

We have looked at different categories of data, and shown how confidentiality and integrity should be treated, with respect to each of these categories. As a client of shared data, the granting of a capability should be seen as bestowing privileged access. With privileges come responsibilities – once access has been granted, the responsibility for policing access has to be accepted also.

Your decision on how to implement secure sharing of your data will depend on its type and the characteristics of that data. We noted that system services should be used where possible, in preference to duplicating their functionality.

The benefits of sharing data safely are clear: in a world where more and more information is stored electronically, and where much of it may reside on or pass through a mobile phone and where the abuse of electronic communications to perpetrate fraud is rapidly increasing, mediated access to your data for trusted clients is paramount.

PART 3

Managing Platform Security Attributes

8

Native Software Installer

by Andy Harker

8.1 Introduction to the Native Software Installer

8.1.1 What the Installer Does

The native software installer is a Symbian OS component which manages the installation of add-on ('after-market') software packages – software which is added to the mobile phone after its manufacture, typically by the phone user, rather than software which is included in the ROM of the phone. A user interface (UI) layer is added by the mobile phone manufacturer, so the controls may look quite different on, say, a Series 60 phone and a UIQ phone, but the same Symbian OS software installer engine is doing the work in both cases.

The software installer is one of the platform security 'gatekeepers', as it is responsible for ensuring that add-on native software is copied to the mobile phone with the correct set of security attributes. Before reading this chapter, which contains frequent references to digital certificates, signatures and chains, you may find it useful to refer to Appendix B for a review of some of the basics of cryptography.

In Symbian OS releases prior to v9, installation could take place from a PC connected to your mobile phone. This is still the case, but the interaction you have during a native software install will now take place with the mobile phone and not with the PC, for reasons of trust and security that we will look at later.

We are using the term 'native' to indicate that the software which is installed runs directly on Symbian OS itself and to differentiate these applications from other, layered, types of software such as Java MIDlets. Java MIDlets do not run directly on the OS – they are managed and run in a Java Virtual Machine. MIDlets also have different security requirements, which are out of the scope of this book. Consequently, MIDlets have a separate install mechanism, which won't be covered here.

Now that it's clear what type of applications we are referring to, we will drop the term 'native' and simply refer to the 'software installer' (sometimes SWI for short) or just 'installer'.

In short, the software installer's key responsibilities are:

- to validate and install native software packages (SIS files) on the mobile phone

- to validate software that is delivered in a pre-installed form on media cards

- to handle upgrades and removals, and provide package management services to the rest of the platform.

The rest of this chapter explains how the installer actually achieves the above responsibilities. First, however, let's take a brief look at how things have changed from a security perspective.

8.1.2   Platform Security and its Impact on the Installer

Inevitably, improving security in any way requires the introduction of new security checks and Symbian OS platform security is no different in this respect.

As an example, previous versions of the Symbian OS installer placed almost no limitations on where a package author could deliver files into the file system. Data caging clearly changes this situation significantly. In brief, here are a handful of new rules, which we will cover in much more detail as this chapter unfolds:

- For a given drive, binaries (EXEs and DLLs) should be placed in one (and only one) designated file area. If it should prove possible to circumvent this rule – perhaps by getting a program to create an EXE or DLL outside the designated area – the binary certainly won't be launched by Symbian OS v9.

- The overwriting of files might not be permitted – especially if the file affected belongs to another package.

- The capabilities an application EXE needs may have to be signed for (that is, there are some things an EXE will not be allowed to do without authorization).

In short, the software installer polices software installations to ensure that they conform to platform security rules and, therefore, contributes towards maintaining the integrity of the mobile phone. The installer itself can, clearly, perform privileged operations (such as the copying of files into restricted areas) based on certain criteria, which we will describe later.

As such, it is appropriate to consider the installer as a 'gatekeeper' since it examines credentials and enforces rules, and only allows software into the OS environment if it passes these tests.

8.1.3 Installer Configuration – a Warning

A large number of software installer rules and behaviors are described in this chapter. Due to the number of configuration options available to the mobile phone manufacturer, it is possible that the behavior described here is not what you may observe on a specific mobile phone model. Some manufacturers may choose to enable a particular behavior while others may not.

8.2 Validating Capabilities

As previous chapters have explained what capabilities are, how they behave, and how they are specified within binaries, it's time to look at the signing requirements. Failing to get a package adequately signed may lead to installations being aborted. This section should help you understand what needs to be done and how everything actually works.

8.2.1 Who Can Grant Capabilities

In Chapter 2, Section 2.4.4 we mentioned that the mobile phone manufacturer might choose to allow some capabilities to be granted to software by the user at install time. The software installer will check for signing approval for system and user capabilities, and may also seek user approval for some user capabilities, as we'll see shortly.

The decision about which capabilities may be granted by the user is in the hands of the mobile phone manufacturer and it's quite possible for them to configure one phone model differently from another (although this is probably unlikely). It's also possible for some capabilities always to be granted to running processes – essentially making them ignored. Again this configuration choice is in the hands of the manufacturer.

Similarly, the mobile phone manufacturer decides which signing authorities will be trusted to approve which capabilities, and the requirements of the signing authority may vary. We expect that in most cases, the Symbian Signed scheme will be included, and the requirements of that scheme are discussed in Chapter 9.

Assuming that you know what capabilities your package as a whole requires, and thus what approval it needs, let's now cover what you will need to do to make it generally installable.

8.2.2   What You Need to Do

Firstly, and most simply, if your package contains no binaries, or only binaries requiring no capabilities, then it is not necessary to have it signed by a signing authority (although you may wish to do so simply to avoid the install-time warning which is shown to the user when untrusted packages are installed). However, the mobile phone may be configured to require all packages to be signed – in this case you can 'self-sign' your package, and this is covered in more detail in Section 8.4.1. Even if this isn't a mandatory requirement, you can still sign it anyway – the software installer won't complain about extraneous signatures as long as you sign it correctly and the validity dates are current.

User-Granted Capabilities

If your package contains binaries requiring only user-grantable capabilities, then again you do not have to have this package signed by a signing authority. You must be aware, however, that the mobile phone user will be asked whether they wish to allow your package to be installed with those capabilities. If the user says no, the installation will be aborted. Note that if you choose to have your package signed by an authority, and the authority endorses your user capabilities then the user will not be asked for verification at install time.

Signature-Granted Capabilities

Finally, we need to cover the situation where your package contains binaries requiring one or more capabilities that the user is not able to grant. Clearly, for your package to be granted the trust required for these capabilities, you will need to submit it to a signing authority. Once verified and signed, your application will be installable and able to access or employ sensitive parts of the system which impinge on device integrity and user privacy.

Situations Which Always Require Package Signing

In addition to the general situations above, there are other reasons why signing your package may become necessary. These are covered later in Section 8.3.1.

8.2.3   An All-or-Nothing Approach to Package Installation

At install time, your package is evaluated for its suitability to be installed, based on:

- the capabilities your package requires
- how (or if) you had your package signed.

This evaluation is based on looking at the signatures that are present, and in some cases asking the user to agree to your package being installed with the capabilities it requires.

From the installer's perspective, binaries that arrive within SIS files are requesting permission to be installed with the capabilities that have been declared within them by the developer. The installer, therefore, is either going to grant permission (that is, install all the files present) or deny permission (fail the install).

Note that there is no halfway solution here – the installer either grants permission for all the binaries present to be installed or rejects the entire package. Similarly, for each binary within the SIS file, the installer will either validate the grant of all the capabilities required or none at all. In short, there's no way that the installer will install some binaries and not others unless conditional statements are present in the SIS file. In addition, the installer will never modify a binary, so there's never a situation where the installer will remove or downgrade the capabilities of a binary.

Any problems with a package will, therefore, result in the entire package installation being aborted. Any partial changes made up to that point will be rolled back. Incidentally, if power fails during a software install operation, rollback may occur on the next invocation of the installer, or after boot – depending on the particulars of the installation.

8.2.4 Certificate Chaining

The signing certificates themselves can be either self-signed, or signed by another certificate – which itself could be self-signed or signed by another certificate, and so on.

Building the Chain

What we essentially have here is the means to build a certificate chain, and we can do this by:

1. Identifying the certificate's issuer.

2. Validating the signature of the current certificate (using the issuer's public key).

3. Checking the current date is within the validity range for the certificate.

4. Going back to step 1, but this time with the certificate of the issuer.

Eventually the chain will terminate either on a self-signed certificate – from which we can go no further – or at some point where we recognize the certificate, trust it and consciously decide to go no further.

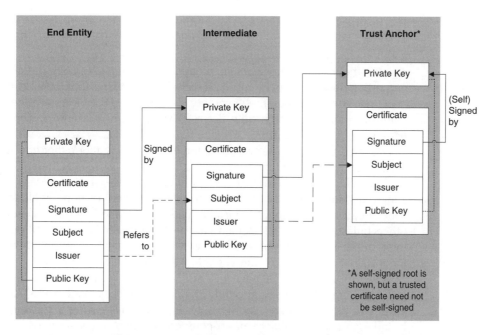

Figure 8.1 How Certificates and Keys Relate to Each Other

A Complete Chain

The certificate terminated on is generally referred to as the 'root' certificate or 'trust anchor' (see Figure 8.1). The certificate we started to build the chain from in the first place is referred to as the 'end entity', and the certificates in the middle which link the 'end entity' to the 'root' are referred to as 'intermediates'.

In summary, nearly all the decision-making by the installer is based on the fact that the chain is proven to terminate on a known or trusted certificate of which the mobile phone itself has a copy, in its own private store.

8.2.5 Why Chaining?

Chaining does seem remarkably complex, but its main advantage is that you can create one or more intermediate certificates and delegate signing to those, rather than sign everything with the root certificate. This means that you can leave the root certificate's private key safe in a vault somewhere and only bring it out again if you need to generate more delegates. A key that spends much of its life in a vault is less open to compromise than one that is in use every day.

If one of the delegates does become compromised, you can revoke it (see Section 8.2.7) and then journey down to the vault to generate a new one! Your root key, therefore, remains in a safer environment. Just imagine the enormous cost of replacing a root certificate in all those shipped mobile phones if it were to be compromised.

In some circumstances, signing may be delegated to you, the developer. You'll be issued with a certificate and a private key so that you can test your applications. You're probably wondering what the security implications of such a scheme are, but we'll look at this shortly when we cover developer certificates (see Section 8.2.12).

8.2.6 Where Do the Certificates in a Chain Come From?

Clearly, there's no way that every mobile phone can keep a database of all known certificates, but it is feasible to provision them with a limited number of root or trust anchor certificates.

As mentioned earlier, it's essential to provide supporting certificates with anything that has been signed, that is, the end entity and any intermediates. The software installer will, however, try to resolve missing certificates by looking in its internal certificate store, and always check its private store for root certificates.

This is why the SIS file-signing tools accept a certificate chain; these entries will be built into the SIS file so that the installer can rebuild the chain and locate a root from the mobile phone.

Figure 8.2 shows the single chain of certificates constructed from those present in the SIS package and one from the mobile phone's store.

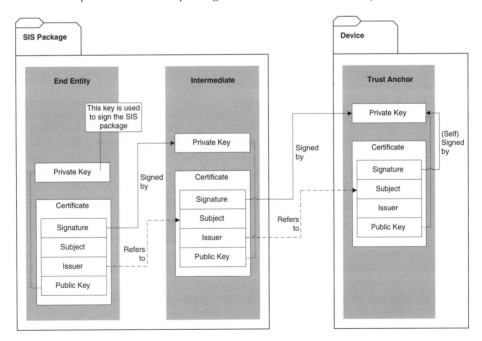

Figure 8.2 Where Different Types of Certificates in a Chain are Found

8.2.7   Additional Certificate Validation – OCSP

We've covered validating certificates (from a tamper protection viewpoint) and building a chain. There is, however, an additional verification step available to the installer and this is a 'revocation check'.

If you've ever had to wait in a shop while the merchant checks out your credit card, then you've been subject to this type of check. There is nothing apparently wrong with your card – your signature matches, the card's date is valid – but a check with the card issuer might be being performed randomly, or, more likely, because you're buying an expensive item.

A revocation check on a certificate is much the same thing. The certificate appears to be valid, but a check is made to see if, in fact, it has been revoked in the meantime. Perhaps the private key has been compromised somehow, and its issuer wishes to prevent signings based on the certificate from being treated as valid. Symbian OS uses a protocol called OCSP (Online Certificate Status Protocol) to achieve this.

Depending on how the mobile phone is configured, the installer might, therefore, connect to the network during an installation to validate certificates. Of course, it is possible for the network to be unavailable, in which case further device configuration comes into play. This controls whether the platform allows package installations to go ahead when an OCSP network service cannot be reached or is unavailable. It's likely that most mobile phones will be configured to allow installations to finish despite transient OCSP problems. This is because the internal software install package registry will remember the validation state of the package, and an application manager – or other application – can always request revalidation at a later date.

Revalidation of an Application

(Note: this is a new feature being introduced in Symbian OS v9.2).

As well as providing information about the contents and state of a package, the SisRegistry interfaces can be used to re-initiate this OCSP check. Beware, some SisRegistry interfaces require ReadDeviceData capability and some are restricted to the software installer alone. Checking revocation may require NetworkServices, so please check the header files for details if you use these interfaces.

If you wish to check the trust status of an application, then some example code follows:

```
Swi::RSisRegistrySession regSession;
Swi::RSisRevocationEntry revEntry;

// connect the session
User::LeaveIfError(regSession.Connect());
```

```
CleanupClosePushL(regSession);

// open the registry entry for package by pUID
User::LeaveIfError(revEntry.Open(regSession, packageUid));
CleanupClosePushL(revEntry);

// check the current trust status
Swi::TSisTrustStatus trustStatusBefore;
trustStatusBefore = revEntry.TrustStatus();

// perform post install revocation (synchronous)
revEntry.CheckRevocationStatusL(tempUriValue);

// check the new trust status
Swi::TSisTrustStatus trustStatusAfter;
trustStatusBefore = revEntry.TrustStatus()

CleanupStack::PopAndDestroy(2, &regSession)
```

8.2.8   Trusted Roots

Certificates can contain their own metadata in the form of certificate
extensions, but Symbian OS certificate stores also contain additional
proprietary certificate metadata that is associated with the certificate
and stored independently. This associated metadata is writable in some
certificate stores but, in the case of certificates used for installation
(and OCSP), there are no APIs that allow the certificates or metadata
to be changed programmatically. In fact, the store employed by the
software installer is part ROM-based and part file-system-based, but the
file-system part can only be updated via a proprietary software installer
mechanism which requires additional signing constraints to be met. This
store is called the Software Install Certificate Store, or 'swicertstore'
for short.

Even though this particular certificate store is readable through the
unified certificate store interfaces, it is the *only* store queried by the
installer during an installation or any activity relating to revocation.
Certificates not in this private store are therefore ignored during the
software installation process.

Installation Certificate Metadata

In general, the associated certificate metadata (see Figure 8.3) relates to
which activities the certificate can be used for. Examples of usage are
TLS server authentication, Java MIDlet installation or OCSP and native
software installation (see below).

In addition, certificates intended for the validation of software installation are also associated with a set of capabilities, which the certificate
will endorse during the software installation process.

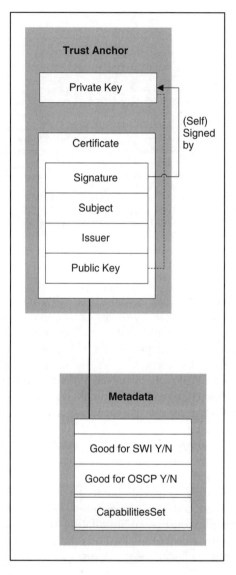

Figure 8.3   Symbian OS Metadata which may be Associated with Certificates

8.2.9   The Trusted Application

Based on what we've covered up to now concerning certificates, chains and metadata we can define a trusted application as follows: if any of the chains present on the SIS package can be shown to correctly chain back to a certificate in the private store which has an applicability setting of 'native software install' then the application is deemed 'trusted'.

It follows, therefore, that any unsigned application, self-signed application, or signed application *not* chaining back to one of these certificates, is 'untrusted'.

Later in the chapter we'll talk generally about what it means to be a trusted application or an untrusted application. We'll see that trusted applications may be somewhat more privileged than untrusted ones when it comes to deciding what to do about upgrade clashes and other software installation features.

8.2.10   The Significance of Multiple Chains

Given that an application can be signed multiple times, multiple chains can now be present within a SIS file, you may be wondering whether an application can have more than one chain resolving to a software install trust anchor. If so, can the capabilities being granted to an application come from more than one trust anchor certificate?

The answer to both questions is yes, so it would be quite possible to split desired capabilities between two root certificates, thus forcing all applications requiring those capabilities to be signed twice – perhaps by two authorities. Although possible in theory, this is unlikely to be the case in practice – it could perhaps be applicable to situations involving Digital Rights Management where separate signings may be required for applications that deal with valuable digital assets that need to be deployed.

The most likely case for multiple signings is where an application, which is currently valid and signed for only one operator domain, could be signed again later to enable it for use in another domain – where the root certificates are entirely different. At least one of the chains present will, hopefully, resolve to one root certificate that will grant most – if not all – of the capabilities required by general applications.

8.2.11   Software Installer Capability Processing

The installer's primary role in life (apart from copying files) is, therefore, to build chains based on SIS file signatures in order to identify the relevant root or trust anchor certificates. Once these have been identified, the metadata associated with each is used to validate a particular install. If you'd like to understand the processing logic this section will provide more details.

Software Install Basic Capability Logic

As we saw earlier, certificates can chain to form a relationship between the End Entity (EE), which was used to sign the SIS file, and a trust anchor certificate which is, we hope, on the mobile phone. We're also now aware that more than one of these chains can be present in a SIS file since it can now be signed multiple times. With this in mind, the installer logic looks something like this:

1. Identify which binaries (EXEs and DLLs) from the SIS file are actually going to be installed. (User selections and SIS conditionals may result in only a subset requiring installation.)

2. Make a list of all the system and user capabilities required by these binaries.

3. Build the chains present in the SIS file and identify the trusted certificates in the software install certificate store that successfully terminate these chains.

4. Make a list of all the system and user capabilities associated with those trusted anchor (or root) certificates.

So, at this point we have a list of all the capabilities required by the package, and a list of all the capabilities endorsed by the certificates. The installer can now check to see if the certificates can effectively endorse the capabilities requested by the application:

5. Discard any capabilities specified as ignored by the manufacturer.

6. Ensure that the certificates specify all the remaining system capabilities required by the package. If they do not, then abort the installation.

7. Ensure that the certificates specify all the remaining user capabilities required by the package. If they do not, then the user is presented with a list of unresolved user capabilities and asked to allow or disallow them in their entirety. If the user fails to allow them, the installation is again aborted.

> The root or trust anchor certificates against which a package is signed must endorse the capabilities required by the EXEs installed by the package.

Nested SIS Files

As in earlier releases, SIS files can be nested within SIS files (now to a bounded depth – currently eight). Although they are nested, they are processed linearly in depth-first order. This means that each time we encounter an embedded SIS file, we open and process it before continuing on with the files in the current package. Any dependency an outer SIS package has on an inner package is automatically resolved by the installer, so there's no need to order packages.

From a signing and capability perspective, each SIS file is processed based on its own merits. This means that there is no inheriting of signatures or capabilities from the containing (outer) package to the contained (embedded) package, or vice versa.

8.2.12   Developer Certificates

In Section 8.2.5, we mentioned that the ability to sign packages could be delegated to you, the developer. The need for this is clear: signing (and testing) authorities just don't have the resource to sign every version of a package that you might ordinarily produce to ensure that your latest application works on real mobile phones.

Allowing developers to sign their own applications does sound a little generous – or risky, depending on your viewpoint – but we must point out that these certificates are highly constrained in their use.

Constraints, Constraints

There's already one significant constraint present in a certificate, and that is the validity date range. Developer certificates are likely to have a significantly reduced lifetime. Please be aware that the point at which an expired certificate becomes clearly noticeable is at install time, so watch out for developer certificate-signed SIS files which suddenly don't install any more.

Other constraints exist within certificate extensions – parts of the standard certificate structure (defined in X.509 and RFC3280) designed to carry additional information about the certificates.

The sorts of things your developer certificate issuer can constrain you to are:

- Installations on one or more listed handsets. You won't be able to install your SIS file on any other handsets as long as it's signed with the developer certificate.

- Certain capabilities, that is, you won't be able to sign for capabilities outside of an agreed set.

There are also additional constraints relating to package and binary UIDs. You may, therefore, be constrained to a set of SIDs, VIDs, or, perhaps, unprotected parts of the identifier ranges (for example, VID = 0). (See Section 8.3.1.)

As an additional safeguard the installer will also raise a UI dialog, warning the user that what they are installing has been signed in a developer context and may not necessarily be of production quality, or even trustworthy.

8.3   Identifiers, Upgrades, Removals and Special Files

8.3.1   Identifier Checking

UID Overload

32-bit UIDs are used for many purposes in Symbian OS, which may lead to some degree of confusion. As an introductory point, it's worth clarifying the role of the three UIDs, which are particularly significant to the software installer:

- the SID or secure ID; allocation of SIDs is discussed in Chapter 2

- the VID or vendor ID; an additional value, which can be assigned to an EXE, also discussed in Chapter 2

- the pUID or package UID; this is a value assigned to a SIS file from the specification in the package file, and is essentially the identifier of a package, or set of files, that forms an installable unit.

To complicate things a little further, these identifier ranges are divided into protected and unprotected ranges, and your use of values from a particular range in a package (or binary within a package) may require your package to be signed.

SID Uniqueness

The most important thing for you to be aware of is that SIDs on EXEs must be unique – at least as far as a single mobile phone is concerned. This means that the installer will reject an installation if it detects an EXE with a SID that is already present on the mobile phone (and this includes OS executables as well).

SIDs on DLLs are not meaningful, and therefore the installer does not enforce uniqueness.

Identifier Ranges

We mentioned at the start of this section that identifiers have ranges. For pUIDs and SIDs, the identifier space is, in fact, divided into two:

- an unprotected range (identified by bit 31 = 1)

- a protected range (identified by bit 31 = 0)

Any identifier greater than or equal to `0x80000000` is therefore part of the 'unprotected' range, and any identifier less than this value is part of the protected range.

> In the case of VIDs, any non-zero VID is in the protected range. The only unprotected VID, therefore, is zero.

Conditions of Use

If the installer comes across a protected range pUID or an EXE with a protected range SID, then it will require that the package is 'trusted' (see Section 8.2.9). This means that signing programs can support the concept of owned identifiers i.e. they will only sign your application if the identifiers present in the package are actually owned by you.

In summary, therefore, if you use a pUID that is less than `0x80000000`, or attempt to install an EXE with a SID less than `0x80000000`, your package *must* be trusted to successfully install. This helps mitigate against SID hijacking, which is the act of deploying EXEs with particular SIDs with the sole purpose of preventing legitimate applications installing later – a form of denial of service attack.

VIDs and Untrusted Packages

Similarly, the installer will reject any untrusted application which installs an EXE or DLL with a non-zero vendor ID. The UI should, if this situation occurs, indicate that some form of VID violation has taken place.

In summary, if you use a non-zero VID in any EXE or DLL in your package, your package *must* be trusted to successfully install.

8.3.2 Special Directories

As you will now be aware, things have been moved around in the file system a little since Symbian OS v8. For example, binaries are in `/sys/bin`, and resource files in `/resource` etc. There are two directories relevant to the software installer, which we cover here.

The Private Directory

Private directories take the form `/private/<SID>` where the SID corresponds to the Secure ID of the EXE (see Section 3.1.1).

What the installer will do is collect all the SIDs of EXEs in the package which are destined for installation and make all of those `/private/<SID>` directories eligible for installation to the current package. For example, if a package were to install two EXEs with SIDs

`0x263A7E40` and `0x123D6758` respectively, then any non-executable (that is, data) file in the package can be installed to either `/private/263A7E40` or `/private/123D6758`, but not `/private/12345678`. Basically, the installer will evaluate the private directories you've specified in the PKG file and make sure you're only using the private directories appropriate to your package.

The Import Directory

The import directory for a given EXE is `/private/<SID>/import`. Any package can install files into the import directory of an EXE it doesn't own – this is in order to deliver files to another package. A third-party delivering map data for a mapping application is a good example of this feature.

Using the example from the previous subsection again: if a package installs EXEs with the SIDs specified above, then it clearly cannot deploy a data file to `/private/12345678`, but it *can* deploy a file to `/private/12345678/import`.

There are three additional points to make clear, here. First, many people assume that `/private/<SID>/import` can be written to by any application using the file server. This is *not* the case. Import directories can only be used in the context of deploying a file into `/private/<SID>/import` via software install. Secondly, please note that file-overwriting rules apply – look out for these in Section 8.3.5 because import directories are subject to the same rules as everyone else. Finally, you can only deliver into someone's import directory if it already exists, so if you wish your application to receive files from other installed packages you must create an import directory to permit it.

8.3.3   Upgrades

The process of upgrading packages has been simplified in Symbian OS.v9. Essentially there are three options available to you. These are described below. (For those of you who are familiar with the PKG header types, this means that several old types – SO, SC and SY – are no longer supported.)

Standard Upgrade

The standard upgrade is essentially the delivery of the same package again. During the upgrade, the original package is actually removed and replaced with the new package. In detail:

- The standard upgrade PKG type is SA.

- The SIS file package UID (see Section 8.3.1), package name and non-localized vendor name must be identical to the original package, but a new version number is required.

- Files not re-delivered in the new SIS package are removed from the installed package.

- Should an EXE be removed and not replaced by the upgrade, the private storage directory will also be removed. If a replacement EXE is delivered, then the private storage directory remains untouched during the upgrade.

Partial Upgrade

The partial upgrade is a way of achieving a standard upgrade, but replaces only those files that need to be modified and adds any new files. For example, a developer does not need to re-deliver all the large map files with an upgrade if only the EXE requires replacing. Some additional points are:

- The partial upgrade PKG type is PU.

- The SIS file package UID, package name and non-localized vendor name must be identical to the original package, but a later version number is usually required. The same version will be permitted, but only as a means of allowing the package creator to deploy configuration changes (in a similar fashion to the old SC package type).

- Files can be replaced or added.

- The contents of the partial upgrade become part of the package itself, so it is not possible to select or remove anything other than the entire package. (The installer would certainly not be in a position to revert the package to its previous version.)

Patching or Augmenting a Package

A patch (or augmentation) is simply a set of new files that adds into the original package. Unlike the partial upgrade, the patch must not conflict with the original package by attempting to replace any existing files. The benefit of a patch is that it can subsequently be identified and uninstalled. The patch is, therefore, a convenient vehicle for delivering, for example, additional game levels to an application where it is envisaged that the user may wish to remove them after playing them.

- The patch PKG type is SP.

- The upgrade package must have the same SIS file package UID and non-localized vendor name.

- The package name should be different from the base package name.

- Files must not conflict with the original package.

Note that it is possible to install a patch to a drive other than the one that the original package was installed to. Assuming, therefore, that the package is capable of identifying that new files are present, this ability ought to extend to other drives, e.g. looking for files in `D:\private\SID` as well as `C:\private\SID`. Smart application writers could, of course, use the SisRegistry interfaces to identify if a patch is present for their pUID and determine where the user chose to install the package:

```
// connect to the SIS Registry and
// look for updates to the
// package 'WoollyJumper'
RSisRegistrySession session;
User::LeaveIfError(session.Connect());
CleanupClosePushL(session);

// open the package entry
RSisRegistryEntry package;
User::LeaveIfError(package.Open(session, Tuid::Uid(KUidWoollyJumper)));
CleanupClosePushL(package);

// retrieve the list of augmentations to the package
RpointerArray<CSisRegistryPackage> augmentations;
package.AugmentationsL(augmentations);

// open the package entry for the augmentation
RSisRegistryEntry aug;
User::LeaveIfError(aug.Open(session, augmentations[0]->Uid()));
CleanupClosePushL(aug);

// retrieve the drive the augmentation was installed on
// note: only applies if a drive wasn't specified in the SIS file.
Tchar driveLetter = aug.SelectedDriveL();

// clean up
CleanupStack::PopAndDestroy(3,&session);
```

Other Issues Relevant to Upgrade

Standard or partial upgrades can bring new EXEs into the package. This implies that the set of eligible private directories for subsequent upgrades can grow over time.

8.3.4 Package Removal

When a package is removed, the installer will always attempt to remove all the files that were originally installed. For a partially upgraded package, this includes all the original files plus any additional files added in the meantime.

If an EXE is removed, the installer will also finish the uninstall process by attempting to remove the contents of `/private/<SID>` and the directory itself. The installer will also clean up `/private/<SID>` directories on other drives (if found).

Import Directories

As a necessary part of cleaning `/private/<SID>`, the `/private/<SID>/import` directory will also be removed, so, if your package delivered files to someone else's import directory, when your package is uninstalled the installer will ignore any missing files.

As a slight twist, please note that removal of a package which deployed files to a third-party `/private/<SID>/import` will result in these files being removed. If, therefore, you're worried about files in your import directory vanishing inexplicably, then you should take ownership of them by moving them up one directory into your `/private/<SID>` area so that they are not removed when the 'donating' application is uninstalled.

This all sounds a bit convoluted, but having explained it, you are free to use this behavior to your advantage depending on your specific situation.

Running Applications

The software installer may attempt to terminate applications that are running at the time of uninstall (or standard upgrade) and that relate to the package being uninstalled. This also includes programs which are run on install and uninstall and do not complete before a predetermined timeout period.

Rollback

The general policy for the system installer in a failure situation is to 'roll-back' immediately. This means that installations revert to the point prior to the installation (the partial package is removed), and un-installations revert to the point prior to the un-installation (i.e. partial removals are restored).

Future versions of the software installer may intelligently roll-forward under some uninstallation circumstances, or perform necessary consistency operations at phone boot-time.

8.3.5   File Overriding Rules

Two problems are now being actively dealt with in the new platform security environment; they are:

- file overwriting (or 'clobbering', if you'd like a technical term for it)
- file eclipsing.

File Overwriting

As an example, suppose package A deploys a file, say `C:\sys\bin\utils.dll`, and package B then attempts to deploy an identically named `C:\sys\bin\utils.dll`.

Clearly we cannot allow packages to arbitrarily replace files in other packages, accidentally or otherwise, because we may be putting the integrity of the device or the user's privacy at risk.

As with any general rule, there are exceptions. In this instance there are two. The first relates to the features described in Section 8.3.3: If package B is an upgrade to package A, then the replacement *will* be allowed. Being an upgrade, package B will have the same pUID as package A. (If you're concerned that using the same pUID sounds easy for a nefarious package creator, then refer back to Section 8.3.1.)

The second feature is a safeguard against untrusted packages that deliberately deploy files known to clash with legitimate applications (a type of Denial-of-Service attack in Security circles): if package B is a trusted package (see Section 8.2.9) and package A is untrusted, then the user can be asked to make a decision about whether to remove the untrusted file.

(Although we state that the user could be queried in this situation, you must consider what was stated in Section 8.1.3 about mobile phone configuration. Although the installer notifies the UI that such a situation has occurred, the mobile phone manufacturer might choose to resolve the issue through the installer configuration or within the UI. This means you may discover that the decision to overwrite or abort has already been made.)

If the above criteria are not met, the installation will not be able to proceed, and the UI should report a clash and indicate the blocking package.

Note that even if the file delivered by B is identical in name and content to the one previously delivered by A, the installer will still report a clash because it does not support files shared by multiple packages. A better approach is to bundle shared files in a separate (or embedded) SIS file and arrange for this to be installed if it is not already present.

File Eclipsing

An 'eclipsed-file' situation can occur when you have the same path and filename existing on two or more different drives. For example, if there is a file `C:\resource\mydata.rsc`, and a package attempts to install `D:\resource\mydata.rsc`, we could have an eclipsing situation if an application which made use of the existing resource file on `C:` started using the new file on `D:` instead.

This might not seem a big problem, but the situation is much more serious if the file in question is a DLL. As in other operating systems, Symbian OS operates a path-based search scheme for DLLs. This means that the loader will load one DLL of a given name and version instead of another based on where it is in the file system. The loader policy is to search for a DLL on drive Y, go backwards through the alphabet to A and then try Z – halting the search if an eligible DLL is found.

As is the situation with overwriting, we can no longer allow arbitrary packages to deploy DLLs that eclipse those in other packages or the OS.

Once again, there are two special cases. Firstly, as is the case for overwriting, if a trusted package attempts to install a file that is eclipsing one from an untrusted package the user can be asked if the file from the untrusted package should be removed.

Secondly, there is an exception to the general no eclipsing rule when OS files are deliberately eclipsed – perhaps by the manufacturer to resolve a software issue. In this case much more stringent rules come into play, based on signing – so, in general, it's probably safe to state that if you try to eclipse an OS file your package will fail to install.

Data file eclipsing is a less serious issue than binary eclipsing, but Symbian has chosen to apply the same rules because there are areas in the OS – and possibly in applications – that employ search path rules to find files and could be duped into finding a file deliberately planted by another package.

How to Avoid It

On first reading, the above rules may appear rather Draconian until you consider that, in earlier versions of the OS, files would simply have overwritten or eclipsed each other silently – perhaps leading to some interesting application failures.

As a general rule, try to avoid both overwriting and eclipsing – allow yourself, instead, to become highly imaginative with your filenames!

8.4 SIS File Changes for Platform Security

Software Install Scripts (SIS files) are used to deliver software packages to mobile phones for installation and they can be installed from a PC, downloaded via a browser, or sent to a phone by MMS. A SIS file could be described as a smart archive – what actually gets installed from the SIS file can depend on certain rules and also on choices such as which language the user selects. The result of installing a SIS file is usually (assuming all is well) one of the following:

- A new package is installed and available on the mobile phone.

- An existing package has been upgraded or modified.

- An existing package has had some new removable components installed (e.g. game levels).

There were some significant new requirements relating to SIS files for Symbian OS v9, so Symbian also took the opportunity to redesign the basic structure of the SIS file to provide additional benefits – these are covered in the following subsection.

Although the internal format of the file has changed, Symbian has kept the extension SIS to maintain some consistency in the development process. New system recognizers associated with this format expect to see *both* the extension SIS and the internal format of the new files.

The most significant point to be aware of about the new SIS file is as follows:

> Pre-Symbian OS v9 SIS files are *not* compatible with the Symbian OS v9 installer.

This may appear to be a big compatibility break, but bear in mind that the binaries in an old SIS file wouldn't be compatible with Symbian OS v9 anyway. You have probably already foreseen the next point, but we'll mention it anyway:

> Symbian OS v9 SIS files are *not* compatible with the installers in earlier OS releases.

SIS File Format Changes

The new SIS file format changes are summarized briefly below:

- **Multiple Signatures**

  The new SignSIS tool allows packages to be signed multiple times. Why? Well, some parties may want to endorse or sign packages only if they have already been signed by another party. Also, some packages may require signing twice to allow the package to obtain the platform security capabilities it requires to run (see Section 8.2.10).

  This leads to some interesting issues relating to how multiple certificate chains are handled and validated. This was covered in more detail earlier (see Section 8.2.11).

- **Larger Package Sizes**

  The theoretical maximum package size has been increased significantly, well beyond the current mobile phone's typical storage capacity – but Symbian likes to think of the future.

- **Streamed Install**

  Large package files may become necessary, but caching them locally on the mobile phone prior to installation is wasteful. The new format (and installer) allows them to be fed to the phone incrementally over a shortlink or network connection. The API for this is covered in Appendix C.3.

- **Future Proofing**
  The underlying structure allows us to be much more flexible with the contents and ordering of a SIS file. This also means we can avoid SIS file compatibility problems in future, even if we enhance the file contents.

Additional Compatibility Note

While we are on the subject of SIS file compatibility, it is worth recalling that the binary format was modified for Symbian OS v8.1b and v9. Since the software installer checks binaries for capability information it should come as no surprise that, if the installer encounters an old-style binary in a new SIS file, the installation will be aborted.

In general it's a good idea to ensure that the binaries present in your package are applicable to the target environment. Look out for the following situations:

- You are packaging emulator binaries for use on a mobile phone or vice versa.

- You're packaging binaries built for the wrong version of Symbian OS for your intended target.

In short, please ensure your binaries are correct for the target environment; this includes having the appropriate binary version for the target version of Symbian OS or the correct choice of emulator and target binaries.

8.4.1 Auto-Signing

It is possible that some operators or manufacturers may require that *all* SIS files be signed. This does not mean an end to unsigned applications in the traditional sense, so there's no need rush off and worry about getting your application signed by a signing authority – perhaps at some cost to you. Assuming the requirement is simply that they are signed, this can include 'self-signing'. We've already seen that makekeys.exe can generate self-signed certificates and keys, so all the tools are present for you to sign your SIS file with the private key associated with your self-signed certificate.

To make things more convenient, the CreateSIS script tool (createsis -h for help) will generate the required self-signed certificate and key – if you choose not to specify any alternative signing material – and will then create and sign a SIS file for you. This ephemeral private key can then be discarded if you do not plan to do any further signing with it.

Those familiar with Makekeys will notice that CreateSIS simply wraps Makekeys, MakeSIS and SignSIS into one command-line operation, and auto-generates some of the field data required along the way.

Why should signing need to be a mandatory requirement? Well, it's simply there to provide additional mechanisms for identifying packages – the public key acts rather like a random car registration plate. Rogue packages, or malware, once identified can be found and removed more quickly, while at the same time making it difficult to 'clone' someone else's public key in an attempt to have their legitimate package removed.

8.4.2   Auto-Execution within SIS Files

If you're familiar with PKG file options, you might know that there are some 'run-at-install' and 'run-at-uninstall' options which have been with us for some time (see RI/RR/RB package file options in the Symbian OS Library).

```
; Exe that is run on installation. SWI
; will wait until Exe has completed.
;flags FILERUN, RUNINSTALL, RUNWAITEND

;Languages
&EN
;Header
#{"testrun_exe"}, (0x1000007A), 1, 2, 3,TYPE=SA

%{"LocalVendor"}
:"UniqueVendorName"
"\epoc32\release\9.1\armv5\nocapability.exe"-
"!:\sys\bin\nocapability.exe", FR, RI, RW
; GJtEFLqAAHAQRVQJOXTCPAAJECAEEAZJUyIU
```

After some considerable deliberation, Symbian decided to maintain support for these in Symbian OS v9, although there are some constraints to be aware of. In future releases, this auto-run ability may be restricted to trusted applications.

Limitations

In previous OS releases, you might have used auto-execution to unpack data in the SIS file, after the installation. An example of this might be a database of chess opening moves.

Now, we need to apply data-caging rules to auto-execution and some limitations become apparent:

• The auto-run EXE has its own SID – by definition.

- The auto-run EXE *can* see data in its own `/private/<SID>` directory.

- The auto-run EXE *cannot* see data in any other EXE's `/private/<SID>` directory.

Sadly, therefore, data-caging rules limit what the auto-run EXE would have been able to do with the file system prior to Symbian OS v9. For example, an auto-run EXE cannot manipulate data files (for example, to unpack chess opening moves) in the private directory of an EXE being installed. The auto-run EXE can still, however:

- manipulate any data in public (non-data-caged) areas

- communicate with servers

- act as a server itself.

Note, also, that the auto-run EXE cannot write into the import directory of the EXE being installed – in fact, as we previously noted, only the installer can write into that directory.

Finally, auto-run executables may not be allowed to run indefinitely. For example, the installer may terminate them after a period of time to allow uninstallation to complete.

8.5 Installing to and from Removable Media

As in previous releases, it's perfectly possible to install a SIS file to a writable, removable media card. Now, with platform security, we have introduced an additional mechanism to prevent binaries installed on removable media from being tampered with when the media is removed from the mobile phone.

The Software Installer and the OS Loader

A deal has been struck between the OS loader and the software install infrastructure. In addition to the rules that the loader observes while finding and loading binaries, there is now an additional step where the loader checks for the presence of a hash (see Appendix B) for any binary on removable media. It should be no surprise that the table of hashes is populated by the software installer.

What this means from a security perspective is that you can always insert media cards containing binaries – but they won't be loadable by the OS loader until the installer generates the hash entry. The installer won't do this until it has validated the installation – this is similar to a SIS-based installation.

'Pre-Installed' Media

It's useful to be able to supply media cards, containing software that can run almost immediately after the card has been inserted and without the need to install from a SIS file.

However, delivering 'pre-installed' software on removable media proves to be an interesting challenge in a platform security environment, and the rest of this section discusses this particular issue. After all, you might imagine that there would be no specific install step required – however, this is not the case.

In fact, just about the only part of the software installation which does not take place for media card based applications is the extraction of the files from the SIS archive, and then the copying of them into their destination directories.

8.5.1   In-Place Installation

A pre-installed media card installation is called an 'in-place' installation, simply because the files are already in place when the card arrives in your hand.

The SIS file, as you'll recall, contains lots of additional metadata such as hashes, signatures and certificates, and this information must be provided with the in-place package so that the installer can validate the package and make the application eligible to be run.

Some New Package Types

In Section 8.3.3, we described the package install types (SA, SP, and PU) which are specified in the package file. At the time, we neglected to mention two *additional* types for pre-installed applications, which we can reveal now:

- type PA – standard pre-installed application

- type PP – pre-installed patch.

Consider the following example:

```
; Pre-installed package example
; Languages
&EN
; Header
#{"PreInstalled_Install"}, (0x11111209), 1, 2, 3,TYPE=PA

%{"LocalVendorName"}
:"UniqueVendorName"

"files\bigvideo.mpg"-"e:\public\bigvideo.mpg"
```

You will notice that the resulting SIS file is rather small. This is because the files specified are not actually included in the SIS package at all. What you have been provided with by MakeSIS is a 'SIS Stub File'.

SIS Stub Files

SIS stub files should be placed on the media card in directory `\private` `\10202DCE`. This specific location is important because it is the private directory of the software installer's daemon process, and it is the job of this process to identify media card insertions and bring them to the attention of the installer UI. There is no naming convention for SIS stub files at the moment other than that the file must have a `SIS` extension and be recognizable as a SIS file.

When the media card is inserted (or soon after), an in-place install takes place. If the certificates and the signings in the stub are valid for the data files and binaries present, and no eclipsing occurs, the installer will enable subsequent loading of the binaries by populating the loader cache accordingly.

Future Enhancements

At the time of writing it was necessary to specify, in the package file, the expected target drive for the in-place files. By the time you read this, it should be possible simply to use the wildcard '!' for the drive, and the installer will validate the installation based on the drive location of the stub SIS file.

8.5.2 Auto-Propagated Packages

As an additional feature, if you should perform a normal installation of a SIS package to a media card, the installer will (if configured to do so) automatically generate a stub SIS file for you on the card. This means you can move your media card to another compatible phone, and an in-place installation will take place.

There are a number of limitations on the way that you should create your package if you want propagations to work. Most importantly:

- Make sure all the required files install to your media card.

- Ensure the application doesn't modify any of the files listed as part of the package.

Deviating from these rules could mean that you have a propagated application that is either missing files or cannot be installed, because the files have been modified and no longer match the hash values stored in the SIS stub file.

8.6   Summary

In this chapter we've looked in some detail at how the Symbian OS v9 software installer behaves, and covered a number of the new rules which will be enforced by the installer prior to allowing packages onto the mobile phone successfully.

As pointed out in Section 8.1.2, the additional security tends to manifest itself as additional restrictions, so it might be useful to recap and list a number of the most common reasons why your new Symbian OS v9 SIS file does not, or may not, install:

- Are you trying to install a pre-v9 SIS file?

- Are the binaries in your package suitable for the target environment? This includes installing emulator binaries on a mobile phone.

- Are you using the correct versions of the tools? MakeSIS, for example, should report a version of at least '4,0,0,1'. Tools from earlier kits will not work correctly.

- Does your operator or manufacturer demand that all applications are signed – even if they are only self-signed? If so, you'll need to use the tools provided to generate a key and a certificate so that you can sign your own package.

- Is there any way the SIS file could have become corrupt? If so, the checksums and digital signatures might no longer match the rest of data in the package.

- Do your package's EXEs and DLLs require any system capabilities (as defined by your manufacturer)? If so, you'll need to have them appropriately signed by a signing authority.

- Does the certificate with which you (or your signing authority) signed your SIS file actually chain to a trust anchor in the swicertstore? (If you are developing for a handset, did you even create a swicertstore in the first place?)

- Is your package already installed? This seems obvious, but can be an occasional oversight.

- Is your package attempting to overwrite a file that was delivered by an earlier package? If so, you may wish to restructure your package or rename your files. Delivering private application data files to a /private/<SID> directory is probably the best idea. If your intention was to upgrade a package, ensure you've used the same pUID (and matched name and vendor fields) otherwise the installer may treat it as a new package.

- Is your package installing files which may eclipse (or be eclipsed by) a file with the same path on another drive (this includes OS files)? Again, you may wish to restructure your package or rename your files.

- Are you trying to install an EXE with a SID that is already in use? This can easily happen if your SID is in the unprotected range. You could contact your signing authority and obtain your own SID range, which can be appropriately signed for.

- Have you employed a reserved range pUID or SID? If so, your package must be signed appropriately for it to be trusted. Similarly, non-zero VIDs must also be signed-for.

- Are you using a developer certificate outside of the context that you agreed with your developer certificate issuer? Perhaps the certificate has expired, or you are trying to install the package on the wrong handset.

- Does your SIS file specify dependencies that cannot be met at the moment? For example, does another package need to be present first?

9

Enabling Platform Security

by Geoff Preston

9.1 Responsibilities in Granting Capabilities

In this chapter we discuss who is able to approve the granting of platform security capabilities to Symbian OS applications, and how they do it. In particular we discuss the Symbian Signed application signing scheme. The scheme has been adopted by the majority of mobile phone manufacturers with Symbian OS-based phones in the market, as well as major network operators and requirements bodies; however, it is important to note that the device manufacturers and operators can choose to support other schemes should they wish to do so.

9.1.1 Granting Capabilities to After-market Applications

Applications may be granted capabilities (that is, they may be authorized to use particular security-related sensitive APIs) either explicitly by the user at the time the application is installed or, prior to application installation, by a digital signature from a trusted authority. As we noted in Chapter 3, Section 3.4.1, the mobile phone manufacturer has the final say on the specific capabilities that can be granted by the user or by signing, but in this chapter we cover Symbian's recommended security policy, which has been developed in consultation with phone manufacturers and network operators.

With this security policy, the capabilities the user can grant are `LocalServices` and `UserEnvironment` (see Appendix A for further details on what these capabilities control). Any application requiring other capabilities will, therefore, need to be signed. Developers submit their application to a testing and certification program such as Symbian Signed. When the signed SIS file is returned, it will be permitted by the software installer to install on a mobile phone with the capabilities requested by the application.

9.1.2   Granting Capabilities for Built-in Code

For applications developed specifically for, or adapted for, inclusion in a mobile phone's firmware, the same basic development processes as outlined in earlier chapters apply. However, with such applications the authority that grants access to capabilities is the mobile phone manufacturer rather than Symbian Signed.

Mobile phone manufacturers will implement their own internal quality and test processes, in order to be assured that an application's performance criteria meet their specific needs (in a similar way to the generic Symbian Signed process and its published test criteria). Several of Symbian's licensees have adopted the generic Symbian Signed criteria and use them in their internal processes, adding any additional tests they feel are required – for example, to help in specifically targeting a brand, device segment or functional focus.

9.1.3   Granting Capabilities for Libraries

When a developer releases a library that may be used by other software (either after-market software or, in the case of plug-ins, the built-in mobile phone software), the library must be trusted with at least the same set of capabilities that are held by the process loading it (the exact rules for this are covered in Chapter 2, Section 2.4.5).

If the library is going to be used by add-on after-market software, one option is simply to distribute the library as a DLL file, which can be included with, and signed at the same time as, the applications using it. That way, the DLL will be trusted with exactly the same set of capabilities that the calling application has. This has some disadvantages, however. If several applications on one mobile phone include the DLL, there will be multiple copies on the phone, which could result in name clashes and version problems. Also, an update to the DLL would have to be distributed separately to all applications which include it.

A more flexible option is to distribute the DLL in a separate, signed SIS file. In this case, the SIS file would be submitted for signing, requesting the maximum set of capabilities that could be held by any of the applications loading it.

9.1.4   Layered Execution Environments

Execution environments, such as Java, Visual Basic and Python, create specific challenges for Symbian's platform security architecture, as they do for all open operating systems. In order to ensure that these environments can offer the richest functionality and the best user experience, they may need to be granted a significant set of capabilities. To ensure that security is not compromised, any such environment needs to enforce a complementary security model to that provided by the native operating system; otherwise there is a danger that applications written for the layered execution environment can bypass the security controls enforced for native applications. Signing authorities need to pay special attention to the trustworthiness of the layered security model when deciding whether to approve granting of sensitive capabilities to the layered execution environment implementation.

9.2   Overview of the Signing Process

Symbian's application certification scheme, Symbian Signed (see Figure 9.1), was launched in March 2004. Since that time it has seen significant industry adoption and endorsement, as well as providing leadership in terms of application certification best practice. The scheme has been adopted by a range of channels as a prerequisite for distribution and provides developers with access to a significant distribution route to market by (optionally) including signed applications in the exclusive Symbian Signed catalog available to licensees and channel partners.

Figure 9.1   Logo for Symbian Signed Approved Applications

With the introduction of Symbian OS platform security, Symbian Signed becomes a key enabler for applications requiring access to sensitive APIs. Changes have been made to the existing program to support the granting of capabilities, and the Symbian Signed portal has been extended to provide a 'one-stop shop' for all the developer's v9 needs. This includes developer certificates and the allocation of UIDs, SIDs and VIDs.

The signing process uses a standardized Public Key Infrastructure (PKI) to provide easy to use, robust security and authentication services. Two certificates are used – the first is the Authenticated Content Signing (ACS) Publisher ID, which has a chain of trust to a public root certificate held by VeriSign. This is used to provide *developer* authentication. On applying for an ACS Publisher ID using the link provided on the Symbian Signed portal, you will be asked to submit information about yourself and your organization, as well as to provide referees who can verify what you submit. VeriSign, as Symbian's Certificate Authority, will validate your identity using this information.

It should be noted that the ACS Publisher ID is only available to companies and recognized organizations. Individual developers or user groups may utilize either Channel or Publisher Certification routes to gain cost-effective access to the signing process. In addition, there are a number of routes to market available for freeware and open source developers. For more information please visit the Symbian Signed portal (**www.symbiansigned.com**).

The second certificate used in the process is the Content ID, which has a chain of trust to a Symbian root certificate held on the mobile phone. This second certificate is used to provide *application* authorization and to approve the granting of capabilities to the application based on the authorization provided by Symbian Signed. A more detailed analysis of how to get access to and make use of these certificates will follow. In short, however, the signing process consists of four key steps:

1. Development.

2. Developer authentication (using the ACS Publisher ID).

3. Testing against industry-agreed defined criteria.

4. Signing against the mobile phone's root certificate (using the Content ID).

9.2.1 Development

As detailed in Chapter 3, Section 3.4.2, there is special provision made for deploying in-house interim development versions of applications needing capabilities on real mobile phones for testing, without the need to constantly submit the application to the full signing process.

Symbian OS developer certificates permit SIS files to be signed by the developer and enable those signed SIS files to be installed on real mobile phones for application testing. The process is managed by tying the signed applications to specific mobile phone hardware. The process works on standard mobile phones and does not require specialized software builds or new hardware. The developer certificates have embedded within them the set of capabilities to which the developer is permitted access, alongside identifiers for the specific mobile phones (using hardware identifiers such as the IMEI or ESN) on which the signed application may be installed. Identifying specific mobile phones ensures that a test build of an application cannot accidentally leak out and be installed by the general public. Details of the process for obtaining and using these certificates are given in Section 9.3.2.

9.2.2   Developer Authentication

Developer authentication provides a mechanism to build trust in your relationship with end-users, publishers and channels by enabling those parties to reliably identify you. This enables them to associate you with reliable applications and builds confidence in the quality and stability of your products through their ongoing commercial relationship with you. Your customers have the assurance that a developer-authenticated application does, in fact, come from you, the trustworthy source. Symbian Signed achieves this through the ACS Publisher ID mentioned above.

The private key of your ACS Publisher ID is your unique developer identity, which is validated using the VeriSign Class 3 public root. The identity verification procedure utilizes industry-recognized processes and database sources. However, if a mistake is made – a fraudulent identity is used or the private key is disclosed – the ACS Publisher ID may be revoked to ensure no further content-signing requests can be made using that ACS Publisher ID.

On completion of your own internal quality assurance and test processes (including validating your application's performance against the Symbian Signed criteria), you sign your SIS file using the private key of your ACS Publisher ID. This is a crucial step before you submit your application to the Symbian Signed portal and your selected test house for testing. A step-by-step guide to this process follows later in this chapter (see Section 9.3). At this stage the application is **not** Symbian Signed. This signature only validates who the submitting developer is and prevents tampering with the SIS file once submitted (any changes would be detected by a change in the unique hash that is part of the digital signature).

9.2.3   Testing Against Defined Criteria

Once submitted through the Symbian Signed portal, the application, signed with your ACS Publisher ID, is forwarded to your selected test house. The test house will provide a quote for the testing of the application in line with their published pricing policy. This policy may be found on the portal under 'Test House Information'.

Once you have accepted the test house's quote, they validate the application against the test criteria (which you can freely download from the Symbian Signed portal to ensure you comply with them) and provide you with a final report. Testing consists of two main elements. The first is generic testing, which is performed on all applications to validate their stability and adherence to required processes (such as the correct use of UIDs, including correct platform identifiers in your SIS file, and efficient memory usage and cleanup). The second element consists of targeted tests based on the specific capabilities used by your application – through the use of such targeted testing the price of the test process can be reduced and provide price point benefits to the developer. It should be noted that the more capabilities you have used, the more testing is required – and hence the more costly the test cycle is likely be.

9.2.4   Signing Against the Phone's Root

Applications which successfully pass the tests are handed on to the Certificate Authority (CA) where your ACS Publisher ID signature is removed and replaced with a Content ID signature with a chain of trust to the Symbian root on the phone. The Content ID is a unique certificate, which has an audit trial back to you, the developer, and also validates against the 'trust anchor' – the Symbian root certificate on the mobile phone. It is at *this* stage that the application is Symbian Signed and can be installed by users with the appropriate capabilities validated by the Software Installer.

Whilst every effort is made to ensure testing is as comprehensive as possible, there is a need to ensure the certification process is affordable to all developers. Hence the level of testing that is possible is an agreed compromise with all major stakeholders in the mobile phone industry. No testing solution can provide a 100% guarantee of quality, especially in the event of any deliberate intent to introduce security threats to the mobile phone. In the unlikely event that such a threat is actually found after testing and release, the uniqueness of the Content ID can be used to revoke an application and hence prevent it from causing further harm. We discuss revocation further in Section 9.4.

9.3   Step-by-step Guide to Signing

9.3.1   Getting your ACS Publisher ID

As mentioned in Section 9.2.2, a key aspect of Symbian Signed is the identification and authentication of the developer. This creates a relationship based on trust with the channels through which you distribute your applications.

Your ACS Publisher ID is essential to the Symbian Signed process and can be obtained via the Symbian Signed portal or directly from the Certificate Authority (CA). We suggest you take advantage of the links on the Symbian Signed portal to take you directly to the correct ACS pages on the CA's portal; this will save time and reduce the risk of applying for the wrong type of ACS Publisher ID. Note that the ACS Publisher ID you receive for Symbian Signed is a generic, standard ID and may be used to sign applications for other platforms where appropriate. Obtaining an ACS Publisher ID suitable for use with Symbian Signed is purely a

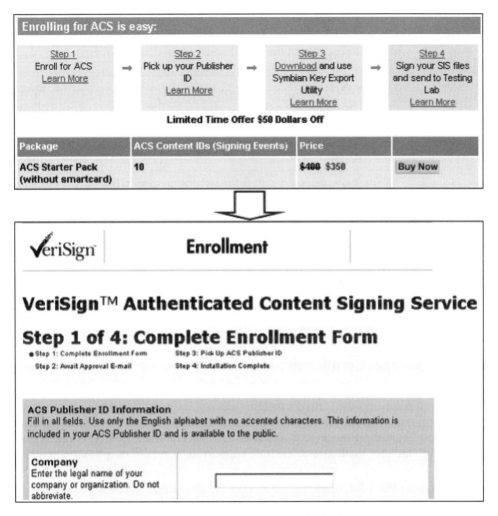

Figure 9.2 Requesting an ACS Publisher ID

software process with no additional hardware tokens to add to the cost, the complexity or the time taken for the ID to be issued.

Selecting 'Prerequisites' from ***www.symbiansigned.com/app/page/ process*** will take you to the ACS Starter Pack page shown in Figure 9.2. Select 'Buy Now' and complete the enrollment form. At the time of writing, the recommended browser is Microsoft Internet Explorer.

Ensure information is entered correctly and accurately, as it needs to be verifiable. Also, ensure you make a careful note of your chosen challenge phrase and keep this somewhere safe – the final certificate cannot be picked up without this. Once your enrollment form data is verified you will be notified of your successful application and provided with a URL to visit to pick up your new ACS Publisher ID.

When you log on to pick up your ACS Publisher ID you will need the PIN number included in the notification email and the challenge phrase you selected as part of the enrollment process shown in Figure 9.3.

> **IMPORTANT:** Do *not* tick the box to protect your private key otherwise you will be unable, in future, to export it for the signing process. Follow the process and your new certificate file will be imported into your browser.

While it is a necessary part of the signing process to have the application signed with an ACS Publisher ID, this does not mean that the small developer, or the freeware or open source developer, needs to purchase one. A range of publishers are able to test applications and they use their own ACS Publisher ID to sign an application, based on commercial terms agreed between the developer and the publisher. This provides the small developer with a low-cost route to signing. In addition, Symbian has worked hard to provide a route to market for free applications, and further details about that process are available at the Symbian Signed portal (*www.symbiansigned.com*).

9.3.2 Developer Certificates

SIS files signed with developer certificates are validated on the mobile phone by the software installer using a different root certificate from the one used for SIS files that are signed going through the regular Symbian Signed procedures. It is, therefore, possible for a mobile phone manufacturer to choose to exclude support for Symbian developer certificates while still supporting applications signed with a regular Symbian Signed Content ID certificate. However, at the time of writing indications are that the majority of Symbian OS-based mobile phones will include both root certificates, and thus support both signing procedures.

Validation for developer certificates includes checks that:

- one of the mobile phone identifiers (IMEI or ESN) in the certificate matches that of the phone the SIS file is being installed upon;

- the certificate has not expired (i.e. it is less than six months old);

- the binaries inside the SIS file are assigned only the capabilities listed in the certificate.

The set of capabilities allowed will vary depending on how the certificate is applied for and issued, as shown in Table 9.1.

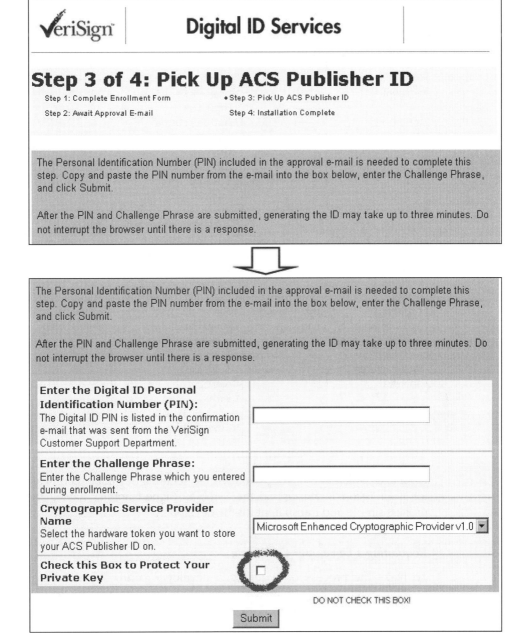

Figure 9.3 Retrieving an ACS Publisher ID

Table 9.1 Classes of Symbian Signed Developer Certificates

Authentication Process	No. of Phones	Capabilities Allowed	Cost

Any Symbian Signed registered account	1	`LocalServices`
		`UserEnvironment`
		`NetworkServices`
		`Location`
		`ReadUserData`
		`WriteUserData`
		`SWEvent`
		`SurroundingsDD`
		`ProtSrv`
		`PowerMgmt`
			Free

Symbian Signed registered account and a valid ACS Publisher ID	1–20	Capabilities above and
		`ReadDeviceData`
		`WriteDeviceData`
		`TrustedUI`
			Free

Symbian Signed registered account, an ACS publisher ID and mobile phone manufacturer approval	As allowed by mobile phone manufacturer	Capabilities above and additional capabilities allowed by mobile phone manufacturer
		`AllFiles`
		`DiskAdmin`
		`CommDD`
		`Drm`
		`MultimediaDD`
		`NetworkControl`
		`Tcb`
			Determined by mobile phone manufacturer

No matter which of the groups you wish to secure a developer certificate for, submission is always via the Symbian Signed portal, making the process simple and transparent for the developer.

Requesting a Developer Certificate

To make the process of acquiring a developer certificate as easy as possible, Symbian has provided a free Windows-based wizard application for developers to download. This is available from the Symbian Signed portal. Once installed, you can run the wizard (see Figure 9.4) and follow a simple five-stage process to obtain your certificate.
Here's a brief run-through of the process:

1. Specify the name for your output certificate request file (CSR) which the wizard will produce. The output from the wizard is a single CSR

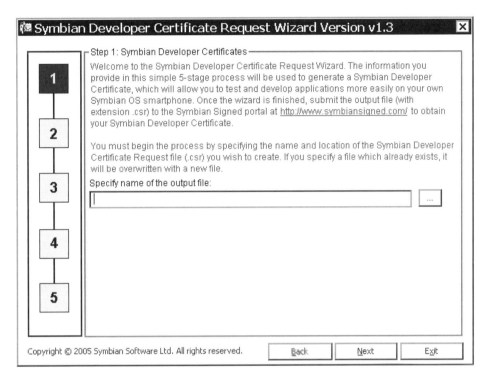

Figure 9.4   Developer Certificate Request Tool

file, which contains all the necessary information for your actual certificate to be created. At the end of the wizard process, you submit your new CSR file to the Symbian Signed portal and you will be sent back a new developer certificate.

2.   At this point you have the option to:

  •   Enter the file names of your ACS Publisher ID and related private key into the entry fields. The application uses the private key to create the CSR file to be used in the creation of your developer certificate. The private key from your ACS Publisher ID is used locally by the application and is not included in the CSR file, which merely uses the certificate data (containing the public key).

  •   Create a private/public key pair using the application and the data entered. Again the private key is used locally by the application and is not included in the CSR file.

  The method you choose here will affect the number of mobile phones that can be included in the final developer certificate – see Table 9.1.

3.   Enter some personal information to be contained in the developer certificate.

4. Specify the mobile phone identifiers (IMEIs) you wish to include in your developer certificate. Here, you can also select which subset of available capabilities you wish to request (again, this is dependent on your actions in Step 2, and Table 9.1, which lists the capabilities available with and without an ACS Publisher ID).

5. Finally, you can review and confirm your choices so far, before either going back to amend them or creating the CSR file.

Once the wizard has completed, you can take the CSR file and upload it to your account on the Symbian Signed portal.

Using a Developer Certificate

When you have submitted your CSR file and it has been verified, a new certificate will be generated and returned to you. This is your developer certificate. You can begin using the new certificate immediately – much as you would use the CER and KEY files generated from your ACS Publisher ID when submitting your final SIS file to be Symbian Signed. You simply build your SIS file with the MakeSIS tool and then sign it with the SignSIS tool (see Chapter 3, Section 3.3.)

9.3.3 Submitting an Application for Certification

Having developed and tested your application – perhaps using the emulator as described in Chapter 3, and using developer certificates to test on a real mobile phone – we recommend that the final stages of your application quality assurance include testing against the test criteria for Symbian Signed. This will save time and money by preventing unnecessary re-submissions because the application was non-compliant in one or more of the tests. The test criteria can be found at **www.symbiansigned.com/app/page/requirements**. The page also provides a link to useful tools that may assist you in your development and testing. Once you have verified your application's behavior against the test criteria, you are ready to submit your application to the Symbian Signed portal or Publisher/Channel process.

Preparing Your ACS Publisher ID Keys and Certificate for Signing

The first step in submitting your application is to export your ACS Publisher ID keys and certificate so they can be used by the Symbian OS packaging tools (you do not need to repeat this step if you have already done it for previous submissions).

The following instructions are for Microsoft Internet Explorer. Go to 'Tools' and select 'Internet Options' (see Figure 9.5). Select the 'Content' tab and under the 'Certificates' section select the 'Certificates' button

Figure 9.5 Internet Explorer Internet Options Dialog

(see Figure 9.6). Look down the list of displayed certificates and select your ACS Publisher ID. This will have your name under the issued-to column and 'VeriSign Class 3 Code Signing 2001 CA' under the issued-by column. Press the 'Export' button. Now select the 'Yes, export private key' option (see Figure 9.7). If you are unable to select this option, or the option is grayed out, you may need to contact VeriSign as this generally means that the private key was protected at pick up (see our warning in Section 9.3.1).

At the Export File format dialog, select PKCS#12. Do *not* select the box marked 'Delete private key if export is successful' – this will remove your certificate from the browser, which will make it unavailable for future signings. We would recommend you password protect, or alternatively, use PGP or a similar form of encryption, to protect the file. Finally, specify a name (for example, ExampleACSPublisherId) and location for the export file and protect access to the file once again. This last step is especially important if you choose not to password protect the keys in the earlier part of the process.

At this point you have a PFX file, which contains both the private and public keys. You now need to export this into file formats recognizable to the Symbian OS tools, using the key export tool (vs_pkcs.exe) that

Figure 9.6 Exporting your ACS Publisher ID Certificate

is available from VeriSign. The simplest way to locate this tool is to use the link provided in the paper 'How do I get my Symbian OS application signed', which may be downloaded from the 'Process' section of the portal (***www.symbiansigned.com/app/page/process***). The link can be found in 'Section 2: Signing your SIS file with your ACS Publisher ID'.

Download the tool and unzip the contents (vs_pkcs.exe and readme.txt) into a new folder on your PC. You can now use the tool to extract the certificate and key files. Note that these will not be password protected and should, therefore, once again be secured using PGP or similar.

Run vs_pkcs using the command line prompt and provide the names you wish to use for the final certificate files. For example:

```
C:\> vs_pkcs -p12 ExampleACSPublisherId.pfx -passwd frederick
       -key ExampleACSKey.key -cer ExampleACSCert.cer
```

In this example we have used the ExampleACSPublisherId.pfx file defined above. The output file names are ExampleACSkey for the key

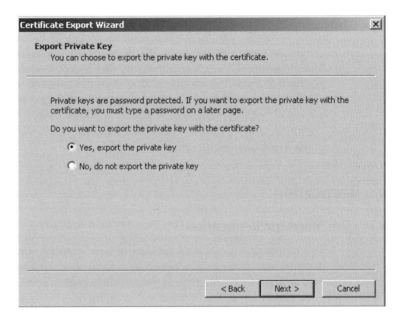

Figure 9.7 Exporting the ACS Publisher ID Keys

file and `ExampleACSCert` for the certificate file. The `-p12` argument recognizes the PKCS#12 format used, and the password used is 'frederick'.

Congratulations! You have your certificate and key file ready to be used with SignSIS (see Figure 9.8).

ExampleACSCert.cer

ExampleACSKey.key

Figure 9.8 Certificate and Key Files for SignSIS

Signing and Submitting the Application

You will now be able to sign the SIS file containing your completed application using the SignSIS tool as described in Chapter 3, Section 3.3.3. Make sure you specify the correct key and certificate files (`ExampleACSkey.key` and `ExampleACSCert.cer` in our example above) – if you use another certificate, for example a developer certificate, your application will not be accepted by Symbian Signed. In most circumstances, you should also make sure the SIS file does not have any previous signatures on it; in particular a SIS file with a developer certificate signature would still be subject to the constraints of only installing on the specifically identified mobile phones (see Chapter 8, Section 8.2.12).

Having used SignSIS, your SIS file will now be signed with your own ACS Publisher ID. Once again, remember this does *not* mean your file is Symbian Signed. The mobile phone does not trust the application at this point – it is trusted by the test house and the CA and is tamper-proofed, but it will not be installable on a mobile phone as it is.

Now you must submit your application on the Symbian Signed portal (***www.symbiansigned.com***).

9.4   Revocation

9.4.1   The Need for Revocation

Revocation provides a final sanction to handle applications that may compromise user, device or network security. There are a number of reasons why an application might be revoked, ranging from security vulnerabilities (either intentional, that is malware, or unintentional) to accidental or unintentional user or network impacts (bugs in the design or implementation).

Although stability and conformance are verified by application testing against the test criteria as part of the Symbian Signed process (or any similar process), testing can never offer a 100% guarantee that all malware, security vulnerabilities or other bugs will be dealt with. With increasingly more expensive processes, such as in-depth source code analysis, higher levels of assurance can certainly be achieved – however, even then there are no guarantees.

A 'fallback' method is, therefore, required to mitigate the effects of any problems and to limit the impact of such attacks or bugs, should they fail to be found during the test process. This is where revocation of the application (through revocation of the Content ID certificate with which the application is signed) can offer a final line of defense and prevent the spread of such applications once they have been identified.

For a developer whose clear intent is to be malicious the option also exists to revoke their ACS Publisher ID, thus preventing them from submitting any further applications for certification.

In order for revocation to work there must be some reference or unique identity for the application, which may be used to identify it and hold its status. This unique identifier is the digital certificate or Content ID certificate in the case of Symbian Signed. Unsigned applications can *not* be revoked, as they do not have a unique identifier.

9.4.2   Revocation Mechanisms

Should a significant security threat or problem be found, a certificate can be revoked by the Certificate Authority (CA) changing its status on a revocation database. When a status query is made for that certificate in future, the signed application can be prevented from being installed or the user warned that the application's status has changed and appropriate action suggested.

As we described in Section 9.3, the developer signs their application with their ACS Publisher ID prior to submission for testing on the Symbian Signed portal. Once the application has been shown to meet the Symbian Signed criteria, the developer's ACS Publisher ID signature is removed and replaced with a unique Content ID signature, using a certificate that has a chain of trust to the root certificate stored on the mobile phone. The Content ID reference is added to the CA's master database and provides the control point for revocation. The database maintains a status history for Symbian Signed applications, which may be queried to confirm whether an application has been revoked, or not.

Two major forms of revocation checking exist; these are Certificate Revocation Lists (CRLs) and the Online Certificate Status Protocol (OCSP). CRLs rely on a database being available that contains a list of all applications that have been revoked – this is not the optimal method for the mobile environment. Firstly, the CRL can consume significant amounts of memory, and secondly, it is likely to be cached for efficiency, which can lead to latency in updates and thus applications installing even though they may have been revoked on the master database.

Symbian OS implements OCSP, as being the best fit for the requirements of a constrained mobile device. The device queries the CA's revocation database directly to seek confirmation of the application status. This is generally initiated at installation (to prevent the application from gaining access to the device) or it may be initiated manually at any time (to validate that an application has not been revoked since installation). Symbian is also implementing a 'push' mechanism that allows

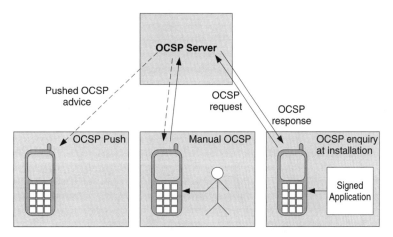

Figure 9.9   OCSP Revocation Checking

notifications to be automatically sent to a mobile phone as soon as an application's status changes.

Figure 9.9 illustrates the various uses of OCSP for revocation checks.

9.5 Summary

In this chapter we have discussed the background to granting capabilities in third-party applications, ROM code and libraries. We have considered the elements involved in working with and signing for platform security. In addition, we have examined in some detail the process of applying for and using your developer certificate and considered the application submission process to the Symbian Signed portal, including related tools. Finally, we have looked at how the signing process enables revocation of signatures. You are now ready to sign your applications!

PART 4

The Future of Mobile Device Security

10

The Servant in Your Pocket

by Craig Heath

10.1 Crystal-Ball Gazing

Predicting the future is a very presumptuous thing to do, and the mobile phone industry as a whole seems to be rather bad at it – the enormous success of SMS text messaging came as a surprise to its developers, and, conversely, a lot of time and money was invested in WAP services, which were much less widely used than was predicted. Nevertheless, we thought it would be interesting to conclude this book with some speculation on how the security features of mobile phones and their associated services might evolve. For the record, this chapter is being written in October 2005; it may be proved wrong even before the book is published!

None of the content of this chapter should be taken as an indication that Symbian intends to offer such features in future releases of Symbian OS, or indeed that we are even aware of work going on in these areas – it merely reflects the authors' interests and occasional flights of fancy.

Security is not an end in itself – it has been said that the best way to secure a computer system is to turn it off, encase it in concrete and bury it! That is certainly a secure system, but it is not suitable for doing anything useful. Security measures must be applied in order to enable useful functionality. Thus, to decide the future direction of mobile phone security, we need to consider how the use of mobile devices is likely to develop.

10.2 Convergence, Content and Connectivity

'Convergence', combining mobile phone functionality with that of other consumer electronic devices, is already happening: camera phones are ubiquitous; music player phones are starting to appear; mobile TV broadcasting to phones is on the horizon. These examples are all to do with adding content (mainly commercial entertainment content) to the mobile phone, but the primary *raison d'être* of a phone remains to connect the user with another person. [Odlyzko 2001] makes the argument that, even for the wired world of the 'Plain Old Telephone Service' and fixed-line Internet, consumers ascribe significantly more value to connectivity than to content – the highest-value application for the Internet being email. This not only indicates that mobile phone manufacturers should make sure that their devices continue to be very effective at making phone calls, but also that successful new functionality on mobile phones is likely to be that which assists people to connect with each other in various ways.

It is interesting to consider what other instances of convergence are likely to manifest in the future. One place to start that consideration is with what people typically carry along with them in their wallet, purse or bag – this could include:

- keys
- money
- tickets
- credit/debit cards
- membership cards/licenses
- loyalty cards.

For many people, the mobile phone has become *the* indispensable item they never leave the house without – this tendency is only likely to become more widespread in future. In a way, the mobile phone is becoming an extension of 'self', and there is an opportunity to offload tasks to the phone that people might otherwise use their brains for! This opportunity could be perceived as a risk; those who believe the advent of the pocket calculator was the death knell for the skill of mental arithmetic might similarly bemoan the tendency for people not to remember phone numbers any more, nor to remember appointments, nor their to-do lists – on the other hand, the more optimistic may view this as releasing brain capacity to do something more useful! (Incidentally, pocket calculators are another example of convergence, where the phone has subsumed another, previously separate, consumer electronics device.) Perhaps the most advanced realization of the mobile phone as an extension of human memory thus far is the Nokia Lifeblog software, which continuously records a diary created from photos, videos, and sent and received messages on the phone.

Returning to the 'connecting people' theme, there are interesting developments in the area of peer-to-peer (P2P) applications. This resonates with the perception of the mobile phone as an enabler of social networks; in some sense, your phone is a way of carrying around your social circle, friends and family in your pocket. P2P is primarily seen in the wired Internet world as a technology used for file sharing, and predominantly for entertainment content (legitimately acquired or more often not, via what is ominously referred to as the 'Darknet' [Biddle 2003]). There are, however, some rather more innovative possibilities for mobile phones, with the phone acting as a sort of social mediator, advertising your interests and 'match-making' with other P2P agents, leading to actual human contact by text, voice or in person. The social side of this is exemplified by a prototype application that is currently being distributed for Symbian OS-based phones, Nokia Sensor, which publishes a home page and selected pieces of content to other similarly-equipped phones within Bluetooth connection range and provides a way for like-minded individuals to make contact. It is likely that commercial use could be made of such social profiles too, for instance by transmitting targeted advertising based on the individual's interests, although for some that may be a little too reminiscent of the obtrusive advertising portrayed in the Stephen Spielberg film 'Minority Report'!

Services delivered on or to the mobile phone are likely to provide more of a 'personal touch' than similar services might do on a PC. Given the mobile phone's association with the user's social circle, it is easier to portray services on the phone as being friendly and helpful. Indeed, the mobility of the phone means that it is always (or mostly) available when it is needed, which will certainly contribute to the 'helpful' part.

10.3   Enabling New Services

Mobile Payments

Mobile payments are an area where there are already several competing standards and technologies. There are two main categories here, one being the use of the phone to pay for things when physically present (for example, groceries or bus fares) and the other being to pay for remote or intangible goods and services (for example, ordering books, downloading music, or paying for an extra life in a game). There is also interest in 'micropayments', amounts of perhaps fractions of a penny that are uneconomical to collect using established payment mechanisms such as credit or debit cards due to the per-transaction overheads.

One of the most interesting challenges is in allowing software running on the mobile phone to generate billing events. For example, protected content could be delivered to a mobile phone in anticipation of the content being used (perhaps a digital newspaper) and the rendering software could arrange for the user to be charged only for the content they actually use (pages actually read).

Symbian OS v9 has a security architecture that allows the operating system to distinguish between trustworthy and untrustworthy processes, but the billing system will be implemented in software running on a remote server – how will it know whether a billing request it receives originated from a trustworthy application or an untrustworthy one (or even if it was sent from a Symbian OS-based mobile phone, or some malware running on a PC)? The best mechanism, at the time of writing, appears to be to use premium-rate SMS numbers, as the application will have to be signed appropriately in order to send the SMS. But there is considerable per-transaction overhead involved (including for the mobile phone user, who may be paying a standard rate SMS charge simply for sending the message, on top of the amount going to the vendor). Establishing the trustworthiness of the source of a billing message is a similar problem to that facing DRM rights issuers establishing the trustworthiness of the recipient of rights – we will return to this later in the chapter when we discuss 'remote attestation'.

Mobile Phone as Access Token

Referring back to our discussion of convergence in Section 10.2, one class of things we carry about with us is keys, whether the old-fashioned mechanical kind, or swipe cards or other forms of access passes. Aside from the convenience of not needing to carry keys separately from the mobile phone, and thus having one less class of things to remember to pick up when leaving home, the phone can provide an additional bene-fit – the 'key' can make sure it is being used by its legitimate owner rather than someone who stole it or just found it lying around. We discuss how the mobile phone might identify and authenticate the person holding it in the next section.

We can also consider the use of the mobile phone as an access token for remote network services – this is already possible to the degree that an Internet browser on the phone can cache passwords used to access web sites, but we can anticipate that this sort of functionality will become more sophisticated and more secure in the future.

Content Protection

The main security challenge in delivering entertainment content to mobile phones is, of course, digital rights management (DRM), or in other words, preventing unauthorized use and duplication of copyrighted con-tent. DRM implementations are already deployed on mobile phones. Somewhat paradoxically, it is easier to protect content on simpler, lower-specification phones which do not allow add-on software, whereas the increased functionality of higher-specification phones which do allow add-on software may make an attacker's job easier, by providing the means to access and make copies of protected content.

Several of the regular features of Symbian OS platform security archi-tecture are helpful to DRM implementations. For example, data caging, which can prevent access to certain data (perhaps the content itself, or encryption keys used in turn to protect the content), and the capability model, which allows processes that can be trusted to respect the rights associated with protected content to be distinguished from untrustworthy processes. There are, however, a couple of security challenges with specific relevance to DRM solutions, which we will cover in the next section: *renewability* and *remote attestation*.

10.4   New Security Technologies

We are already seeing some security technologies being added to Symbian OS-based phones by Symbian's licensees and successfully marketed to mobile phone users. Figure 10.1 shows the Fujitsu F900iC phone, which includes both biometric user authentication using a fingerprint sensor, and mobile payment functionality using a Near-Field Communication (NFC) technology developed by Sony called FeliCa.

Figure 10.1   Fujitsu F900iC

In some cases, new security functionality will be invisible to the phone user. This is appropriate where the security configuration is being managed by an entity that the user trusts, such as a network operator, or an enterprise IT department – increased security can be provided without burdening the mobile phone user with responsibility for making security decisions. In other cases, security functionality will be visible to the user, where the goal is to provide the user with more control. It may be appropriate to provide more control over financial costs or over the disposition of the user's personal data, but developers still need to be careful not to increase the burden on the user. The default security policy should be carefully chosen to minimize the number of explicit decisions the user needs to make.

Renewability

Providing for 'renewability' is accepting the inevitable imperfection of any security solution. However much time and effort is put in to developing a security system, it is always possible that there is an attacker with more time and effort available (or perhaps many attackers whose cumulative time and effort exceeds that of the defender) who will be able to find a flaw in the system and exploit it. In the case of such a successful attack, one potentially effective response is to replace components of the security system with new ones – this particularly applies to secret and private keys, trust anchors (root certificates) and, in extreme cases, to entire cryptographic algorithms (both encryption and hash algorithms). This technique has been widely and successfully employed in what are called 'conditional access' systems, as used in set-top boxes providing Pay TV services. The keys used to protect services and content are regularly changed – in some cases they may only be used for a period of seconds, thus making it pointless for an attacker to spend any effort in discovering the key currently in use. As applied to mobile phones, our main challenge is to ensure that the renewal mechanism does not introduce security holes itself; to enable remote *management of security*, we must first ensure that we have *security of management*.

Remote Attestation

The topic of this book is a security architecture, implemented in software, that puts in place a number of controls designed to maintain and improve trust in the services provided in and via a mobile phone. You might legitimately ask the question 'who guards the guardians' (in the original, 'quis custodiet ipsos custodes' [Juvenal 100]) – how can any tampering with the logic of the security-enforcing code (the Trusted Computing Base) be detected? One relatively straightforward means of doing this is checking the integrity of the operating system image when it is loaded in to the mobile phone at boot time (otherwise simply known as 'secure boot'). Secure boot is implemented in some mobile phones today, and detects attacks which reprogram the phone memory while the operating system is not running (such attacks may be attempted using commercially-available service hardware). A mobile phone with secure boot would, therefore, refuse to start up if it had been reprogrammed with an unauthorized operating system image. This helps improve security, but there is still a gap: a service running on a remote server may need assurance that the mobile phone it is communicating with (perhaps to receive billing messages or to deliver rights to protected content) is a genuine phone, running an integrity-checked version of the secure operating system. The operating system itself has no way of reliably reporting this to the remote server, as it is not able to tell the difference between legitimate hardware, with secure boot performing a successful integrity check, and a carefully crafted simulator running on some other hardware that merely reports plausible, but fictitious, results. (The philosophically inclined might like to ponder the analogous problem posed by [Bostrom 2003] – how can humans know whether they are real or simulations?) In order to remotely report the integrity of a piece of software, we need an independently authenticated trustworthy source to make the assertion – such functionality is known as 'remote attestation'.

For remote attestation to be useful, it is necessary for the entity generating the integrity report to be *more* trustworthy (that is, better protected) than the software being measured. If it was no more secure it would be equally easy to attack and nothing would have been gained. In practice, this means that the reporting entity must be protected by hardware security mechanisms. The Trusted Computing Group (TCG) publishes a specification for a Trusted Platform Module (TPM) that has been implemented on several PC platforms in the form of a separate microcontroller on the motherboard. The TPM monitors the software running on the main processor, stores a record of integrity measurements, and contains an embedded private key that can be used to authenticate the reports that it generates. The TCG includes several working groups, one of which (the Mobile Phone Working Group) is working on a specification adapting the TPM concept to the specific needs and constraints of mobile phones. It is likely that the specification will allow a greater part of the TPM to be implemented as software on the main processor, but, as noted above, not all hardware security requirements can be removed as that would weaken the protection to the point that it provided no benefit.

Preventing Denial of Service

As Symbian restricts the damage that malware can do by implementing measures such as the security architecture described in this book, malware authors are likely to turn to other, less well defended avenues. One such avenue is to use Denial of Service (DoS) attacks. Denying access to a particular service is not likely to result in immediate damage to the end user, such as financial loss or loss of privacy, but such attacks can still result in significant inconvenience – they have been used, for example, as a means to blackmail service providers. DoS attacks, performed by software running on a mobile phone, are particularly difficult to defend against as the rogue process isn't actually performing an operation it shouldn't be allowed to – it's just doing more than we would like it to (using more than its fair share of resources such as memory, file store, CPU, network bandwidth, battery power and so on). There are methods for addressing this – such as the concept of 'quotas' in multi-user operating systems, which prevent users consuming more than their allocated share of disk space – but the overhead of monitoring processes for such behavior makes them impractical for use on today's mobile phones. Perhaps as phones become more powerful to support more demanding uses (3D games, video playback and recording) and battery technology improves to keep pace (perhaps using fuel cells), there will be sufficient spare capacity to implement such controls.

User Authentication

The increasing use of mobile phones to perform services on behalf of the phone user leads to an increasing need for the phones to be able to verify that, at a particular time, they are still in the possession of their legitimate user. Most mobile phones already have functionality for authenticating the user via a PIN, both for locking the user interface of the phone so that it cannot be used by others and for authenticating the user to the SIM in order to enable network functionality. Typically, the implementation of PIN checking is closely integrated with the function that it is protecting, and it is not possible for it to be used by other functions on the mobile phone. This can lead to the user having to remember several PINs for different functions, which is clearly an unnecessary burden when they all have the same essential purpose: to verify that the legitimate user is in possession of the mobile phone.

One way to address this might be to split off the authentication into a separate system service, which can then be invoked by the individual functions that need to check the user's status.

- The same authentication token (for instance, a PIN) could be used by several different functions.

- The authentication service could ensure that, if the user has recently authenticated themselves, they are not immediately asked to do so again because a different function is being used.

- The authentication service could also provide a single point for implementation of alternative authentication mechanisms.

One class of alternative mechanisms to the conventional PIN is biometrics (that is, measuring a physical characteristic of the user). Biometrics differ in their accuracy but, even if the absolute security is no better than a PIN, the improved convenience of, for example, swiping your finger over a sensor versus remembering a string of digits is likely to encourage wider use. A security mechanism which users choose not to turn on benefits nobody. (Biometrics include facial recognition, voice-print recognition and fingerprint recognition.)

Labeling

Sharing, or otherwise publishing, user data from the device – as we discussed in the context of P2P applications – gives rise to a number of concerns relating to user privacy. The most important property a security technology needs to address this is simplicity (referring back to Chapter 2, Section 2.1.2, this is the principle of 'economy of mechanism' [Saltzer and Schroeder 1975]). As we mentioned at the start of this section, we must minimize any burden on the mobile phone user, so that any decisions they are expected to make have the virtue of clarity. A clear decision point with clear consequences is likely to provide the user with a useful degree of control, whereas unnecessary complexity either results in a security feature not being used at all, or worse, used incorrectly.

One security technology that has a venerable history in security systems but is currently rather out of fashion is the notion of 'labeling'. This has mainly been used in the context of multi-level secure systems implementing mandatory access controls to classified data – typically 'classified' in the sense of government or military security controls. Briefly, every *object* on the system (typified by a file, but also other collections of allocated data) has associated with it a *label* describing its *sensitivity*; this sensitivity label is then processed by the TCB to ensure that the data is only made available to processes that have the necessary *clearance*.

Instead of using such labels for mandatory access controls enforced by the TCB, they could be used in an advisory way to help trustworthy applications make the right decisions about what to do with a user's personal data (including photos, videos, voice recordings, text notes, and so on). The system would simply need to ensure that the label stayed with the data as it was moved or copied around. Instead of using hierarchical classifications such as 'Secret', 'Confidential' and 'Unclassified', labels could be, for example, 'Private' or 'Shared'. Such labels could subdivide the current set of data to which access is controlled by the `ReadUserData` and `WriteUserData` capabilities. Applications with those capabilities would be trusted to respect the advice of the labels, such as a file sharing application only sharing files with the 'Shared' label, and the contacts application refusing to transmit any contact marked as 'Private' from the device.

Going further, it might be possible in future to agree standards for transmitting these labels along with data when it is sent from the mobile phone, for example to a web site as part of making an e-commerce purchase. This could go hand-in-hand with privacy profiles, which would express the mobile phone user's intent in supplying that data to the remote server (such as prohibiting it from being used for marketing purposes). There is an existing standard developed by the Platform for Privacy Preferences Project (P3P), but this works in reverse (the server tells the user what the privacy policy is) and the more sophisticated (and hence more interesting) features of the P3P specification are not widely implemented in browsers today.

Auditing

The final area where we may anticipate some additional security technology in mobile phone operating systems is in the area of auditing. In 'traditional' secure computer systems, there is a lot of attention is paid to making sure that all security-relevant events can be recorded for future analysis, but somewhat less attention is paid to making sure that what is recorded can actually be made sense of. It seems to be forgotten that the word 'auditing' refers more to the analysis of data than it does to the recording of it.

Clearly, given the limited storage available on most mobile phones today, it would not be practical to record all security-related events just in case that log might prove useful in the future. Nevertheless, some means to analyze what it going on in the phone would be of considerable benefit in analyzing any security incident that occurred. Such data is almost certainly going to be meaningless to the majority of mobile phone users, but could be used by, for example, a network operator or enterprise IT department responding to a support call. It is, therefore, likely that auditing functionality would be mainly, if not exclusively, accessed remotely, perhaps using existing device management infrastructure. We want to stress again here though, that before enabling *management of security*, it is necessary to be confident of the *security of management*. It would certainly not be good if an attacker could turn on the audit log and effectively perpetrate a DoS attack, nor would it be good if an unauthorized entity could use the audit log to discover personal data about the user, authentication codes, and so on.

The hooks that would enable logging of security-related events could also potentially be used by security software running on the mobile phone, perhaps to detect abnormal behavior and raise an alert, or for other forms of intrusion detection.

10.5 Summary

This final chapter discusses some of the ways in which security technology on mobile phones may evolve in the coming years.

We considered how the use of mobile phones may evolve, as the purpose of new security technology should be to help people use their phones more effectively. This usage is likely to increasingly include the functions of other consumer electronic devices such as cameras, music players or TVs. New services are also likely to be provided on mobile phones, including payment services, use of the phone for access control to physical or network resources, and protection of digital content.

We concluded by examining some new security technologies which may be implemented on mobile phones to support these new uses and services: renewability, remote attestation, preventing denial of service, user authentication, labeling, and auditing.

We hope this book has proved useful, and that the Symbian OS platform security architecture will be a sound basis for both improving security and enabling more and better services to be provided by all participants in the mobile phone industry. By ensuring secure and happy users, we should all benefit!

Appendix A

Capability Descriptions

A.1 System Capabilities

Tcb

Write access to executables and shared read-only resources

Tcb allows write access to \sys and \resource directories. This is the most critical capability as it allows write access to executables, which contain the capabilities that define the security attributes of a process. No third-party code should be allowed to do this. The TCB processes run with at least this capability.

AllFiles

Read access to the entire file system and write access to other processes' private directories

Similarly to Tcb, this capability is very strictly controlled and it is not granted lightly. Nevertheless, phone manufacturers' test software might reasonably have it.

For instance, the backup and restore server might need it to backup data on behalf of programs.

Unlike Tcb, AllFiles permits read and write in \private.

The system capability AllFiles can be used in the following circumstances:

- By mobile phone manufacturers wishing to have a powerful shell or file manager. In this case, the user would be allowed to destroy or modify some servers' private files. Symbian therefore highly discourages such a facility being made publicly available

- For test utilities to retrieve files in order to audit them to validate the behavior of a subsystem.

CommDD

Direct access to all communications equipment device drivers

This includes for example, WiFi, USB and serial device drivers.

DiskAdmin

Access to file system administration operations that affect more than one file or directory (or overall file-system integrity and behavior, etc.)

This includes, for example, mounting and unmounting a drive partition.

Drm

Access to DRM-protected content

DRM agents use this capability to decide whether or not a program should have access to protected content. Symbian OS trusts that software granted Drm capability will respect the rights associated with this content.

MultimediaDD

Access to critical multimedia functions such as direct access to associated device drivers and priority access to multimedia APIs

This includes sound, camera, video, etc.

NetworkControl

The ability to modify or access network protocol controls

Typically when an action can change the behavior of several existing and future connections, it should be protected by NetworkControl.
    For example, forcing all existing connections on a specific protocol to be dropped or changing the priority of a call.

PowerMgmt

The ability to kill any process, to power-off unused peripherals and to cause the mobile phone to go into stand-by, to wake up, or to power down completely

Note that this doesn't control access to anything and everything that might drain battery power.

ProtServ

Allows a server process to register with a protected name

Protected names start with a '!'. The kernel will prevent servers without ProtServ capability from using such a name, and, therefore, will prevent protected servers from being impersonated. All servers in the TCE have this capability.

ReadDeviceData

Read access to confidential network operator, mobile phone manufacturer and device settings

Settings that are not confidential (such as the system clock) do not need to be protected by this capability.

Examples of confidential device data include the list of installed applications and the device lock PIN code.

SurroundingsDD

Access to logical device drivers that provide input information about the surroundings of the mobile phone

Good examples of drivers that require this capability would be GPS and biometrics device drivers. For complex multimedia logical device drivers that provide both input and output functions, such as a sound device driver, the MultimediaDD capability should be used where it is impractical to separate the input from the output calls at its API level.

SwEvent

The ability to simulate key presses and pen input and to capture such events from any program

Note that, when it has the user input focus, normal software does not need SwEvent in order to be dispatched key and pen events.

TrustedUI

The ability to create a trusted UI session and, therefore, to display dialogs in a secure UI environment

Trusted UI dialogs are rare. They must be used only when confidentiality and security are critical: for instance for password dialogs.

Normal access to the user interface and the screen does not require this. Code implementing a trusted UI dialog would need `SwEvent` capability.

Note that trusted UI dialogs are not implemented in Symbian OS v9.1.

WriteDeviceData

Write access to settings that control the behavior of the device

This setting is not always symmetrical with `ReadDeviceData`, i.e. just because data important to maintaining the integrity of the system is protected from being written, does not mean that it needs to be protected against being read.

Examples of this type of setting are device lock settings, system time, time zone, alarms, etc.

A.2   User Capabilities

LocalServices

Access to services over 'short-link' connections (such as Bluetooth or infra-red). Such services will not normally incur cost for the user

The location of the remote service is assumed to be well known to the user. A program with this capability can normally send or receive information through a serial port, USB, IR and point-to-point Bluetooth profiles. Examples of local services are synchronization of data with the user's PC, file transfer, etc. This capability does not allow use of IP or any routable Bluetooth profiles, or spending of a user's money by dialing a telephone number.

Location

Access to data giving the location of the phone

This capability supports the management of a user's privacy regarding the mobile phone's location.

NetworkServices

Access to remote services (such as over-the-air data services or Wi-Fi network access), which might incur cost for the user

This capability allows access to a remote service without any restriction on its physical location. Typically, this location is unknown to the user. Voice calls, SMS and Internet services are good examples of such network services. This capability controls access to services delivered via GSM, CDMA and all IP transport protocols including IP over Bluetooth ('PAN profile').

ReadUserData

Read access to confidential user data

This capability supports the management of a user's privacy.

Typically contacts, messages and appointments are always seen as the user's confidential data. For other content, such as images or sounds, there could be a choice to be made by the user.

UserEnvironment

Access to live data about the user and their immediate environment

This capability protects the user's privacy.

Examples of services protected using this capability are audio, picture and video recording, and biometrics (such as fingerprint) recording. Please note that the location of the device is excluded from this capability and is instead protected by using the dedicated capability Location.

WriteUserData

Write access to confidential user data

This capability supports the management of the integrity of user data.

Please note that this capability is not always symmetric with Read-UserData. For instance, one might wish to prevent rogue software from deleting music tracks but not wish to restrict read access to them.

Software developers creating programs (whether system servers or applications) may use this capability to control access to their data when it is stored in private directories.

It is not always obvious whether to treat data as confidential and the choice will depend on the UI implementation.

Appendix B

Some Cryptography Basics

For additional background reading, we recommend *Applied Cryptography* by Bruce Schneier [Schneier 1996] and *Understanding PKI* by Carlisle Adams and Steve Lloyd [Adams and Lloyd 1999].

B.1 Asymmetric Key Pairs

Unlike symmetric cryptography, where the same key is employed to decrypt data as was used to encrypt it, asymmetric cryptography is based on a related *pair* of keys. You can then use one key to encrypt the data, and the other to decrypt it – and vice versa. The generally followed scheme is for you to publish one key (referred to as a *public key*) and keep the other key (the *private key*) secret. This means that the following mechanisms can be used:

1. Using *your* public key, I can encrypt data, safe in the knowledge that only you can decrypt it.

2. Using *my* private key, I can encrypt data that anyone can decrypt using my public key.

Mechanism 2 doesn't sound too useful at first. However, if the data does decrypt correctly (and you'll need to recognize this – perhaps by seeing readable text) then you'll know that I (and nobody else) encrypted it.

Hard-core cryptographers will argue over the rather general statements made above, and quite rightly point out that everything depends on the fact that private keys remain private and public keys are always correctly associated with the correct owner. Also, as time goes on, technological advances in cryptanalysis and mathematical wizardry mean that mechanisms 1 and 2 above become less reliable – which is why cryptography continuously evolves as well (e.g. by employing increasingly larger key sizes).

B.2   The Cryptographic Hash

A hash function takes some variable-length input data and produces a fixed-length output, which is usually called the *hash* or *message digest*. The idea here is that it's extremely costly or time-consuming to find – or concoct – another input that produces the same hash value. It should also be effectively impossible to determine anything about the original input from the hash output.

B.3   How Signing Works

Signing a piece of data is a two-step process. First I calculate the hash of the data I wish to sign. Second, I encrypt the hash with the private key from my own asymmetric key pair. I can then send, post, or publish this data and signature. (Note that the data itself is not encrypted – only the hash.)

You, the recipient, by using my public key, are able to decrypt the hash and **also** run the same hash operation yourself to confirm that you come up with the same hash value. If the hash values match, then you can be reasonably sure (within cryptographic guarantees) that:

- The data hasn't been tampered with.

- I constructed the data and I am the source.

There are things you are going to need to know to 'verify' the signature, and I didn't draw attention to them in the paragraph above. The first is the ability to identify or obtain *my* public key (as opposed to anyone else's). As I said earlier, this can be a little tricky to resolve. The second is the hash algorithm I used to calculate the hash (of which there are quite a few), and the third is the encryption algorithm, which I used to encrypt the hash. Standards exist which specify how these things go together to form a signature (for example, see the PKCS#7 and other related standards at ***www.rsasecurity.com/rsalabs***).

B.4   The Digital Certificate

The digital certificate is an amalgamation of a number of useful things into a signed data container. The two key pieces of information present are:

- a public key

- Some information which can help to identify the owner or subject. In particular, this information should help differentiate the owner from others, and give you some idea that the public key belongs to that person and that the data therein matches your knowledge of the real person (name, country, company, e-mail address, etc.).

Other information is present too – in particular a date validity period and information about who issued (and signed) the certificate.

Appendix C

The Software Install API

This section will mainly be of interest to UI developers who are developing an installer application. Some of these APIs might not be fully documented in public SDKs due to the limited audience for them.

C.1   The Software Installer Launcher

The basic installer API can be found in the `Launcher` class in `%EPOCROOT%\epoc32\include\swi\launcher.h`.

The first method you'll encounter there is:

```
static IMPORT_C TInt Install(MUiHandler& aUiHandler,
        const TFileName& aFileName, const CInstallPrefs& aInstallPrefs);
```

You'll notice immediately that a reference to an abstract UI interface is required. This is how the installer communicates back to the UI when questions need to be asked of the user, or certain conditions and events are reported. These call-backs are defined in `MUiHandler` which itself is an amalgamation of the `MCommonDialogs`, `MInstallerUi-Handler`, and `MUninstallerUIHandler` abstract interfaces. These are all declared in the header `%EPOCROOT%\epoc32\include\swi\msisuihandlers.h`.

Given that the caller provides a concrete implementation of the `MUi-Handler` class, the software installer will call back to this code on the same thread which called the above `Install()` method.

C.2   TrustedUI Capability

Another key point about the installer API is that the caller must have the `TrustedUI` capability. Being charged with this capability means that the calling code has been deemed responsible enough to accurately broker important information between the user and the installer and not, for example, to subvert the user's choice *not* to continue with an installation by itself returning *'continue'* to the software installer call-back.

If you're not going to find yourself in a position where you're writing installer UIs, but you still wish to install a package, then the best way to initiate the process is to use `RApaLsSession::StartDocument()` to launch whatever application is registered to handle SIS files on your mobile phone.

C.3   The SISDataProvider Interface

SIS files might be present in the mobile phone's file system and, therefore, accessible by filename or file handle. Symbian didn't want to have to restrict installations to having the entire package present, and recognized that packages might simply be too large to cache locally and leave enough space left for the installation.

By allowing you, the caller, to provide your own data provider implementation, Symbian allows you to provide the support for wherever the SIS file data needs to come from. For example:

- You read the file via the network.

- You compressed a SIS file using a proprietary algorithm.

Note, however, that you will need to provide some form of `seek()` operation as the installer might wish to move forwards (and backwards) through the SIS file.

`SISDataProvider` call-backs come from a different thread, but one which is set up to share the same heap as the thread calling the `Install()` method. If you manage memory within your `SISData-Provider` object, then please create this object on the install thread so that the object doesn't end up owning memory in different heaps.

A brief synopsis is given below, but full details can be found in the Developer Library or in `sisdataprovider.h`.

```
class MSisDataProvider
{
public:

virtual TInt Read(TDes8& aDes)=0;
virtual TInt Read(TDes8& aDes, TInt aLength)=0;
virtual TInt Seek(TSeek aMode, TInt64& aPos)=0;
virtual ~MSisDataProvider() {}
virtual void OpenDrmContentL (ContentAccess::TIntent aIntent);
virtual TInt ExecuteDrmIntent (ContentAccess::TIntent aIntent);
};
```

C.4   Install Preferences

You may also have noticed that you can pass preferences into the installer, and this class – `CInstallPrefs` – is also defined in `launcher.h`.

These preferences are primarily concerned with run-time configuration issues, such as whether the installer should perform a revocation check on the software being installed, and where it might go to perform this check in default circumstances.

```
Class CInstallPrefs : public CBase
{
public:
void SetPerformRevocationCheck(TBool aCheck);
Tbool PerformRevocationCheck() const;
const TDesC8& RevocationServerUri() const;
......
```

It's worth pointing out, however, that a ROM-build setting could override any preferences which the caller attempts to set. For example, the manufacturer might have chosen to mandate revocation checks, in which case the caller's preference will be ignored. Alternatively, the manufacturer might choose to give control of a parameter to the caller.

Note that `CInstallPrefs` might change over time, so please refer to `launcher.h` for the options available to you.

C.5   Asynchronous Installation

If you would prefer to drive the software installation process via a `CActive` object running within an active scheduler, then you'll find that Symbian has provided an alternative installer API that is defined in `security\swi\inc\swi\asynclauncher.h`.

Glossary

AppArc The Symbian OS Application Architecture framework, which defines the application structure and basic user interface handling.

attack surface The complete set of resources and interfaces exposed to potential attackers trying to compromise a system's security.

binary A file containing compiled native executable program code.

BLOB Binary Large OBject: a collection of binary data held in a file store or database. Commonly used to represent multimedia objects such as images, sounds and video.

CONE The Symbian OS CONtrol Environment, the framework responsible for graphical interaction.

CSR Certificate Signing Request: an unsigned certificate, used to create a valid certificate by signing it with the private key of a certificate authority.

CSY Symbian OS plug-in communications server module.

DLL Dynamically Linked Library: a binary which can be loaded into a running process to make code available for use.

DoS Denial of Service: an attack on the security of a system which results in it being unavailable for use.

DRM Digital Rights Management: the administration of rights in a digital environment. Rights may include controls on the use and redistribution of digital content.

ECOM Symbian OS object factory framework used to manage and instantiate plug-in implementations.

ESN	Electronic Serial Number: a unique number used to identify a mobile phone on CDMA mobile phone networks.
ESOCK	Symbian OS network socket server process.
ETEL	Symbian OS telephony server process.
EXE	A type of binary which when loaded is used as the basis for a new process.
F32	The Symbian OS file server process.
FEP	Symbian OS Front End Processor: allows implementation of character input mechanisms as an alternative to the phone keypad.
firmware	Programs stored in semi-permanent storage such as ROM.
GSM	Originally 'Groupe Spéciale Mobile', rechristened 'Global Standard for Mobile Communications': the most widely used standard for mobile phone networks.
hard reset	Restarting a system from scratch, a 'cold boot', as opposed to a 'soft reset' which preserves the system state.
hashing	Using a one-way function to produce a short but effectively unique value representing a longer block of data.
IETF	Internet Engineering Task Force: a body that develops and ratifies standards for network data interchange (see **www.ietf.org**).
IMEI	International Mobile Equipment Identity, a unique number used to identify a mobile phone on GSM (and UMTS) mobile phone networks.
IPC	Inter-Process Communication: communication across thread and process boundaries. Symbian OS has supported two versions of IPC interface. IPC v2 was introduced to support platform security.
ISV	Independent Software Vendor, also referred to as a third-party developer: a software author using publicly available development tools.
kernel object	An object that is created and managed in the address space of the OS kernel, rather than of an individual process.
keyspace	In Symbian OS, a subsection of the central repository that contains the settings managed by one particular application.

LDD	Logical Device Driver: part of a kernel device driver which includes the logical functions of a device e.g., on and off, and read and write.
malware	Malicious software designed to damage or interfere with the operation of a computer system.
MIME type	Multipurpose Internet Mail Extensions media type, defined in IETF RFC 2046.
MMU	Memory Management Unit: a hardware component which maps kernel and user process virtual memory addresses on to physical memory.
OCSP	Online Certificate Status Protocol, defined in IETF RFC 2560.
opcode	Short for 'operation code', a short code used to represent one of a set of functions.
OTA	Over the Air refers to data arriving via the mobile phone network rather than local data from a physically connected source.
P2P	Peer to Peer: network services which involve direct data connections between two or more client devices. A canonical P2P application is file sharing.
PDD	Physical Device Driver: part of a kernel device driver which includes interfaces to specific hardware functions of a device.
PIN	Personal Identification Number: a simple authentication mechanism requiring the user to enter a string of digits that only they know.
PKCS#10	One of the Public Key Cryptography Standards, which defines the format of a certificate signing request (CSR).
process	The Symbian OS unit of memory protection: one user process may not access another's memory. A process may contain one or more threads.
race condition	An undesirable condition when two or more operations may be attempted simultaneously, and the system behavior depends on which is processed first.
recognizer	Symbian OS plug-in code that can examine sample data, and return, if recognized, its data type. The data type is represented as a MIME type.
RFC	Request For Comments: an IETF standard.
ROM	Read-Only Memory (often loosely used to include flash memory which is reprogrammable, but effectively read-only in normal operation).

SIM	Subscriber Identity Module – a secure means of storing the key identifying a mobile phone service subscriber and a small amount of other information.
SIS	Symbian OS Software Install Script – a package format for delivering applications to the phone in installable form.
SMS	Short Message Service: a mechanism for sending text messages on GSM mobile phone networks.
spoofing	A technique for attacking security systems by masquerading as another user, process or device.
SSL	Secure Sockets Layer: a network security protocol for data connections between two end points providing confidentiality, integrity and authentication.
SWInstall	The Symbian OS Software Install subsystem.
TCB	Trusted Computing Base.
TCE	Trusted Computing Environment.
TLS	Transport Layer Security: a network security protocol defined by IETF RFC 2246. Developed from SSL.
TOCTOU	Time of Check, Time of Use: a mnemonic describing the risks of race conditions when operations may affect security attributes between the time the security check is made and the time the result of the check is acted upon.
UI	User Interface. On Symbian OS-based mobile phones, the graphical user interface is a separate component such as S60 or UIQ.
UIKON	Symbian OS common APIs for graphical user interfaces.
UMTS	Universal Mobile Telecommunications System – a third-generation (3G) mobile phone network standard, the next generation of GSM.
URL	Uniform Resource Locator: the address of content on the World-Wide Web.
vtable	Virtual method table: in C++, contains pointers to all the virtual member functions defined in a class.
WAP	Wireless Application Protocol: a network protocol designed for delivering OTA content to mobile phones.
X.509	A standard format for digital certificates, defined by the International Telecommunication Union.

References

Adams, Carlisle, and Lloyd, Steve (1999) *Understanding PKI: Concepts, Standards and Deployment Considerations*, 2nd edition, Addison-Wesley.

Anderson, James P. (1972) *Computer Security Technology Planning Study*, ESD-TR-73-51, US Air Force Electronic Systems Division, October.

Anderson, Ross (2001) *Security Engineering: A Guide to Building Dependable Distributed Systems*, Wiley.

Biddle, Peter, *et al.* (2003) 'The Darknet and the Future of Content Protection', in *Digital Rights Management: Technological, Economic, Legal and Political Aspects*, Springer-Verlag.

Bostrom, Nick (2003) 'Are You Living in a Computer Simulation?', *Philosophical Quarterly* 53:211.

Computer Industry Almanac, Inc. (2005) Press Release, ***www.c-i-a.com/pr0305.htm***, 9 March.

Dennis, Jack B., and Van Horn, Earl C. (1966) 'Programming Semantics for Multiprogrammed Computations', in *Communications of the ACM* 9:3, March.

Gowdiak, Adam (2004) *Java 2 Micro Edition Security Vulnerabilities*, presented at Hack-in-the-Box Security Conference, Kuala Lumpur, October.

Harrison, Richard (2003) *Symbian OS C++ for Mobile Phones*, Wiley.

Harrison, Richard (2004) *Symbian OS C++ for Mobile Phones, Volume 2*, Wiley.

Holmes, Phil (2002) *An Introduction to Boundaryless Information Flow*, electronic publication, The Open Group, July.

Juvenal (c. 100CE), *Satire VI*.

Kerckhoffs, Auguste (1883) 'La Cryptographie Militaire', in *Journal des Sciences Militaires* IX, January/February.

McGraw, Gary, and Felten, Edward W. (1999) *Securing Java*, Wiley.

Miller, Stanley A. (2005) *When nature calls, cell phone owners should answer carefully*, Associated Press, 4th April.

Odlyzko, Andrew M. (2001) 'Content is Not King', in *First Monday* 6:2, ***www.firstmonday.org/issues/issue6_2***, February.

Sales, Jane (2005) *Symbian OS Internals: Real Time Kernel Programming*, Wiley.

Saltzer, Jerome H., and Schroeder, Michael D. (1975) 'The Protection of Information in Computer Systems', in *Proceedings of the IEEE* 63:9, September.

Schneier, Bruce (1996) *Applied Cryptography: Protocols, Algorithms and Source Code in C*, 2nd edition, Wiley.

Schneier, Bruce (2000) *Secrets and Lies: Digital Security in a Networked World*, Wiley.

Sellar, Walter C., and Yeatman, Robert J. (1930) *1066 and All That*, Methuen.

Shirey, Robert W. (2000) *Internet Security Glossary*, RFC 2828, Internet Engineering Task Force, May.

Simmonds, Paul (2004) *De-perimeterisation – This Decade's Security Challenge*, presented at Black Hat Briefings, Las Vegas, July.

Stallman, Richard M. (2002) 'Can you trust your computer?', in *Free Software, Free Society: Selected Essays of Richard M. Stallman*, Free Software Foundation, October.

Stichbury, Jo (2005) *Symbian OS Explained: Effective C++ Programming for Smartphones*. Wiley.

United States Department of Defense (1985) Trusted Computer System Evaluation Criteria, DOD 5200-28-STD, December.

Virgil (19BCE), *The Aeneid*.

Index